ESSENTIAL COLLEGE ENGLISH

A Grammar and Punctuation Workbook

ESSENTIAL COLLEGE ENGLISH

A Grammar and Punctuation Workbook

THIRD EDITION

Norwood Selby

Surry Community College

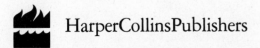 HarperCollinsPublishers

Sponsoring Editor: Jane Kinney
Project Manager: Patti Brecht/Spectrum Publisher Services, Inc.
Cover Design: Viviani Productions
Production: Michael Weinstein
Compositor: Compositors Corporation
Printer and Binder: R.R. Donnelley & Sons Company
Cover Printer: New England Book Components

Essential College English: A Grammar and Punctuation Workbook, Third Edition
Copyright © 1991 by Norwood Selby

Library of Congress Cataloging in Publication Data

Selby, Norwood.
   Essential college English: a grammar and punctuation workbook/
Norwood Selby.—3rd ed.
     p. cm.
   Includes index.
   ISBN 0-673-46231-5
   1. English language—Grammar—1950- —Problems, exercises, etc. 2. English
language—Punctuation—Problems, exercises, etc. I. Title.
PE1112.S37 1991

428.2–dc20
                                          90-44009
                                             CIP

ISBN 0-673-46231-5 (Student's Edition)

ISBN 0-673-53585-1 (Teacher's Edition)

90 91 92 93 9 8 7 6 5 4 3 2 1

Contents

Preface

Essential College English was written to fill a need. For years my students had been using one of the freshman English handbooks. However, because these books did not devote enough time to the basics of grammar and punctuation, I found myself teaching a grammar course. This was not what I wanted to do in a freshman composition class. As I tell my students, grammar and punctuation are merely tools to use in the composition process, just as mathematics is a tool used by the physicist.

Many of the grammar and punctuation texts on the market either included unnecessary detail on grammar or lacked adequate coverage of punctuation. For these reasons, I decided to write my own text. *Essential College English* presents enough basic grammar for students to understand how the language works and how sentences are structured. Naturally, problem areas such as pronoun case and subject-verb agreement are discussed. But more significantly, the basics of grammar are presented in a logical way by moving from smaller to larger units. Each step is explained and sufficient exercises are provided so that students can master one unit before going on to the next. Definitions and explanations are repeated when necessary; readers who don't go through the text from front to back will not be lost. Unnecessary cross-references have been avoided. Furthermore, punctuation is explained in clear-cut rules, without numerous and confusing exceptions. An index is included to make the book easier to use. I have tried to make *Essential College English* thorough but understandable, complete but straightforward. The result is a book that is quite conservative, but one that is easy for students to understand and use.

Essential College English can be used in many different ways. Some teachers may want to employ the text as the primary subject matter, having the students compose sentences illustrating the principles being discussed. Other teachers may prefer to use the text as a supplement to a composition rhetoric that discusses style and the composition process. One class period a week could be used to discuss grammar and punctuation. Or, because the answers to all Practice Sentences are provided in the back of the book, the text could be used entirely outside of class on a self-instructional basis, allowing more time in class for writing and discussing the principles of composition.

Essential College English is appropriate for *all* levels of freshman college English. It can be used as a main or supplementary text in some classes and as a parallel or reference book in others. An Instructor's Manual is available which includes two comprehensive tests with answers for grammar and two for punctuation, individual chapter tests with answers, and the answers to all of the Review Exercises that appear at the end of each chapter in the text. Note that the text is perforated so that students can submit the Review Exercises as graded assignments.

I want to thank Jackie Atkins of Penn State (Du Bois Campus), Helen C. Covington of North Harris County College, Muriel Harris of Purdue University, C. Jeriel Howard of Northeastern University, Randall L. Popken of Tarleton State University, Audrey J. Roth of Miami Dade Community College, Judith Stanford of Merrimack College, Margaret A. Strom of George Washington University, Janice Townley-Moore of Young Harris College, and Denise Weber-Watts of the University of Texas, all of whom offered constructive suggestions for this third edition. Finally, I would like to thank the administrative staff of Surry Community College, my students, and my colleagues in the English Department.

Norwood Selby

PART 1

GRAMMAR

1

Verbs, Subjects, and Complements

You are beginning a study of your language. What you learn will help you better understand how the English language works and give you more confidence in yourself when communicating with others. Think about how important communication is in all phases of day-to-day life and how you can benefit from having confidence in your use of language. If you couldn't communicate, how could you get a date, order a pizza, or pass your English course? Without communication you would be isolated.

As you know by this point in your education, every field of study has names for things. Automobile mechanics know not only what a carburetor is but what the names of the parts are that make up a carburetor. Physicians know the names of bones, muscles, nerves, etc. The names given to things make it easier for people talking about a subject to know exactly what is being discussed. Language also has names for things, such as the terms *subjects*, *verbs*, and *complements* mentioned in the title of this chapter. These terms provide a kind of shorthand that allows us to learn more easily. Once we are familiar with the concepts the terms represent, we can better understand and more easily analyze the writing. Do not allow yourself to be bothered by the various terms you will encounter. Just consider them as tools to use in learning about language. Other terms could just as easily be used and, in fact, often are. There is nothing sacred about the terminology.

In this book we break the study of language down into basic steps. Study each step until you feel you understand it before moving on to the next.

Subjects and Predicates

A normal English sentence contains both a **subject** and a **predicate**. A **subject is what is talked about in a sentence**.

John drives a 1966 Mustang.
> *John* is the subject of the sentence. He is being talked about in the sentence.

3

A predicate says something about the subject. In the sentence above, *drives a 1966 Mustang* is the predicate. It says something about John.

A sentence can be composed of just a subject and a predicate.

> <u>Mary</u> sews.
>> *Mary* is the subject. She is being talked about in the sentence.
>> *Sews* is the predicate. The word *sews* says something about Mary.

More often, however, a sentence contains more than just a subject and predicate.

> A tall man with red hair walked into a restaurant.
>> The subject of the sentence is *man*. He is being talked about.
>> *Walked* is the predicate in the sentence. It says something about the man (subject).

The sentence is said to have a **complete subject** and a **complete predicate**. The complete subject contains the basic subject *man* (called the **simple subject**) and all the words that relate to the subject. Thus, the complete subject is *A tall man with red hair*. *A, tall,* and *with red hair* all relate to *man*. The complete predicate contains the predicate itself *walked* (called a **simple predicate**) and all the words that relate to it. Thus, *walked into a restaurant* is the complete predicate. *Into a restaurant* relates to *walked*.

> The fat cat ate the lasagna.
>> The complete subject is *The fat cat.*
>> The complete predicate is *ate the lasagna.*

> The tired student stretched out for a nap.
>> The complete subject is *The tired student.*
>> The complete predicate is *stretched out for a nap.*

The key word in the complete predicate is the verb. *Stretched* is the verb in the sentence above because it is the key word that says something about the subject.

Recognizing Verbs

Action Verbs

Verbs are often the most important words in sentences. When you can recognize them, you are on your way. Everything else in a sentence relates to the verb either directly or indirectly. The easiest verbs to recognize are those which show action. Words such as *run, jump, play, sing,* and *drive* can clearly show action.

> The men <u>run</u> three miles every day.
>> *Run* is the verb.

The boxer <u>jumps</u> rope for fifteen minutes every day.
Jumps is the verb.

The girl <u>played</u> basketball for thirty minutes.
Played is the verb.

Not all action verbs show physical action. Many verbs in English express mental action; these include *think, believe, imagine,* and *wonder.* They are also action verbs; they just express a different kind of action. As you know, thinking can be hard work; it is an active process.

The executives <u>think</u> about the company's problems every morning.
Think is an action verb.

They <u>believe</u> in the potential of the company.
Believe is an action verb.

Practice Sentences 1-1

Identify the action verbs in the following sentences by underlining them.

Example: The students <u>raided</u> the school supply room.

1. They found towels, pens, soap, and many other things.

2. However, they sought one item in particular.

3. Then one student shouted to his friends.

4. He showed them a case of bathroom tissue over in the corner.

5. They loaded up.

6. Each student took at least three or four rolls.

7. They went straight to the main part of the wooded campus.

8. They threw paper to the top of every tree.

9. Unfortunately for them, the night watchman caught them in the act.

10. The next day in the rain they removed the entire mess.

Linking Verbs

Action verbs are easy to recognize: just look for the word that tells what is being done. Some verbs, however, do not show action. Instead they link the subject to another word, phrase, or clause that names or describes it. Thus they are known as linking verbs. The various forms of the verb *be* are the most common linking verbs. The verb *be* is very irregular and takes many forms (for example, *is, was, are, am, were, being,* and *been*). By examining a few examples, you will see how forms of the verb *be* link parts of sentences together.

> Jane is tall.
> > *Is* is a linking verb.

The word *is* does not show action. Instead, *is* establishes a connection, or equivalency, between *Jane* and *tall*. It links the woman to an attribute describing her, and so it is known as a linking verb.

> I am a student.
> > *Am* is a linking verb.

Notice that the verb *am* links the word *I* to the word *student*. It is a linking verb.

Practice Sentences 1-2

Identify the linking verbs in the following sentences by underlining them.

Example: Jane Dunnigan is an artist.

1. Her specialty is oil painting.

2. She is partial to seascapes.

3. Her favorite is a view of whitecaps at dusk.

4. However, as an artist she is versatile.

5. Her productions in watercolor, acrylics, and even ceramics are famous.

6. Last year she was Artist of the Year.

7. This year is a new challenge for her.

8. Sculpture is the goal.

9. Her bust of Queen Elizabeth is currently on display at the Denver Museum.

10. The only limit on Jane's career is her own imagination.

Though forms of *be* are the most common linking verbs, they are not the only ones. Many verbs that refer to the senses are linking verbs.

Words such as *feel, taste, sound, smell,* and *look* can be linking verbs, though they do not always have to be (see the section on correct usage of adjectives and adverbs, Chapter 10). Other linking verbs are *become, seem,* and *appear*. Here are some linking verbs:

is		feel
am		taste
was	any form	sound
were	of the	smell
been	verb *be*	look
being		become
		seem
		appear

The pie <u>tastes</u> sour.
  Tastes links *pie* to *sour*.

The girl <u>became</u> a champion fiddler.
  Became links *girl* to *fiddler*.

The man <u>seems</u> confident.
  Seems is a linking verb. What does it link?

Auxiliary Verbs

Besides action verbs and linking verbs, there is another type of verb—the auxiliary verb. An auxiliary verb precedes the main verb and helps it do its job. The auxiliary verb may make the main verb more precise in describing and telling when things happen. It may indicate obligation, possibility, emphasis, or permission.

The man <u>will complete</u> the project.
  The main verb is *complete*, and the auxiliary verb is *will*. The auxiliary verb tells you that the action has not yet been completed. It will be completed, however, sometime in the future.

Ralph <u>has ended</u> his five-year probation.
  The main verb is *ended*, and the auxiliary is *has*. The auxiliary verb tells you that the action has been completed.

I <u>have noticed</u> the change in policy.
  The main verb is *noticed*, and the auxiliary is *have*. The auxiliary verb tells you that the action has been completed.

You <u>must complete</u> the assignment.
  The main verb is *complete*; the auxiliary is *must*. The auxiliary indicates that the act of completing is an obligation.

I <u>do know</u> the answer to that question.
  The main verb is *know*; the auxiliary is *do*. The auxiliary emphasizes the act of knowing.

Some common auxiliary verbs are *may, might, must, do, did, could, should, is, am, are, was, were, has, had, have,* and *will.* Sometimes only one of these auxiliaries will be used with the main verb. Sometimes more than one will be used.

> Jane Davis is working behind the counter this afternoon.
> I am working behind the counter this afternoon.
> You are working behind the counter this afternoon.
> Evelyn Smith will be working behind the counter next week.
> John Coppleton is being assigned behind the counter next week.

In each of the examples the last word in the word group (*working* and *assigned*) is the main verb. The other words underlined as part of the verb are auxiliaries. The auxiliaries formed from *be* help to identify the time of the action.

Note: Forms of *be* can be auxiliaries of other verbs. A form of *be* is a linking verb if it is the main verb in the sentence. Example: This sentence is short. *Is* is a linking verb that links the word *sentence* to the word *short.* There is no other verb in the sentence, so *is* cannot be an auxiliary verb.

> My professor is teaching me English.
> > *Is* is not a linking verb because it is not the main verb in the sentence. It is an auxiliary verb that precedes the main verb *teaching* and tells when the teaching is being done.

Auxiliary verbs do not always occur side by side with main verbs. In fact, when an auxiliary is used to form a question, the auxiliary occurs earlier in the sentence than the main verb.

> Are the engines performing properly?
> > *Are* is the auxiliary of the main verb *performing.*

> Has the man completed the cabinets?
> > *Has* is the auxiliary of the main verb *completed.*

Sometimes the auxiliaries themselves are separated:

> Is the movie being filmed today?
> > *Is* and *being* are auxiliaries of the main verb *filmed.*

> You should not have played an ace just then.
> > *Should* and *have* are auxiliaries of the main verb *played.*

When auxiliaries are used to introduce questions, the easiest way to analyze the sentence is by turning the question into a statement:

> **Question:** Are the engines performing properly?
> **Statement:** The engines *are performing* properly. (Now the auxiliary and main verb are together.)

Question: Has the man completed the cabinets?
Statement: The man *has completed* the cabinets. (Auxiliary and main verb are now together.)

Practice Sentences 1-3

Underline the auxiliary verbs in the following sentences.

Example: Mary <u>is</u> working on her science project.

1. She is building a functional volcano.
2. The frame of the volcano was made of wood.
3. The cone was constructed of papier mâché.
4. When dry, the cone will be sprayed with paint.
5. She has even thought about some moss or even Easter-basket grass on the slopes.
6. She has left a hole in the center of her volcano.
7. A small jar has been placed inside the hole.
8. Mary has placed a mixture of baking soda and water inside the jar.
9. A little vinegar will be added to the baking soda and water.
10. With this chemical mixture her volcano will actually erupt.

Practice Sentences 1-4

Identify the verbs (auxiliaries and main) in the following sentences by underlining them.

Example: I <u>am going</u> to college for a degree in accounting.

1. At first I was planning a career as clerk in a local department store.
2. But I could never earn a good salary in such a position.
3. I would never be promoted in the family-owned business either.
4. So, what can I do?
5. I have always enjoyed working with numbers.
6. In college I could study accounting.
7. An accountant can make a good living.
8. Accountants can help people with their financial problems as well.

9. Would I enjoy a career in accounting?

10. My teachers and my heart are telling me, "Yes."

Practice Sentences 1-5

In the blanks provided, write out the verbs in the following sentences.

Example: Have you read *Walden*?

verb *Have read*

1. I have heard about the book at school.

verb _____

2. What did you hear?

verb _____

3. Thoreau's book is considered good, but difficult.

verb _____

4. I was told the same thing.

verb _____

5. Have you read it?

verb _____

6. I have just finished it.

verb _____

7. Did you enjoy it?

verb _____

8. I was very pleased with Thoreau's masterpiece.

verb _____

9. Did you find it difficult?

verb _____

10. A little, but the book would not have been as good otherwise.

verb _____

Recognizing Subjects

The second step in learning the basics of English grammar is to be able to recognize the subject. After you have found the verb, you should then find the subject. The subject is rather easy to recognize. You find it by asking Who or What? in front of the verb.

> John swept the sidewalk.
> > Who or what swept? **John**

> Jane considered the problem for three hours.
> > Who or what considered? **Jane**

> The robot set the table.
> > Who or what set the table? **robot**

> The computer saved the company a fortune.
> > Who or what saved the company a fortune? **computer**

Obviously, **the subject is a naming word.** The subject of an action verb names the doer of the action. In the sample sentences just presented, John does the action of sweeping, Jane does the action of considering, the robot does the action of setting, and the computer does the action of saving.

Practice Sentences 1-6

Find the action verbs in the following sentences. Then ask Who? or What? in front of the verb. The word that answers the question is the subject. Underline it.

> **Example:** <u>Curt</u> likes fine furniture.

1. He owns several books about furniture styles and periods.

2. Recently he developed an interest in the construction of furniture.

3. This interest led to an interest in woodworking equipment.

4. Now his basement contains numerous tools.

5. Unfortunately his shop has poor ventilation.

6. Sawdust covers everything, including the washer and dryer.

7. His wife prefers to buy her furniture from a store.

8. Curt built a beautiful oak cabinet.

9. The cabinet cost him over $300 to make.

10. His wife saw one just like it in a display window for $195.

As you know, not all verbs are action verbs. Linking verbs do not express action, but they do take subjects. Since a linking verb does not express any action, the subject of a linking verb cannot be the doer of any action. Like any other subject, however, the subject of a linking verb is a naming word. Also like any other subject, the subject of a linking verb can be found by asking Who or What? in front of the verb.

Gene Caudill is president of the Exeter Company.
Who or what is? **Gene Caudill**

The machine is a constant source of trouble.
Who or what is? **machine**

Practice Sentences 1-7

Find the linking verbs in the following sentences. Then ask Who or What? in front of the verb. The word that answers the question is the subject. Underline it.

Example: The <u>vase</u> was exceptionally beautiful.

1. It had been in Conrad's family for more than a hundred years.

2. The vase had become an antique.

3. The design was now out of fashion.

4. Mythological figures were all around the vase.

5. Conrad became the sole owner in 1963.

6. He was a collector of fine vases.

7. This was his first piece.

8. The out-of-fashion design seemed unique to him.

9. The vase was on a table in his hallway.

10. The vase is still there—after three bumps and one fall.

You may have found the subjects in the preceding sentences by just underlining the first naming word in the sentence. Underlining the first naming word worked in all the sample sentences because those sentences followed the most common order an English sentence takes: subject-verb. However, not all sentences in English follow the subject-verb order. Sentences beginning with the word *there* usually alter the subject-verb order. Don't mistake the expletive *there* for the subject. It merely indicates that the subject will follow the verb. (An expletive like *there* only serves as a filler and does not contribute to the meaning of the sentence.)

subject
There are four girls on the Little League team.

If you get in the habit of finding the verb and then asking Who or What? in front of it, you should have no trouble with sentences that are not in the subject-verb order. In the preceding example sentence, if you know that *are* is the verb and ask Who or What are? you will easily see that the subject is *girls*.

subject
Is Robert making a new piece for the machine?

The sentence is not in the subject-verb order. It is in the auxiliary-subject-verb order. If you ask Who or What is making? you will see that the answer is *Robert*, the subject. The easiest way to find the subject and verb in such a sentence is to turn the question *Is Robert making a new piece for the machine?* into a statement: *Robert is making a new piece for the machine.* Now the sentence is in the subject-verb order.

Practice Sentences 1-8

Identify the subjects in the following sentences by underlining them.

Example: Have you ever owned a Volkswagen beetle?

1. There have been three in our family.

2. My father once collected them.

3. I like the shape of the old beetles myself.

4. Which do you like best, the convertible or the hardtop?

5. Beetles are a little touchy, though.

6. The valves must be adjusted frequently.

7. Did you know that Volkswagen engines are often rebuilt?

8. Nevertheless, beetles have carried many people many miles.

9. Do you remember what people used to call them in the sixties?

10. They referred to VW's as pregnant roller skates.

Now that you can recognize subjects and verbs, it is time to apply your knowledge. In the following exercise you will be expected to identify both subjects and verbs. You should have no difficulty if you find the verb first and then ask Who or What? to find the subject.

Practice Sentences 1-9

In the blanks provided, indicate the subjects and verbs, including auxiliary verbs.

Example: Lachine wants a career as a nurse.

subject __Lachine_____

verb _____wants_____

1. She has already taken all her general college courses.

subject _____

verb _____

2. Last quarter she took pharmacology.

subject _____

verb _____

3. Wow! Did that course have a lot of math in it?

subject _____

verb _____

4. She felt lucky with a C in that course.

subject _____

verb _____

5. After pharmacology came med-surg (medical surgery).

subject _____

verb _____

6. Her main complaint was with the long hours.

subject _____

verb _____

7. But late into the second quarter she began clinical work.

subject _____

verb _____

8. Now she is a real nurse.

subject _____

verb _____

9. She is responsible for three patients every day.

subject _____

verb _____

10. All the classroom work has been worth it.

subject _____

verb _____

Recognizing Compound Subjects and Compound Verbs

The next step in being able to recognize subjects and verbs is realizing that they may be compounded; that is, two or more subjects or two or more verbs may be joined together by the words *and, or, nor, but.*

> John, Bob, and Ralph went to the game together.
> The compound subjects are *John, Bob,* and *Ralph.*

> Tony Arrowsmith sings well but dances clumsily.
> The compound verbs are *sings* and *dances.*

> Jane said she would either trade the car or sell it.
> The compound verbs are *trade* or *sell.*

Practice Sentences 1-10

Identify all the compound verbs in the following sentences by underlining them.

> **Example:** The hamster <u>runs</u> on the wheel in his cage and <u>climbs</u> the ladder up to his house.

1. Freddy can weld his plow and overhaul the engine on his tractor.

2. Norma drives a school bus and operates her own real estate business.

3. John prepared supper and servied it to Marie in the sun room.

4. Aunt Martha neither hears nor sees as well as mother.

5. Jeff handles the ball well but shoots poorly.

6. Does Reverend Brown still visit the hospitals and talk with ill members of the congregation?

7. I dictated and transcribed my own history notes this summer.

8. Andrea always drives the fastest car and spends the most money.

9. The accountant saves his money and keeps excellent records.

10. Can you enjoy a nice evening out and not spend a lot of money?

A compound subject is no more trouble than a compound verb. You still must find the verb first and ask Who or What? in front of it.

Bob Smith, Elaine Frank, and John Bartlett are competent engineers.
> Who or what are? The compound subject is *Bob Smith, Elaine Frank*, and *John Bartlett.*

Television, radios, newspapers, and magazines help to keep people well informed.
> Who or what keep? The compound subject is *television, radios, newspapers*, and *magazines.*

Practice Sentences 1-11

Identify all the compound subjects in the following sentences by underlining them.

Example: Jackie and Paula are sisters.

1. Paula and Jackie both have boyfriends.

2. The girls' mother and father don't mind.

3. Gary and Kevin are nice young men.

4. Gary and Paula have been dating for over two years.

5. Jackie and Kevin have only been going together for eight months.

6. Paula and her boyfriend enjoy bowling.

7. Jackie and Kevin much prefer cruising.

8. New people and neat cars capture their attention on the strip.

9. Bowling balls and scorecards interest the other couple more.

10. But the boys and girls prefer their own company to bowling or cruising.

Finally, in some sentences, both subjects and verbs are compound.

Joan Burger and Tony Arrowsmith sing and dance well together.

The compound subject is *Joan Burger* and *Tony Arrowsmith*, and the compound verb is *sing* and *dance.* Of course, sentences with compound subjects and compound verbs can vary from the subject-verb order like any other sentences.

There are three men and four women on the committee.
The compound subject is *men* and *women*. The verb is *are*.

Are Ed Shoenbaum and Lorraine Chute entering or leaving?
Ed Shoenbaum and *Lorraine Chute* is the subject, and *are entering* and *leaving* is the verb.

Recognizing Complements

Once you can recognize subjects and verbs, you can move on to the next step in sentence analysis, recognizing complements. A complement is a word that completes the meaning of the subject and the predicate. The four most important complements are (1) **direct objects**, (2) **indirect objects**, (3) **predicate nominatives**, and (4) **predicate adjectives**.

Direct Objects

Although the direct object is a common element in many sentences, not all verbs take direct objects. The direct object receives the action of the verb, and so the verb must express action before there can be a receiver of the action. When a verb has a direct object, the object generally appears in a sentence after the subject and verb. Remember: you find the verb first; then you find the subject. Just as you asked Who or What? *before* the verb to find the subject, you ask Whom or What? *after* the verb to find the direct object.

Mary made a mistake.
Clearly, *made* is the verb in the sentence. Now ask Who or what? in front of the verb: Who or what made? Mary. *Mary* is the subject. To find the direct object, ask whom or what after the verb: Mary made whom or what? mistake. *Mistake* is the direct object.

The following chart indicates which questions to ask, where to ask them, and which order to ask them in.

Mary made a mistake.

```
    2                 1                        3
Subject (Who? ←  Verb  →  (Whom?) → Direct Object
        (What?            What?)
    ↓                 ↓                        ↓
   Mary             made                   mistake
```

Be very careful to ask your questions before the verb when looking for the subject and after the verb when looking for the direct object. Since both subjects and direct objects are naming words, a direct object will answer a subject's question and vice versa. Therefore, if you ask the right question in the wrong place, you will get the wrong answer.

In looking for direct objects you must consider other things besides the questions they answer, however. One of the main points to keep in mind is that not *all* sentences have direct objects. Note the following example:

John swims every day.
>   *John* is the subject and *swims* is the verb.
>   There is no direct object.

Clearly, not all action verbs take direct objects.

Remember, too, that only action verbs can take direct objects. Note the following example:

The animal is a deer.
>   There cannot be a direct object since the verb is the linking verb *is* and not an action verb.

On the other hand:

This company produces ten cars an hour.
>   The verb *produces* is an action verb; it can and does take a direct object—*cars*.

It is easy to remember that only action verbs can take direct objects when you understand what direct objects are. Direct objects receive the action of the verb. Clearly then, as we said earlier, there must be action before there can be a receiver of the action.

In the sentence *Mary made a mistake*, a mistake receives the action of being made. In the sentence *The company produces ten cars an hour*, the cars receive the action of being produced. In the sentence *John loves Beth Henson very much*, Beth Henson receives the action of being loved. In all these sentences the receiver of the action is the direct object. Of course, all of the direct objects answer the question Whom or What? asked after the verb:

Mary made what?
>   *Mistake* is the direct object.

The company produces what?
>   *Cars* is the direct object.

John loves whom?
>   *Beth Henson* is the direct object.

Notice that the most common pattern for sentences containing direct objects is subject-verb-object.

s.   v.   d.o.
Mary made a mistake.

s.   v.   d.o.
The company produces ten cars an hour.

s.   v.   d.o.
John loves Beth Henson very much.

Practice Sentences 1-12

In the following sentences write d.o. *above the direct objects. Be sure to get in the habit of finding the verb first, then the subject, and then the direct object. Caution: You may find that some of the sentences do not contain direct objects.*

                           d.o.
Example: Bill and Brian play basketball for their school.

1. Bill shoots an accurate shot from the outside.

2. Brian, on the other hand, prefers the dunk.

3. They can be an awesome combination at times.

4. Coach Smith usually wants Brian as the shooter, though.

5. He likes the high-percentage shot.

6. Last week, however, Bill hit one from twenty-three feet.

7. That basket won the game.

8. Bill was the school's instant hero.

9. He describes the shot to Brian every evening coming home.

10. Bill and Brian are brothers.

Though the most common pattern for sentences containing direct objects is subject-verb-object, do not assume that is the only pattern.

Does John play golf often?
    Notice *does* is an auxiliary, *John* is the subject, *play* is the main verb, and *golf* is the direct object. The pattern is auxiliary-subject-verb-object.

aux.   s.   v.   d.o.
Do computers solve problems quickly?

Like verbs and subjects, direct objects can also be compound.

        d.o.   d.o.   d.o.
John loves golf, tennis, and skiing.

          d.o. d.o.   d.o.
Jane loves Bob, John, and Roy.

> *A Checklist for Direct Objects*
> A direct object must:
> 1. Be a naming word.
> 2. Be in the predicate.
> 3. Follow an action verb.
> 4. Answer the questions: "What?" or "Whom?"

Indirect Objects

After learning to recognize subjects, verbs, and direct objects, the next sentence part you need to look for is the indirect object. Like subjects and direct objects, indirect objects are naming words. You can find an indirect object if it is present by asking To or for whom? or To or for what? after the direct object.

      s.   v.   d.o.
Bruce gave Martha a ring.
    Bruce gave a ring to or for whom? *Martha* is the indirect object.

       s.   v.   d.o.
The philanthropist gave the museum a million dollars.
    The philanthropist gave dollars to or for what? *Museum* is the indirect object.

Remember: The indirect object is the fourth sentence element you try to find. Be sure you ask the right question in the right place.

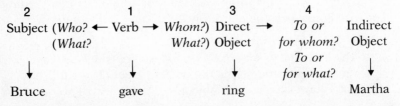

Most sentences will not contain indirect objects, because only a few verbs can take them. Here are examples of some of the verbs that can take indirect objects: *give, bring, buy, present, throw,* and *award.*

    Even though the indirect object is the fourth sentence part you try to find, it is generally located in the sentence before the direct object. The most natural order is subject-verb-indirect object-direct object. Note the following examples:

s.   v.   i.o.   d.o.
The quarterback threw his receiver a perfect pass.

s.   v.   i.o.   d.o.
The committee awarded Sara the prize.

Of course, when the sentence is a question, the order may change.

aux.   s.   v.   i.o.   d.o.
Did the executive buy her office a new typewriter?

But such a sentence fits the pattern of subject-verb-indirect object-direct object if you turn it around into a statement.

s.   v.   i.o.   d.o.
The executive did buy her office a new typewriter.

One thing to remember when studying indirect objects is that you must mentally supply the words *to* or *for* before the *whom* or *what*. If the sentence has the *to* or *for* expressed, the word cannot be an indirect object.

The quarterback threw a perfect pass (to) his receiver.

Since the *to* is expressed, the word receiver cannot be an indirect object. Which of the following sentences contains an indirect object?

1. The team presented the coach a new trophy case.
2. The team presented a new trophy case to the coach.
    Sentence 1 contains the indirect object since you mentally supply the missing *to*: The team presented (to) the coach a new trophy case.

A Checklist for Indirect Objects
An indirect object must:
  1. Be a naming word.
  2. Be in the predicate.
  3. Follow an action verb.
  4. Answer the question: "To whom?" "To what?" "For whom?" "For what?"

Practice Sentences 1-13

Identify the indirect objects in the following sentences by writing i.o. *over the correct word. Caution: Some sentences may not contain indirect objects.*

                                    i.o.
Example: The teacher gave the class a pop quiz.

1. One student gave his buddy the thumbs up sign.

2. Two others immediately turned in their papers with nothing on them but a name.

3. The teacher gave the class a lecture on the importance of homework.

4. One student told the teacher his view of pop quizzes.

5. Mr. Harper gave that student a lecture on discretion and silence.

6. Mr. Harper then gave his class a choice.

7. I will not give you any more pop quizzes.

8. But you must be prepared for each class.

9. Several of the students did not like the choices.

10. Nevertheless, most students showed Mr. Harper big smiles.

Predicate Nominatives

As you have noticed, only action verbs can take direct and indirect objects. However, linking verbs take complements. One such complement is the predicate nominative. A predicate nominative is a naming word (noun or pronoun) that follows a linking verb and renames the subject.

p.n.

Jane Martinez is a psychologist.
> *Psychologist* is a naming word that follows the linking verb *is* and renames the subject *Jane Martinez. Psychologist* is a predicate nominative.

p.n.

John Smith was an explorer.
> *Explorer* is a naming word that follows the linking verb *was* and renames the subject *John Smith. Explorer* is a predicate nominative.

Since the predicate nominative is linked to the subject by the verb, sentences containing predicate nominatives have linking verbs rather than action verbs.

p.n.

The Eagles are a good team.
> The verb *are* links the predicate nominative *team* to the subject *Eagles.*

Of course, not all linking verbs have predicate nominatives, just as not all action verbs have direct objects.

John Tybalt is handsome.
> There is no other word in the sentence that renames the subject *John Tybalt*. Therefore, the sentence does not contain a predicate nominative.

A Checklist for Predicate Nominatives

A predicate nominative must:
1. Be a naming word.
2. Be in the predicate part of the sentence.
3. Follow a linking verb.
4. Mean the same or rename the subject.

Practice Sentences 1-14

In the following sentences, identify the predicate nominatives by underlining them. Caution: Not all sentences contain predicate nominatives.

Example: Kareem is an avid <u>reader</u>.

1. Books are his hobby.
2. He has always been a collector of good books.
3. His room is a mess.
4. There are books in his closet, on his bed, and on the floor.
5. Kareem's parents were not usually complainers.
6. But this was the limit.
7. Kareem became a carpenter.
8. He built shelves for all his books.
9. Clutter was a thing of the past.
10. However, Kareem became the proud owner of thirty-six additional books yesterday.

Predicate Adjectives

A predicate adjective is a word (adjective) that usually follows a linking verb and qualifies, limits, or describes (modifies) the subject.

p.a.

Jane is happy.

> *Happy* is an adjective that follows the linking verb *is* and modifies the subject *Jane*. *Happy* describes *Jane*. *Happy* is a predicate adjective.

p.a.

The computer is expensive.

> *Expensive* is an adjective that follows the linking verb *is* and modifies the subject *computer*. *Expensive* is a predicate adjective.

A predicate adjective is linked to the word it modifies by a linking verb. Remember: Both predicate adjectives and predicate nominatives are used with linking verbs.

A Checklist for Predicate Adjectives

A predicate adjective must:

1. Be an adjective.
2. Be in the predicate part of the sentence.
3. Follow a linking verb.
4. Modify the subject.

Practice Sentences 1-15

In the sentences below, underline each predicate adjective. Caution: Some sentences may not contain predicate adjectives.

Example: The Case knife on the shelf is <u>old</u>.

1. It is also very valuable.

2. The pearl handles are genuine.

3. The tang is stamped Case Bros. Cut. Co., Little Valley, N.Y.

4. Knife collectors are aware of its value.

5. But they must be careful.

6. Older Case knives are often not genuine.

7. Some people in the knife business are not honest.

8. Fortunately, most dealers are very reputable.

9. This knife seems genuine to me.

10. I bought it for $850.

Review Exercise 1-A   Recognizing Subjects and Verbs

In the blanks provided, identify all subjects and verbs in the following sentences.

Example: The big basketball game is planned for tonight.

subject(s) _game_

verb(s) _is planned_

1. UNC plays Duke in Durham, N.C.

subject(s) _____

verb(s) _____

2. Currently, Duke is number one in the polls.

subject(s) _____

verb(s) _____

3. One of UNC's starters has been sidelined with a bad ankle.

subject(s) _____

verb(s) _____

4. The oddsmakers and the fans favor Duke by five points.

subject(s) _____

verb(s) _____

5. However, Duke has not played as difficult a schedule as UNC.

subject(s) _____

verb(s) _____

6. Many basketball coaches across the country favor UNC.

subject(s) _____

verb(s) _____

7. Do you really think the game will be close?

subject(s) _____

verb(s) _____

8. In the first half Duke outrebounded the Tar Heels 25 to 11.

subject(s) _____

verb(s) _____

9. But in the second half the Tar Heels turned the game around.

subject(s) _____

verb(s) _____

10. UNC won the game 95 to 88.

subject(s) _____

verb(s) _____

Review Exercise 1-B   Using Subjects and Verbs

1. Make up two sentences containing verbs that express action.

   a. _____

   _____

   b. _____

   _____

2. Make up two sentences containing linking verbs.

   a. _____

   _____

   b. _____

   _____

3. Make up two sentences containing compound verbs.

   a. _____

   _____

   b. _____

   _____

4. Make up two sentences containing compound subjects.

   a. _____

   _____

   b. _____

   _____

5. Make up two sentences containing compound subjects and compound verbs.

a. _____

_____

b. _____

_____

Review Exercise 1-C   Identifying Types of Complements (I)

In the following sentences, indicate whether the italicized word is a direct object (d.o.), indirect object (i.o.), predicate nominative (p.n.), or predicate adjective (p.a.) by writing your answer in the space provided.

Example: Wayne collects *tools* of all kinds.

_____*d.o.*_____

1. He has a *set* of woodcarving tools.

   _____

2. Each tool is *beautiful*.

   _____

3. The handles are *American Rock Maple*.

   _____

4. He also owns a *set* of engraver's tools.

   _____

5. He found a *catalog* with the tools of every trade.

   _____

6. How many people have a wide *assortment* of stonecutter's chisels?

   _____

7. He has collected quite a few knifemaking *tools*.

   _____

8. He owns a belt *sander*, a band *saw*, a *buffer*, and at least thirty *files*.

   _____

9. Wayne is definitely an avid *collector*.

   _____

10. Unfortunately, he is not very *good* with tools.

    _____

Review Exercise 1-D   Identifying Types of
Complements (II)

*In the following sentences, indicate whether the italicized word is a direct object (*d.o.*), indirect object (*i.o.*), predicate nominative (*p.n.*), or predicate adjective (*p.a.*) by writing your answer in the space provided.*

Example: John and his brother bought *themselves* a restaurant.

_____*i. o.*_____

1. John is the *waiter*.

_____

2. Dennis is the *cook*.

_____

3. Business has been *good* most of the time.

_____

4. Customers apparently like the *food* at Dennis and John's restaurant.

_____

5. They leave John big *tips* with every meal.

_____

6. Naturally, John shares this *money* with Dennis.

_____

7. Unfortunately, John and Dennis enjoy the *food* also.

_____

8. John gained thirty *pounds* in the first month.

_____

9. But John seems *tiny* in comparison with Dennis.

_____

10. The money from the tips pays their *dues* at Weight Watchers.

_____

Review Exercise 1-E   Using Complements

1. Make up two sentences that contain direct objects but not indirect objects.

   a. _____

   _____

   b. _____

   _____

2. Make up two sentences that contain compound direct objects and no indirect objects.

   a. _____

   _____

   b. _____

   _____

3. Make up two sentences that contain direct and indirect objects.

   a. _____

   _____

   b. _____

   _____

4. Make up two sentences that contain predicate nominatives.

   a. _____

   _____

   b. _____

   _____

5. Make up two sentences that contain predicate adjectives.

a. _____

_____

b. _____

_____

2

Parts of Speech

In every field there are names for everything pertinent to that field. Every piece in a telephone has a name. Similarly, everything in a sentence has a name. Each "piece" in a sentence is used as a certain part of speech. The part of speech of a word depends on the way the word is used in a particular sentence. Therefore, the same word can be any of several parts of speech. For example:

<u>Blue</u> is my favorite color. (noun)
My father drives a <u>blue</u> truck. (adjective)
Mark is <u>blueing</u> his gun barrel. (verb)

Before you can understand the parts of speech, however, you must be familiar with their definitions. The definitions tell you how the word may be used. If you know the part of speech of every word in a sentence, then you know what every word in that sentence does. There are eight parts of speech: *nouns, pronouns, adjectives, verbs, adverbs, prepositions, conjunctions,* and *interjections.*

Nouns

Nouns are naming words. They name people, places, things, and ideas—*Robert, England, tire,* and *justice.*

<u>Robert</u> names a person.
<u>England</u> names a place.
<u>Tire</u> names a thing.
<u>Justice</u> names an idea.

Subjects are naming words as well. A noun, however, is merely a way of identifying how a word is used in a sentence. A subject, on the other hand, is a word that tells what is talked about in a sentence. Clearly, most subjects will be nouns. However, there may be many nouns in a sentence that don't tell what is being talked about. For instance,

Bob lent <u>Mary</u> the <u>key</u> to the <u>car</u>.
Only the noun *Bob* is the subject. But the underlined words <u>Mary</u>, <u>key</u>, and <u>car</u> are all nouns.

Some nouns name more specifically than others. *Ms. Smith, woman, lady, person, mother, wife, Jane Everette Smith* are all nouns that might identify the same person. *Ms. Smith* and *Jane Everette Smith* both name more specifically than the other words; they are known as proper nouns. A *proper noun* is capitalized and names a specific person, place, or thing. *Chicago* is a proper noun and so is *Mississippi River*. *Woman, lady, person, mother,* and *wife* are all common nouns. A *common noun* names a general class of people or things and is not capitalized. Words such as *city* and *river* are common nouns. As you can see, nouns are quite versatile. They can also name things as concrete as *sand* and *wood* and as abstract as *freedom* and *justice*.

Practice Sentences 2-1

In the following sentences underline all the nouns.

Example: <u>Beverly</u> and <u>Tom</u> own a craft <u>store</u>.

1. Customers like the variety of items in the store.

2. Oils, acrylics, pastels, and charcoal can be found in the artist's corner.

3. Watercolor lessons are available for beginners.

4. Tom teaches these lessons and handles the art supplies.

5. Beverly prefers the crafts.

6. She does needlepoint, cross-stitch, candlewicking, and knitting.

7. She displays her own pillows and sweaters and aprons in the shop.

8. The customers, of course, want to buy these beautiful, handmade items.

9. But Beverly would prefer they buy yarn, thread, material, and needles for their own projects.

10. Beverly and her customers want different things from a craft store.

Pronouns

Pronouns are naming words that are used to take the place of nouns. *John* is a noun; *he* is a pronoun. *Team* is a noun; *they* is a pronoun. Pronouns name in an even more general manner than common nouns. By the way, you probably remember that the subjects, direct objects, and indirect objects you were identifying earlier were also naming words. Subjects, direct objects, and indirect objects are either nouns or pronouns. You may be wondering why pronouns are even needed in English. Perhaps the following paragraphs will illustrate why pronouns are used.

> John left John's apartment and got into John's car. John went over to Sally's house. John and Sally listened to Sally's stereo. Sally's parents came in and asked John and Sally to turn the music down low. John got irritated at Sally's father, and John suggested that John and Sally leave Sally's house.

There are no pronouns in that paragraph—but there should be. Pronouns are important in making sentences easier to read. Without them English sentences would be choppy and repetitious.

Since pronouns take the place of nouns, it is not difficult to understand their function. However, many people have trouble identifying pronouns because there are so many kinds. Rather than worrying about all the different kinds, refer to the following list of words commonly used as pronouns:

I	they	anyone	whom
my	them	anybody	whoever
me	their	everyone	whomever
you	we	everybody	myself
your	us	no one	yourself
he	our	none	himself
his	many	each	herself
him	some	this	itself
she	few	that	ourselves
her	both	these	themselves
it	several	those	all
its	one	who	

Practice Sentences 2-2

Underline the pronouns in the following sentences.

Example: Sherrie loves her relatives and thinks of <u>them</u> at Christmas.

1. She gave an uncle in Phoenix a beautiful sweater.

2. The Indian designs on it just seemed to suit him.

3. She gave each of his children a pair of slippers.

4. Sherrie gave everyone in the family a poinsettia.

5. Aunt Leda received a vase with Greek markings on it.

6. John Keats would have been proud of it.

7. She shopped in all of the stores in town for her brother's present.

8. Several of the clerks thought she was crazy.

9. "What is a Hoola Hoop?" they asked her.

10. The hoop she found was listed as a football-throwing target.

Practice Sentences 2-3

In the spaces provided, rewrite the following paragraph, replacing the unnecessarily repetitious nouns with appropriate pronouns.

Marty recently purchased an expensive assortment of camping supplies for Marty and Marty's family. Marty and Marty's wife plan to go camping on the riverfront property Marty and Marty's wife bought recently. To have ready access to their property, Marty and Marty's wife also bought a four-wheel-drive truck. The truck enables Marty and Marty's family to drive all the way to the riverbank. Marty and Marty's wife's children enjoy fishing and swimming in the river. Last week, however, Marty and Marty's family got stuck on the land in the four-wheel-drive truck.

_____

_____

_____

_____

_____

_____

_____

_____

_____

Adjectives

Adjectives are words that describe, clarify, or limit (modify) a noun or pronoun. They are usually easy to recognize because they answer the questions Which one? What kind? How many? One-word adjectives generally come before the words they modify.

adj. n.
big car
  Which car? big

 adj. n.
Siamese cat
  What kind of cat? Siamese

 adj. n.
three men
  How many men? three

One kind of adjective is extremely easy to identify—the *article*. The articles are *a, an*, and *the*. Remember, however, "article" does not name a part of speech. *A, an*, and *the* are adjectives.

Practice Sentences 2-4

Underline the adjectives in the following sentences.

 Example: The car in the corner lot is old.

 1. It is not an antique, just old.

 2. The red top has several holes in it.

 3. The passenger door is barely attached to the rest of the car.

 4. The paint job on the car is Postimpressionism.

 5. The "chrome" grille looks like the smile of an eight-year-old.

 6. The interior looks like something from a Poe room.

 7. Of course, little of the original interior remains.

 8. The battered dashboard has large holes where instruments used to be.

 9. The steering wheel has little plastic still on it.

 10. Believe it or not, however, the old bomb still runs.

 Some adjectives can be confusing. Words such as *his, your, my, her, our, their*, and *its* are as much pronouns as adjectives.

John keeps *his* car in good shape.
The girls made *their* entrance.

In the first sentence *his* is a pronoun taking the place of the noun *John*. At the same time, however, *his* is an adjective modifying the subject *car*. In the second sentence, *their* is a pronoun taking the place of girls as much as it is an adjective modifying *entrance*. Some people call words like these pronominal adjectives; others call them adjectival pronouns. It is not important which part of speech you prefer to call them; the important thing to remember is that they fit the definitions of both pronouns and adjectives at the same time.

Practice Sentences 2-5

Underline the adjectives in the following sentences.

   Example: Bill gave <u>nice</u> presents to <u>his</u> mother, father, and sister.

   1. He gave his mother her first dishwasher.

   2. His sister received six wine glasses in her pattern.

   3. He gave his father a table saw.

   4. Of course, he didn't forget about his interests.

   5. Bill bought himself a shiny, new Thunderbird.

Verbs

The first thing you did in Chapter 1 was to recognize verbs. By now you should be able to recognize them easily. However, you should know other things about verbs besides how to recognize them. You should realize that **verbs are either regular or irregular and that they have tense, voice, number, and mood.**

Regular and Irregular Verbs

Look at the following model:

   1. I _____ today.

   2. I _____ yesterday.

   3. I have _____.

   4. I am _____-ing.

Fill each blank with the appropriate form of the same verb; the forms are known as the principal parts of the verb. The first principal part is called the *simple present*. The second is the *simple past*. The third principal part is called the *past participle*; notice that the third principal part must be preceded by an auxiliary, such as *have*. The fourth principal part is known as the *present participle* and is also preceded by an auxiliary, such as *am*.

A *regular verb* forms the simple past and past participle by adding *-ed* to the simple present, and it forms the present participle by adding *-ing* to the simple present.

I *play* today.	simple present
I *played* yesterday.	simple past
I have *played*.	past participle
I am *playing*.	present participle

An *irregular verb* usually forms its simple past and past participle by changing a vowel of the simple present. The present participle of an irregular verb is formed in the same manner as a regular verb, by adding *-ing* to the simple present.

I *begin* today.	simple present
I *began* yesterday.	simple past
I have *begun*.	past participle
I am *beginning*.	present participle

If you are not sure you can correctly fill in the blanks of the model with the appropriate form of a verb, refer to the following partial list of irregular verbs or, preferably, to a dictionary.

Simple Present	Simple Past	Aux. + Past Participle	Aux. + Present Participle
am	was	been	being
begin	began	begun	beginning
bite	bit	bitten	biting
blow	blew	blown	blowing
break	broke	broken	breaking
bring	brought	brought	bringing
burst	burst	burst	bursting
choose	chose	chosen	choosing
come	came	come	coming
draw	drew	drawn	drawing
drink	drank	drunk	drinking
drive	drove	driven	driving
eat	ate	eaten	eating
fall	fell	fallen	falling

forsake	forsook	forsaken	forsaking
hear	heard	heard	hearing
lay	laid	laid	laying
lead	led	led	leading
lie	lay	lain	lying
ring	rang	rung	ringing
rise	rose	risen	rising
see	saw	seen	seeing
set	set	set	setting
show	showed	shown	showing
sit	sat	sat	sitting
slay	slew	slain	slaying
steal	stole	stolen	stealing
throw	threw	thrown	throwing
wake	woke (waked)	waked	waking
wear	wore	worn	wearing
write	wrote	written	writing

Practice Sentences 2-6

In the following sentences underline the correct principal part of the verb.

Example: I (<u>did</u>, done) the assignment last night.

1. I would have (did, done) it earlier if possible.

2. But my little brother (had threw, had thrown) my papers away.

3. He (threw, throwed) them in the hamper.

4. Then he (gone, went) to visit a friend.

5. Fortunately, my mother (saw, seen) the papers.

6. She (ask, asked) me about them.

7. The sight of mother and the papers (brought, brung) a smile to my face.

8. Within an hour I (had drunk, had drank) three beers and (ate, eaten) two pizzas.

9. In this happy condition I (begin, began) work on the assignment.

10. Later I (showed, shown) the F grade to my little brother.

A common error in using principal parts is failing to put the final -*d* on a word. Though the final -*d* may not always be noticed in speech, its absence in writing is readily apparent.

Incorrect: I use to be a good speller.
Correct: I used to be a good speller.
Incorrect: I was suppose to finish my lab report.
Correct: I was supposed to finish my lab report.

Also, do not use the past participle as though it were the simple past: *I done the job* and *I seen that movie.* Though such sentences rarely cause confusion, they can be very distracting to your readers. Correcting such sentences is easy. Simply use the proper form of the verb:

I did the job.
I saw that movie.

Practice Sentences 2-7

Correct the errors with principal parts in the following sentences by rewriting the sentences in the space provided.

Example: Jason drawed a colorful picture of a race car.

Jason drew a colorful picture of a race car.

1. Some intoxicated people have saw pink elephants.

   _____

2. Robert throwed the ball to first base.

   _____

3. Laura become very nervous as the clock kept on ticking.

   _____

4. The phone rung fifteen times before Mother finally answered it.

   _____

5. I have wrote three letters to that company in the last three months.

   _____

6. On that hot day Lorraine drunk a liter of gingerale, swallowing continuously.

   _____

7. Calvin has rewrote his paper six times.

_____

8. Ryan's teacher has teached him a lot of English.

_____

9. Someone has stole the dean's fall schedule.

_____

10. Joshua has fell out of the tree house.

_____

Tense

The tense of a verb indicates time. There are only six basic tenses: present, past, future, present perfect, past perfect, and future perfect.

The *present tense* indicates an action that is going on at the present time or that occurs habitually.

> The man <u>looks</u> off into the distance.
>> *Looks* reflects an action going on at the present time.

> The seasons <u>change</u> four times a year.
>> *Change* reflects an action that occurs habitually.

Sometimes the present tense indicates future action.

> My plane <u>leaves</u> at 5:00 P.M.
>> *Leaves* indicates an action that will occur in the future.

The present tense is also used to express general truths.

> Water <u>freezes</u> at 32 degrees Fahrenheit.

The *past tense* indicates an action completed at a specific time in the past.

> Luis Astorga <u>broke</u> his arm last week.
>> *Broke* indicates a completed past action.

The *future tense* indicates an action which will take place in the future.

> Ms. Jones <u>will repair</u> the television set tomorrow.
>> *Will repair* indicates an action to be performed in the future.

The "perfect" tenses always contain a form of the verb *have (have, has, had)* and the past participle.

The *present perfect tense* is formed from the appropriate present tense form of the verb *have (has* or *have)* plus the past participle and indicates an action that is completed at the present time or that is continuing into the present.

> B. F. Skinner <u>has completed</u> the research for his new book.
> *Has completed* indicates an action completed at the present time.

> I <u>have played</u> golf for many years.
> *Have played* indicates an action continuing into the present.

The *past perfect tense* is formed from the past tense form of the verb *have (had)* plus the past participle and indicates an action completed before a specific time in the past.

> The girl <u>had broken</u> the vase before her mother could get there.
> *Had broken* indicates an action completed before the mother's arrival.

The *future perfect tense* is formed from the future tense of the verb *have (will have* or *shall have)* plus the past participle and indicates an action that will be completed before a specific time in the future.

> The teacher <u>will have graded</u> the papers before class tomorrow.
> *Will have graded* indicates an action that will be completed before class time tomorrow.

Practice Sentences 2-8

In the blanks provided, indicate the tenses of the italicized verbs.

Example: *Have* you ever *played* basketball?

present perfect

1. I *enjoy* the sport myself.

_____

2. I once *played* for the Metropolis Muppets.

_____

3. Each player *had been* individually *recruited*.

_____

4. The coach *was paid* a big salary.

_____

5. The city *will have rolled* out the red carpet for the return of its victorious heroes.

_____

6. People *will believe* anything.

_____

7. The Muppets *lost* the first game.

_____

8. They *were defeated* in all the other games as well.

_____

9. In fact, no Muppet team *has* ever *won* a game.

_____

10. They *are* the most consistent team in basketball.

_____

Some writers unnecessarily shift from one tense to another. For example, in the sentence *During the meeting Mr. Oliver explained the need for a tax increase while Mr. Leer explains the disadvantages*, there is no reason to shift from the past tense used for Mr. Oliver to the present tense used for Mr. Leer. Such shifts are very distracting to readers and can greatly confuse them.

Practice Sentences 2-9

Correct all needless shifts in tense in the following sentences by rewriting each sentence in the space provided.

Example: Every school morning Freddy Haymore gets out of bed and washed his face.

Every school morning Freddy Haymore gets out of bed and washes his face.

1. He fries the eggs and plugged in the coffee maker.

   _____

   _____

2. He sits down and ate.

   _____

   _____

3. He has now poured his coffee and goes back to the bedroom.

   _____

   _____

4. He lays out his clothes and shaved.

   _____

   _____

5. After he completes this, he took a bath.

   _____

   _____

6. The bath felt good and is relaxing.

   _____

   _____

7. When he finished his bath, he dresses for school.

   _____

   _____

8. One shoe is brown and the other was black.

   _____

   _____

9. His tie does not match the suit he was wearing.

   _____

   _____

10. Freddy gets out of bed in the morning but waked up in the afternoon.

   _____

   _____

Voice

Each verb tense can be either in the *active voice* or the *passive voice*. In the active voice the subject is the doer of the action. In the passive voice the subject is the receiver of the action. The passive voice is composed of a form of the auxiliary verb *be (am, are, is was, were)* followed by a past participle.

> Nelson played the game.
>> The verb *played* is in the active voice because the subject *Nelson* is doing the action.
>> Who or what played? Nelson

> The game was played by Nelson.
>> The verb *was played* is in the passive voice because the subject *game* is the receiver of the action.
>> Who or what was played? Game

The passive voice is formed from the active voice first by making the direct object of the active sentence become the subject of the passive sentence:

Original Sentence: Nelson played the game. → The game . . .

Next, by inserting the form of the auxiliary *be* that is the same tense as the original sentence followed by the past participle of the original active verb:

Nelson played the game. → The game was played . . .

Finally, by making the original subject of the active sentence come after the past participle and after a word such as *by* in the passive sentence:

Active: Nelson played the game. →
Passive: The game was played by Nelson.

With a little practice, you will find that the passive voice is easy to understand and use. Though good writers consider the active voice to be stronger and therefore better than the passive voice, you need to know both. Because the passive voice deemphasizes the doer of the action, it is often used to soften the effect of a complaint. In speaking to the letter carrier, you are much more polite when you say *My magazine was torn* than when you say *You tore my magazine.* Also, there are times when the doer of the action is unknown, as in the sentence *The letter was not signed.* Nevertheless, try to keep your writing in the active voice. The active voice is much more direct since the subject clearly performs the action.

Practice Sentences 2-10

In the blanks provided, indicate whether the verbs in the following sentences are in the active or passive voice.

Example: The little girl's dress was soiled by the ice cream cone.

_____*passive*_____

1. The bat was made by the Louisville Slugger Company.

_____

2. The girl outran the shortstop's throw.

_____

3. Michael Jordan plays basketball for the Chicago Bulls.

_____

4. My mother works with an accounting firm in Atlanta.

_____

5. The company car was sold by the business manager.

_____

6. Andrew drove his mother's car into the driver's door of my car.

_____

7. The bill was padded by the mechanic.

_____

8. The batteries in the child's toy ran down in just one week.

_____

9. The teacher talked to the student about his sloppy work.

_____

10. The entire crew was blamed by the supervisor.

_____

Practice Sentences 2-11

In the space provided, rewrite the passive sentences to make them active and the active sentences to make them passive.

Example: The truck was driven by a student.

A student drove the truck.

_____

1. The *Mona Lisa* was painted by Leonardo da Vinci.

_____

_____

2. Richard Petty drove a victory lap.

_____

_____

3. William Shakespeare wrote *The Rape of Lucrece.*

_____

_____

4. The Ponderosa was owned by Ben Cartwright.

_____

_____

5. *The Thinker* was sculpted by Rodin.

_____

_____

6. Jerry bought Angela a huge box of Valentine candy.

_____

_____

7. The lasagna was prepared by Chef in a Box.

_____

_____

8. John Dillinger was betrayed by the "woman in red."

_____

_____

9. An angry student stole a copy of the test.

_____

_____

10. Mary made her bed at three o'clock this morning.

_____

_____

Be sure to avoid needless shifts from active voice to passive voice and vice versa.

John <u>played</u> football for three years in high school, but the sport <u>was</u> not <u>enjoyed</u> by him.

There is a needless shift from the active voice to the passive voice. Rewrite the sentence to say: John *played* football for three years in high school, but he *did* not *enjoy* the sport.

Practice Sentences 2-12

Correct all needless shifts in voice in the following sentences by rewriting each sentence in the space provided.

Example: Let's do well on this project, so honors will be won by all.

Let's do well on this project, so we can all win honors.

1. I ordered my wife's Christmas gift in July, but it has not been received.

_____

_____

2. Danny dunked the basketball, but his finger was broken on the rim.

_____

_____

3. Greg prepared many different dishes, but only one was eaten by Martha.

_____

_____

4. The player declared his innocence, but a drug test was refused by him.

_____

_____

5. Heather said she really admired Jim, but his ring was refused by her.

_____

_____

6. The appraiser looked over the car carefully, and it was declared a total loss by him.

_____

_____

7. The Express Mail was lost in Chicago, but it was delivered by the postman on time.

_____

_____

8. The ad campaign was rejected by the company, so it was redesigned by Fred.

_____

_____

9. The radio was dropped by Morris, and he repaired it.

_____

_____

10. The manager submitted the proper requisition form, but no action was taken by the boss.

_____

_____

Person and Number

The *number* of a verb simply indicates whether the verb is singular or plural.

The boy sings. (singular)
The boys sing. (plural)

The *-s* on *sings* indicates that it is singular. Do not be confused. Most nouns form their plurals by adding an *-s: chair* becomes *chairs.* Verbs are just the opposite.

The singular and plural forms of the verb are often arranged by *person.* Person indicates the speaker, the person or thing spoken to, or the person or thing spoken about. There are first person, second person, and third person. The *first person* indicates the person speaking:

I will do the assignment.

The *second person* indicates the person or thing spoken to:

You should repair the bicycle immediately.
Batteries, you had better not give out on me during a test.

The *third person* indicates the person or thing spoken about:

The ⟨lawnmower⟩ is ready now.

The first person singular pronouns are *I, my, mine,* and *me.* The first person plural pronouns are *we, our, ours, us.* The second person singular and plural pronouns are *you, your,* and *yours,* used when addressing both one individual and when addressing more than one individual. The third person singular pronouns are *he, him, his, she, her, hers, it,* and *its.* The third person plural pronouns are *they, them, their,* and *theirs.*

Pronouns

Person	Singular	Plural
First	I, me, my, mine	we, us, our, ours
Second	you, your, yours	you, your, yours
Third	he, him, his, she, her, hers, it, its	they, them, their, theirs

Agreement in Number

Person	Singular	Plural
First	I choose	we choose
Second	you choose	you choose
Third	he chooses	they choose

As you can see, the third person singular form of the present tense verb is the one that ends in *s.* In your writing, do not make needless shifts in person and in number.

One expects praise when they succeed.
> *One* is the third person singular *(he, she),* but *they* is the third person plural. There is a needless shift in number.

A person should be modest when we are successful.
> *A person* is the third person singular, but *we* is the first person plural. There is a needless shift in both person and number.

Practice Sentences 2-13

Correct all needless shifts in number and person in the following sentences by rewriting each sentence in the space provided.

Example: Every employee must sign their own check.

Every employee must sign his or her own check.

1. One of the students spent their evenings working.

   _____

   _____

2. One of the second graders lost their spelling book.

   _____

   _____

3. If a person wants to cash their check, you should endorse it on the back.

   _____

   _____

4. We should all write our papers the best one is able.

   _____

   _____

5. The man repaired the door of their house by himself.

   _____

   _____

6. A person should always strive to do the best they can.

   _____

   _____

7. The students did her best on the exam.

   _____

   _____

8. An individual should consider all the factors before they make a decision.

   _____

   _____

9. The men lost his shoe.

_____

_____

10. The women did a nice job on her own project.

_____

_____

Conjugation

To conjugate a verb means to arrange the verb's forms in an orderly manner according to tense, person, number, and voice. The verb *choose* is conjugated below.

Active Voice	*Singular*	*Plural*
Present tense	1. I choose	1. we choose
	2. you choose	2. you choose
	3. he, she, it chooses	3. they choose
Past tense	1. I chose	1. we chose
	2. you chose	2. you chose
	3. he, she, it chose	3. they chose
Future tense	1. I will (shall) choose	1. we will (shall) choose
	2. you will choose	2. you will choose
	3. he, she, it will choose	3. they will choose
Present perfect tense	1. I have chosen	1. we have chosen
	2. you have chosen	2. you have chosen
	3. he, she, it has chosen	3. they have chosen
Past perfect tense	1. I had chosen	1. we had chosen
	2. you had chosen	2. you had chosen
	3. he, she, it had chosen	3. they had chosen
Future perfect tense	1. I will (shall) have chosen	1. we will (shall) have chosen
	2. you will have chosen	2. you will have chosen
	3. he, she, it will have chosen	3. they will have chosen

Passive Voice

Present tense	1. I am chosen 2. you are chosen 3. he, she, it is chosen	1. we are chosen 2. you are chosen 3. they are chosen
Past tense	1. I was chosen 2. you were chosen 3. he, she, it was chosen	1. we were chosen 2. you were chosen 3. they were chosen
Future tense	1. I will (shall) be chosen 2. you will be chosen 3. he, she, it will be chosen	1. we will (shall) be chosen 2. you will be chosen 3. they will be chosen
Present perfect tense	1. I have been chosen 2. you have been chosen 3. he, she, it has been chosen	1. we have been chosen 2. you have been chosen 3. they have been chosen
Past perfect tense	1. I had been chosen 2. you had been chosen 3. he, she, it had been chosen	1. we had been chosen 2. you had been chosen 3. they had been chosen

Active Voice	*Singular*	*Plural*
Future perfect tense	1. I will (shall) have been chosen 2. you will have been chosen 3. he, she, it will have been chosen	1. we will (shall) have been chosen 2. you will have been chosen 3. they will have been chosen

Mood

Besides having tense, voice, person, and number, verbs are also said to have mood. **The mood indicates the way the speaker views the action or state of the verb.** Is the speaker making a statement of fact, asking a question, or expressing doubt?

There are three moods in English: indicative, imperative, and subjunctive. The *indicative* mood makes a statement or asks a question. It is the most frequently used mood in English.

The tractor <u>is</u> a John Deere.
   The sentence makes a statement.

<u>Is</u> the typewriter an IBM?
   The sentence asks a question.

The *imperative* mood gives a command or makes a request.

<u>Open</u> the book!
<u>Open</u> the book, please.

A speaker using the imperative mood is speaking directly to one or more people.

<u>Close</u> the door, John.
   The speaker is addressing one person.

<u>Close</u> all books, class.
   The speaker is addressing a group of people.

In either case the speaker is addressing the second person—*you*—either singular or plural. Thus it is generally understood that the subject of a verb in the imperative mood is *you*.

(You) <u>open</u> the book.
(You) <u>close</u> the door.

The *subjunctive* mood is the least commonly used mood in English. It reflects doubt, indicates a wish, or expresses a condition contrary to fact.

My wife wishes I <u>were</u> a millionaire.
   The verb *were* follows the indication of a wish.

If I <u>were</u> a millionaire, I would not spend my money foolishly.
   The verb *were* expresses a condition contrary to fact.

Practice Sentences 2-14

In the blanks provided, indicate whether the italicized verbs are in the indicative, imperative, or subjunctive mood.

Example: *Put* all the dishes in the cabinet, Jeremy.

imperative

1. If I *were* an author, I would write the "great American novel."

_____

2. *Clear* a wide area around the campfire.

_____

3. Carolyn *worked* both the second and third shifts last night.

_____

4. I *wish* I could afford Herman's house on Mockingbird Lane.

_____

5. Becky *studied* until 3:00 A.M. for her nursing test.

_____

6. *Keep* your eye on the ball and your left elbow straight.

_____

7. Amy, *did* you *catch* anything in the rabbit gum yesterday?

_____

8. *Send* the children outside to play.

_____

9. If I *were* a police officer, I would work in Hawaii.

_____

10. Juan *ran* the mile in under four minutes.

_____

Just as with tense, voice, person, and number, you should be careful to avoid needless shifts in mood.

Save your money, and you should buy a house.
> There is a needless shift from the imperative mood to the indicative. Rewrite the sentence to say: *Save* your money and *buy* a house.

If I were a freelance reporter and was not working at a desk eight hours a day, my life would be more interesting.
> There is a needless shift from the subjunctive mood to the indicative. Rewrite the sentence to say: If I *were* a freelance reporter and *were* not working at a desk eight hours a day, my life would be more interesting.

Adverbs

Like adjectives, adverbs are modifiers. Unlike adjectives, which modify nouns and pronouns, however, adverbs modify verbs, adjectives, and other adverbs. As we will see later, adverbs can also modify entire sentences. Adverbs answer the questions How? Where? When? Why? To what extent? and On what condition?

v.   adv.

Jackie Joyner-Kersy runs gracefully.
> *Gracefully* is an adverb modifying the verb *runs*. It answers the question *How?* Runs how? gracefully

v.   adv.   adv.

Jackie Joyner-Kersy runs very gracefully.
> Now *gracefully* still modifies the verb *runs*, but is itself modified by the adverb *very*. *Very* also answers the question *How?* How gracefully? very gracefully. *Very* modifying *gracefully* is an example of an adverb modifying another adverb.

Jackie Joyner-Kersy ran an extremely graceful race.
> *Extremely* is an adverb modifying the adjective that modifies the noun *race*. How graceful? extremely graceful.

Now you have examples of adverbs modifying verbs, other adverbs, and adjectives.

Many adverbs, like *extremely* and *gracefully*, end in *-ly*. But many adverbs do not.

adv. adv.

Joan Caterman swims quite well.
> Swims how? well (*well* modifies the verb *swims*) How well? quite well (*quite* modifies the adverb *well*)

There is the book.
> *There* is an adverb telling where the book is.

Do the assignment now.
> *Now* is an adverb telling when.

Henri will not lie.
> *Not* is an adverb that modifies the verb *will lie* by restricting its meaning.

In a sentence with the word *cannot*, remember *can* is a verb (auxiliary), but *not* is an adverb.

v. adv. v.

Tanya cannot swim.

With practice you will be able to identify adverbs easily.

Practice Sentences 2-15

Underline all the adverbs in the following sentences.

Example: Jane is <u>extremely</u> intelligent.

1. She does well in all her classes at school.

2. She easily won the Latin award.

3. Her physics instructor said she did her work efficiently and accurately.

4. In English class she organizes her papers well and expresses herself clearly.

5. Unfortunately, she does not do well in certain activities away from school.

6. She learned painfully that she would not be a famous ballerina.

7. Her first pirouette concluded ungracefully on all fours.

8. Jane ended her dancing career then and there.

9. Where could Jane go from here?

10. She went back to school immediately.

Prepositions

Prepositions show the position (pre*position*) of one word in relation to another. They are usually short words such as *in, by,* and *to.* Think of a chair, and then think of a preposition as a word that shows the position of various objects in relation to the chair.

The chair is <u>on</u> the carpet.
The chair is <u>in</u> the truck.
The chair is <u>by</u> the fireplace.
The chair is <u>behind</u> the sofa.
The chair is <u>beside</u> him.
The chair is <u>against</u> the wall.
The chair is <u>near</u> her.

The underlined words are all prepositions. Notice that *carpet, truck, fireplace, sofa, him, wall,* and *her* are all either nouns or pronouns.

A **preposition**, then, **shows the relationship between a noun or pronoun and some other word in the sentence.** The noun or pronoun referred to is generally the one that follows the preposition and is called the object of the preposition.

n.

That man with the hat always dresses well.

> *With* is a preposition that shows the relationship between the noun *hat* and the word *man*. *Hat* is the object of the preposition *with*.

n.

The driver crashed through the guardrail.

> *Through* is a preposition that shows the relationship between the noun *guardrail* and the word *crashed*. *Guardrail* is the object of the preposition *through*.

pro.

John gave the book to her.

> *To* is a preposition that shows the relationship between the pronoun *her* and the word *gave*. *Her* is the object of the preposition *to*.

Here is a list of words that are commonly used as prepositions.

*according to	from
about	*in
above	*in addition to
across	*in back of
after	*in spite of
against	instead of
along	into
among	like
around	of
at	off
*because of	*on
before	on account of
behind	over
below	past
beneath	till
beside	through
besides	throughout
between	to
beyond	toward
**but (when it means *except*)	under
by	underneath
*by means of	until
despite	up
down	upon

* Multiword prepositions are sometimes called phrasal or group prepositions.
** See page 68.

during   with
except   within
for   without

Practice Sentences 2-16

Underline the prepositions in the following sentences.

Example: The students converted an old house <u>into</u> a haunted house.

1. They took all the curtains off the wall.

2. Behind the front door they placed a loud buzzer.

3. They loosened the front step with a hammer.

4. It creaked at the least amount of pressure.

5. Before Halloween the students installed a powerful sound system.

6. The tape they played was filled with scary sounds.

7. The students supplied themselves with makeup from the drama department.

8. Strobe lights contributed to the eerie effect.

9. On Halloween night young children were frightened in the house.

10. Some parents were also unnerved in the haunted house.

Practice Sentences 2-17

In the space provided, construct sentences of your own using the prepositions listed.

Example: except *Although everyone except Helen had finished writing, she kept going until she had said what she wanted to say.*

1. under _____

_____

2. around _____

_____

3. without _____

_____

4. above _____

_____

5. between _____

_____

Conjunctions

Conjunctions are connecting words. They connect words and word groups.

> Carol and Ted have an ideal relationship.
>> *And* connects the words *Carol* and *Ted*.

> Either Renée or Barbara will be married by the end of the year.
>> *Either . . . or* connects the words *Renée* and *Barbara*.

> Eddie will go to the game if it doesn't rain.
>> *If* connects *Eddie will go to the game* to *it doesn't rain*.

Conjunctions are classified as either coordinate or subordinate.
>> *Coordinate conjunctions* connect words of equal grammatical units.

> Maples and oaks are good shade trees.
>> *And* connects the equal grammatical units *maples* and *oaks* (noun subjects).

> I drove through the city and into the desert.
>> *And* connects the equal grammatical units *through the city* and *into the desert* (prepositional phrases).

> Alfred loves his dog Pug, but Pug bites him at every opportunity.
>> *But* connects the equal grammatical units *Alfred loves his dog Pug* and *Pug bites him at every opportunity* (main clauses).

The coordinate conjunctions are *and, or, but, for, yet, nor,* and sometimes *so. Correlative conjunctions* are coordinate conjunctions that are used in pairs.

> My watch is either in the cabinet or on the table.
>> *Either . . . or* connects the equal grammatical units *in the cabinet* and *on the table*.

Common correlative conjunctions are *both . . . and, either . . . or, neither . . . nor,* and *not only . . . but also.*

The other type of conjunction is subordinate. The *subordinate conjunction* connects unequal grammatical units (see Chapter 4).

> Although I studied diligently, I could not make an A on the test.
> *Although* connects the unequal grammatical units *Although I studied diligently* and *I could not make an A on the test.*

Conjunctions will be explained in more detail in Chapter 4, on clauses. Nevertheless, you may find the following partial list of subordinate conjunctions helpful.

after	as though	since	until
although	because	so that	when
as	before	than	whenever
as if	if	though	wherever
as much as	in order that	unless	while
as long as			

Notice that some subordinate conjunctions can also be prepositions. If such a word introduces a group of related words that does not contain a subject and a verb, it is a preposition. If it introduces a group of related words that does contain a subject and a verb, the word is a subordinate conjunction.

> After the dance everyone went home.
> *After* is a preposition introducing the group of related words not containing a subject and a verb: *after the dance.*

> After the dance came to an end, everyone went home.
> *After* is a subordinate conjunction introducing the group of related words containing a subject and a verb: *After the dance came to an end.*

Practice Sentences 2-18

Underline the coordinate conjunctions in the following sentences.

Example: I attended the board meeting, <u>but</u> I was not impressed.

1. The company president droned on and on.

2. He said production was up, but sales were down.

3. He threatened that either sales would increase or some sales personnel would be eliminated.

4. He was straightforward and factual.

5. But he was also repetitious.

6. He brought up the same points time and time again.

7. Some of the sales personnel had been slack and they knew it.

8. Some of them already had new jobs, and they were just waiting until their positions became available.

9. Some just listened to the president and laughed.

10. They knew that a $3.5 million profit and a huge untapped market wasn't bad for a small, family-owned business.

Practice Sentences 2-19

Underline the subordinate conjunctions in the following sentences.

Example: <u>Before</u> you buy your son an official NFL football, take him to see a game.

1. Mark each part as you remove it from the engine.

2. If you get your tackle together, we can go fishing.

3. Although I made a good grade on the last test, my average is still low.

4. My roommate will be ready to go when he finds his shoes.

5. My printer continues to run paper through it after the power is turned off.

6. Unless you are willing to work hard, do not apply for a job at Western Iron Works.

7. Please do not talk so much while I am trying to think.

8. Jack probably paid too much for that lamp since it is not a genuine antique.

9. Arlene turned Ronnie down when he proposed to her.

10. Although Roy was wearing snake chaps, he was bitten on the hand.

Interjections

Interjections are words or groups of words that express strong emotion. Although they add little to the meaning of a sentence, they are considered a part of speech. Generally they come at the beginning of a sentence, but not always.

Heavens! How could you make such a mess?
    Heavens is an interjection.

Gee whiz, that is a good paint job.
    Gee whiz is an interjection.

Damn! That hammer didn't do my finger any good at all.
    Damn is an interjection.

I'll do the best I can, by golly.
    By golly is an interjection.

Practice Sentences 2-20

Underline the interjections in the following sentences.

    Example: Holy Toledo! That pan was hot!

1. Good heavens, Bob, let me help you with that.

2. Ouch! I dropped a hammer on my sore toe!

3. Good grief, Ed, why don't you just ask her if she will go out with you?

4. At least pick up a drill and look like you're doing something, for heaven's sake!

5. Gee, after three days of rain I hope we can finally have our picnic.

Identifying Parts of Speech

You should realize that the part of speech of a word depends on how the word is used in a sentence. The same word can be one of several parts of speech, depending on its context or use in a particular sentence. The word *but*, for instance, is commonly used as a conjunction, as in the sentence *Mary went to the beach, but I stayed home.* On the other hand, the word *but* is a preposition in the sentence *Everyone went to the championship game but me.* Look at these different uses of the word *yellow*:

Yellow is my favorite color. (noun)
Mary has a yellow car. (adjective)
The shirt yellowed in the washing machine. (verb)

Do not be misled into thinking that what you call a preposition in one sentence will always be used as a preposition. When in doubt, consult a dictionary. A good dictionary will classify a word according to the various parts of speech the word can be and give examples of usage.

Review Exercise 2-A   Using Verb Tense, Mood, and Voice

Make up one sentence that contains each of the following verbs.

Example: A verb in the third person singular, past tense

Mary broke her arm yesterday.

1. a verb in the passive voice

   _____

   _____

2. a verb in the indicative mood

   _____

   _____

3. a verb in the first person, present tense

   _____

   _____

4. a verb in the active voice

   _____

   _____

5. a verb in the imperative mood

   _____

   _____

6. a verb in the first person plural, present perfect tense, active voice

   _____

   _____

7. a verb in the third person singular, past perfect tense, passive voice

   _____

   _____

8. a verb in the subjunctive mood

_____

_____

9. a verb in the future present tense, passive voice

_____

_____

10. a verb in the past tense, active voice

_____

_____

Review Exercise 2-B   Using Verbs Correctly (I)

In the space provided, rewrite these sentences to correct any errors in tense, voice, person, number, or mood.

Example: Regina and Tim talk and planned to get married.

Regina and Tim talked and planned to get married.

1. They was both excited about the wedding.

_____

_____

2. Tim had always suppose he would be more nervous about marriage.

_____

_____

3. Regina cries when she saw the ring.

_____

_____

4. She wishes she was a bride already.

_____

_____

5. Tim has done gone to six different realtors.

_____

_____

6. Tim and Regina both were use to working with realtors and lawyers.

_____

_____

7. One man came as far as 300 miles.

    _____

    _____

8. He was a flat-foot dancer, and a special routine had been worked out by him.

    _____

    _____

9. However, he wished he would not have eaten so much.

    _____

    _____

10. He had dance beautifully in the past, but his performance this year was awful.

    _____

    _____

Review Exercise 2-C   Using Verbs Correctly (II)

In the space provided, rewrite these sentences to correct any errors in tense, voice, person, number, or mood.

Example: If he could dance, he will try out for the school play.

If he could dance, he would try out for the school play.

1. The Belton County Historical Society has held its annual historical celebration last week.

_____

_____

2. Musicians and craftsmen was on hand for entertainment.

_____

_____

3. One folklorist sung several ballads.

_____

_____

4. Several of the needleworkers displayed her quilting techniques.

_____

_____

5. If you were at the celebration, you would have had a good time.

_____

_____

6. Some delicious food was served, and everyone enjoyed eating it.

_____

_____

7. They talk to each other and decided to buy the house on Elm Street.

   _____

   _____

8. Regina and Tim paid the realtor and the house was owned by them.

   _____

   _____

9. However, they spend more than they planned to.

   _____

   _____

10. They paid $30,000 more than they were suppose to according to their budget.

    _____

    _____

Review Exercise 2-D Identifying Parts of Speech (I)

In the blanks provided, indicate the part of speech of each word in the sentence (noun, pronoun, adjective, verb, adverb, preposition, conjunction, or interjection).

Example: The rabbit died.

died   *verb*

Although the sewing machine is old, parts are still available.

1. Although   _____

2. the   _____

3. sewing   _____

4. machine   _____

5. is   _____

6. old   _____

7. parts   _____

8. are   _____

9. still   _____

10. available   _____

Review Exercise 2-E   Identifying Parts of Speech (II)

In the blanks provided, indicate the part of speech of each word in the sentence (noun, pronoun, adjective, verb, adverb, preposition, conjunction, or interjection).

Example: Pour the nitroglycerine carefully.

carefully   _____*adverb*_____

Gee, my chemistry experiment in the laboratory went poorly today.

1. Gee   _____

2. my   _____

3. chemistry   _____

4. experiment   _____

5. in   _____

6. the   _____

7. laboratory   _____

8. went   _____

9. poorly   _____

10. today   _____

Review Exercise 2-F   Using Parts of Speech

Compose a sentence that contains each of the following parts of speech. Underline the featured part of speech.

Example: an adverb

Micky hit the ball well.

1. a pronoun

_____

_____

2. an adjective

_____

_____

3. a preposition

_____

_____

4. a passive verb

_____

_____

5. a possessive pronoun

_____

_____

6. a coordinate conjunction

_____

_____

7. a verb in the subjunctive mood

_____

_____

8. an interjection

_____

_____

9. a pronoun in the third person plural

_____

_____

10. a verb in the present perfect tense

_____

_____

3

Phrases

A phrase is a group of related words that does not contain a subject and a verb. Phrases also act as particular parts of speech. That is, the words that make up a phrase may act together as one part of speech. For example, in the sentence *Dave Kingman hit the ball over the fence*, the phrase *over the fence* functions as an adverb because it answers the question Where? The two main types of phrases are prepositional phrases and verbal phrases.

Prepositional Phrases

A prepositional phrase begins with a preposition, ends with the noun or pronoun object, and contains all the modifiers in between, if any. In the earlier phrase *over the fence, over* is the preposition, *fence* is the noun object, and *the* is the modifier. Prepositional phrases almost always function as either adjectives or adverbs.

> The man in the wool suit is uncomfortable.
> > *In the wool suit* modifies the noun *man* and is therefore an adjective phrase. Which man?

> The cassette recorder with a built-in radio is expensive.
> > *With a built-in radio* modifies the noun *recorder* and is thus an adjective phrase. Which recorder?

> The principal ran the banner up the flagpole.
> > *Up the flagpole* modifies the verb *ran* and is therefore an adverb phrase. Ran where? up the flagpole

> There was no game because of the rain.
> > *Because of the rain* modifies the verb *was* and is thus an adverb phrase. Why was there no game? because of the rain

Clearly, then, prepositional phrases are groups of related words that do not contain subjects and verbs and that function as adjectives or adverbs.

Practice Sentences 3-1

Review the list of prepositions on pages 62 and 63 before beginning this exercise. Underline the prepositional phrases in the following sentences.

Example: Gary went <u>to the woods</u>.

1. He was hunting for squirrels.

2. One ran across the road immediately.

3. He could not get his gun ready in time.

4. Gary hunted diligently for two more hours.

5. He didn't see any squirrels in the trees.

6. Neither did he spot any on the ground.

7. At sundown he walked to his truck and smoked a cigarette.

8. He put the gun in the truck and relaxed.

9. Then a squirrel walked slowly between his feet.

10. Frustrated, Gary threw a rock at the squirrel and went home.

Verbal Phrases

A verbal is a word that is derived from a verb but that functions as another part of speech. A verbal phrase consists of a verbal and all its modifiers and objects. There are three types of verbals: infinitives, participles, and gerunds.

Infinitives

An infinitive begins with the word *to* and is followed by a verb form.

> <u>To conserve</u> energy is a wise policy.
> > *To conserve* is an infinitive. It begins with the word *to* and is followed by a verb form, *conserve*.

> John took his date <u>to the movies</u>.
> > *To the movies* is not an infinitive. Though the phrase begins with the word *to*, it is not followed by a verb form. *To the movies* is a prepositional phrase.

Like verbs, infinitives may have auxiliaries that indicate tense and voice: *to conserve, to have conserved, to be conserved, to have been conserved, to be conserving, to have been conserving.*

> The office building <u>to have been auctioned</u> burned last week.
> > *To have been auctioned* is the present perfect tense, passive voice form of the infinitive.

Infinitives also retain enough verb qualities to take objects.

> The group <u>to present the play</u> is well trained.
>> The infinitive is *to present*. To present what? play. *Play* is the object of the infinitive.

An infinitive phrase consists of the infinitive, its object if it has one, and its modifiers if it has any.

> <u>To elect a qualified president</u> is our goal.
>> *To elect* is the infinitive, *president* is the object of the infinitive, and *a* and *qualified* are modifiers.

One of the modifiers may be another phrase.

> <u>To elect a qualified president for next year</u> is our goal.
>> The prepositional phrase *for next year* is another modifier in the infinitive phrase. Thus, the infinitive phrase contains a prepositional phrase within it.

Infinitive phrases can function as either nouns, adjectives, or adverbs.

> <u>To run the mile under 3:50</u> is every miler's dream.
>> *To run the mile under 3:50* is an infinitive phrase used as a noun since it is the subject of the sentence. It answers the question Who or What? asked in front of the verb. Who or what is? to run the mile under 3:50

Notice that the whole phrase functions as a one-word noun. If the sentence read *Speed is every miler's dream*, then the subject would be the one-word noun *speed* rather than the phrase *to run the mile under 3:50*.

As adjective phrases, infinitives usually follow the noun or pronoun they modify.

> The obstacle <u>to be overcome</u> is nothing to a man of his ability.
>> *To be overcome* is an infinitive phrase used as an adjective modifying the noun *obstacle*. Notice the phrase follows the word it modifies.

Finally, infinitives can function as adverbs.

> Jack married the banker's daughter <u>to get a job at the bank</u>.
>> *To get a job at the bank* is an infinitive phrase functioning as an adverb. The phrase modifies the verb *married* and answers the question *why*.

Occasionally, infinitives come at the beginning of sentences and modify the whole sentence rather than any particular word in the sentence. Since the most important word in a sentence is generally the verb, however, such infinitive phrases are said to function as adverbs.

To be frank about it, I haven't had any luck with your TV set.
> *To be frank about it* modifies the whole sentence and is therefore considered an infinitive phrase functioning as an adverb.

Practice Sentences 3-2

In the blanks provided, indicate whether the italicized infinitive phrases function as adjectives, adverbs, or nouns.

Example: The tooth *to be pulled* is badly infected.

_____*adjective*_____

1. Michelle wants *to move this afternoon.*

   _____

2. Albert married the banker *to get a job at the bank.*

   _____

3. The telephone *to be installed* costs $450.

   _____

4. *To start as middle linebacker* is Jeff's goal.

   _____

5. Dee plans *to be president of her own company within six years.*

   _____

6. *To be perfectly honest,* the food at the new restaurant is terrible.

   _____

7. Geneva was interested in all the property *to be sold at the auction.*

   _____

8. Brad wants *to be nominated president of the senior class.*

   _____

9. The man *to be tried next month* is my neighbor.

   _____

10. *To make money for his tuition*, Rodney works at McDonald's.

Participles

Participles are two principal parts of the verb: either the past participle or the present participle. The past participle of the verb is the form that belongs in the blank: I have _____. If the verb is a regular verb, then the past participle will end in *-ed*.

> I have <u>stopped</u>.
> I have <u>looked</u>.
> I have <u>intended</u>.

If the verb is an irregular verb, then the past participle will end in something other than *-ed*, the most common endings being *-en* or *-t*.

> I have *chosen*.
> I have *bitten*.
> I have *slept*.
> I have *bent*.

The present participle of the verb is the form that belongs in the blank: I am _____*ing*. The present participles of both regular and irregular verbs end in *-ing*.

> I am <u>stopping</u>.
> I am <u>looking</u>.
> I am <u>intending</u>.

> I am <u>choosing</u>.
> I am <u>biting</u>.
> I am <u>sleeping</u>.
> I am <u>bending</u>.

Remember, the preceding examples are verbs, not verbals. In the sentences *I have done* and *I am stopping*, *have done* and *am stopping* are verbs; they express action. To be a verbal, a verb form must function as another part of speech. Participles as verbals must function as adjectives.

> I am working.
> > *Am working* is a verb.

> John Draughn, working in his garden, spotted a rattlesnake.
> > *Working in his garden* is not a verb. *Working* is a verbal functioning as an adjective modifying the noun *John Draughn*. *Working* is a participle.

In summary, the most common endings of participles are *-ed, -en, -t,* and *-ing.* But remember, any verb form that belongs in the blank *I have* ____ can be a participle; thus a few participles will end in something other than *-ed, -en, -t,* or *-ing.*

I have <u>blown</u>.
I have <u>done</u>.
I have <u>rung</u>.
I have <u>heard</u>.

Participles as verbals always function as adjectives. That is all they can ever be. Like infinitives, participles are derived from verbs and therefore can have objects and modifiers. A participial phrase usually begins with a participle, ends with its object, and contains all the modifiers.

<u>Selecting Ann Abrams for the job</u>, the executive feels confident of his choice.
> *Selecting* is the participle, *Ann Abrams* is the object of the participle, and *for the job* is a modifying phrase. The whole participial phrase *selecting Ann Abrams for the job* is used as an adjective modifying the noun *executive.*

Since participles are derived from verbs, they can have different tense forms just as infinitives can.

<u>Having been elected to the board</u>, Carlos was elated.
> The entire participial phrase is underlined. The participle itself is *having been elected.* This is the perfect passive participle form. The whole phrase *having been elected to the board* functions as an adjective modifying the noun *Carlos.*

When participial phrases come at the beginning of sentences, they should modify the first noun or pronoun that comes after the comma that sets off the introductory participial phrase. In the last example, *having been elected to the board* modifies the noun *Carlos.* **Participial phrases that do not modify the first noun or pronoun that follows them are said to be dangling.**

<u>Blowing the litter everywhere</u>, the street was a mess due to the wind.
> *Blowing the litter everywhere* is a participial phrase, but it cannot modify the noun *street.* The street cannot blow the litter around. The sentence should be rewritten to avoid the dangling participle: Blowing the litter everywhere, the wind made a mess of the street.

<u>Working with her hair for hours</u>, the dryer scorched Sharon's scalp.
> As written, the sentence says the dryer was working on Sharon's hair for hours, a truly talented dryer.

Can you rewrite the preceding sentence so that it no longer contains a dangling participle?

Practice Sentences 3-3

Each of the ten sentences in this exercise contains a dangling participle. Rewrite each sentence so that the participle is not dangling.

> **Example:** Cleaning the house thoroughly, the refrigerator gave Albert the most trouble.
>
> *Cleaning the house thoroughly, Albert had the most trouble with the refrigerator.*

1. Racing down the hill, a tree stopped the children's sled.

   _____

   _____

2. Having studied diligently for the test, a good grade was Craig's reward.

   _____

   _____

3. Sleeping outside on a cold January night, the new sleeping bag still wasn't enough to keep Angela warm.

   _____

   _____

4. Having purchased a new tennis racket, Jason's game showed no improvement.

   _____

   _____

5. Having been married for six years, the ring on Adrian's finger began to seem like a burden.

   _____

   _____

6. Finished with the test, the papers were turned in by the students.

_____

_____

7. Being scientists, the white mice were studied by the professors.

_____

_____

8. Repaired by the jeweler for $45, Mary still could not get the watch to keep good time.

_____

_____

9. Determined to do a good job, the house was painted slowly by Paulette.

_____

_____

10. Spayed at the local animal clinic, Shannon now had a "safe" pet.

_____

_____

Participial phrases do not necessarily have to come at the beginning of sentences. When one does not, it will generally come immediately after the noun or pronoun it modifies.

The car being repaired with body filler is on the back lot.
   Being repaired with body filler modifies the noun _car_.

Van Adler is the teller making all the mistakes.
Making all the mistakes is the participial phrase modifying the noun _teller_.

Occasionally, however, participial phrases are tacked on to the end of sentences, far removed from the words they modify. The sentence you just read is an example. _Far removed from the words they modify_ is a participial phrase that modifies the noun _phrases_. Here is another example:

The old veteran can be seen every morning, shuffling his feet and hanging his head.

> The two participial phrases *shuffling his feet* and *hanging his head* are tacked on to the end of the sentence and modify *veteran*.

Such sentences can be effective if used sparingly.

Practice Sentences 3-4

In the blanks provided, indicate the noun or pronoun that the italicized participial phrase modifies.

> **Example:** Reba, *having lived on a farm all of her life*, was frightened when she first saw New York City.

<u>   *Reba*   </u>

1. Thad, *selected by his classmates*, represented the student body at the convention.

   _____

2. The old man left the police station in disgust, *mumbling and grumbling at every step.*

   _____

3. The woman *chosen office manager* was well qualified for the job.

   _____

4. *Going on break with the class at last*, Missy learned that the other students wouldn't harm her.

   _____

5. Kristy, *dressed in a formal gown*, was shocked to find everyone else wearing jeans.

   _____

6. *Driving his father's Cadillac*, Bobby was embarrassed when the car wouldn't start in his girlfriend's driveway.

   _____

7. *Sounding as though he were just learning to talk,* Freddy left the dentist's office with his new set of false teeth.

_____

8. David, *having slept for eleven hours,* was rudely awakened by his father.

_____

9. Rebecca, *missing her boyfriend away at college,* got in her car and drove five hundred miles to see him.

_____

10. After the performance, the circus janitor cleaned up the mess, *turning up his nose in disgust.*

_____

Gerunds

The third type of verbal is called a gerund. Gerunds are personal participles and thus always end in *-ing*. A gerund always functions as a noun. Though both participles *and* gerunds can end in *-ing*, participles can function only as adjectives and gerunds can function only as nouns.

Like other nouns, gerunds are generally either subjects, direct objects, or objects of prepositions.

Running is a good way to stay trim.
> *Running* is the subject of the verb *is*.

Maria enjoys running.
> *Running* is the direct object of *enjoys*.

Robert Hamstring stays in shape by running.
> *Running* is the object of the preposition *by*.

Like participles and infinitives, gerunds can also take objects and modifiers. A gerund phrase consists of the gerund, its object if there is one, and any modifiers. In the gerund phrase *doing the laundry, doing* is the gerund, *laundry* is the object of the gerund, and *the* is the modifier.

Read the following sentence:

Jogging five laps leisurely is good exercise.
> *Jogging five laps leisurely* is the gerund phrase. *Jogging* is the gerund, *five* is an adjective modifying the noun *laps*, which is

the object of the gerund, and *leisurely* is an adverb modifying the gerund *jogging* telling how. But don't gerunds function as nouns? Yes, they do, and adverbs are not supposed to modify nouns. The reason the adverb *leisurely* can modify the gerund *jogging* is that gerunds are verbals. Since verbals are derived from verbs, a verbal used as a noun can retain enough qualities of a verb to be modified by an adverb. In a similar manner adverbs can modify infinitives used as nouns.

To shoot accurately is every hunter's desire.

    Accurately is an adverb modifying the infinitive *to shoot*, which is the subject of the verb *is*.

Practice Sentences 3-5

In the blanks provided, indicate whether the italicized gerund phrases function as subjects (subj.), *direct objects* (d.o.), *or objects of prepositions* (o.p.).

Example: *Watching The Today Show* is a ritual with Norbert.

        subj.

1. Jim really enjoys *hunting deer.*

        _____

2. The astronomer passed his time by *looking through a telescope.*

        _____

3. *Looking at girls* is a pleasant way to pass the time.

        _____

4. Some, however, may prefer *looking at guys.*

        _____

5. Alicia has become a successful lawyer by *preparing her cases thoroughly.*

        _____

6. *Washing clothes* always seems to be done on Wednesdays.

        _____

7. Upon *receiving the award*, Herman was so emotional he couldn't speak.

———————————————

8. Billy likes *working for charitable organizations*.

———————————————

9. *Cleaning fish afterward* is not the best part of a fishing trip.

———————————————

10. Becky often thinks about *operating a day-care center*.

———————————————

You should not have trouble with participles and gerunds if you remember that participles (which do not always end in -*ing*) are always used as adjectives and that gerunds are always nouns. Just because a verbal ends in -*ing*, do not immediately think "gerund." Remember, the -*ing* verbal could be either a participle or a gerund. Look to see if the verbal is used as an adjective or as a noun. If the verbal ending in -*ing* is not the subject, direct object, or object of a preposition (the most common functions of a noun), it is probably a participle. Also, if a gerund appears at the beginning of a sentence, it is usually the subject of a sentence.

Getting the car ready for the race was an expensive project.
Getting the car ready for the race is the subject of the verb *was*.

If a participle comes at the beginning of a sentence, it should modify the first noun or pronoun following the verbal.

Mowing the lawn every Saturday, John established a ritual for himself.
Mowing the lawn every Saturday is a participial phrase modifying the noun *John*. *Participial* is the adjective form of the noun participle, and thus the term used to describe this type of phrase.

Notice that a participial phrase appearing at the beginning of a sentence is set off from the main clause with a comma. On the other hand, a gerund at the beginning of a sentence is not generally set off with a comma, because it is undesirable to separate the subject from the verb with a comma.

The main thing to remember, however, is that participles are always adjectives and gerunds are always nouns. Look to see whether the verbal names (gerund) or modifies (participle). In your own writing, participles and gerunds should be no problem. Use them in your writing. Though no technique should be used too often, verbal phrases—especially introductory participial phrases—can make your writing lively.

Without verbal phrase: Elaine is ready to serve and sees her opponent is not in position for a backhand return.

With verbal phrase: Seeing her opponent is not in position for a backhand return, Elaine plans to put her serve in the corner.

Notice how the introductory participial phrase alters the subject-verb pattern and immediately gets the reader's attention with the action word *seeing*.

Practice Sentences 3-6

In the blanks provided, indicate whether the italicized phrase is a participle or a gerund.

Example: *Playing in the band* supplements Danny's income.

_____*gerund*_____

1. *Watching so much TV,* the children seem to be in poor shape.

_____

2. They enjoy *looking at all types of programs.*

_____

3. Cartoons, *being their favorites,* seem to be on all day.

_____

4. *Watching detective shows and situation comedies* entertains them in the afternoons.

_____

5. They are seldom seen *viewing soap operas or westerns.*

_____

6. *Running and playing around the neighborhood* seem to be things of the past.

_____

7. *Sitting in front of the tube all day,* the children get no exercise.

_____

8. *Watching TV programs*, however, is not the only entertainment provided by the set.

   _____

9. *Playing computer games like Atari and Nintendo*, the children can stay in front of the tube when there are no programs on of interest.

   _____

10. To further prevent them from *getting any exercise*, there are, of course, movies and shows on videotape.

    _____

Review Exercise 3-A   Identifying Types of Phrases (I)

In the blanks provided, indicate whether the italicized phrase is a preposition, infinitive, participle, or gerund.

Example: Tim earned money *by cutting trees down with a chain saw.*

preposition)

1. *Working from 6:00 A.M. to 6:00 P.M. every day* was very hard on him.

   _____

2. *Not being an early riser,* Tim had difficulty getting to the job site on time.

   _____

3. *To teach him a lesson,* his boss gave him the heaviest chain saw to operate.

   _____

4. Tim, *being a fast learner,* caught on quickly.

   _____

5. He decided that getting up early was a good habit *to develop.*

   _____

6. *Having worked hard at the job for a couple of months,* Tim noticed he was getting in good physical shape.

   _____

7. Unfortunately, Tim didn't want *to get in good physical shape.*

   _____

8. Tim preferred *to eat pizza and watch television.*

   _____

9. *Running a chain saw,* however, leaves little time for pizza and TV.

   _____

10. Besides this, the job was miserably hot as the trees *to be cut* had to be removed during the summer.

_____

Review Exercise 3-B   Identifying Types of Phrases (II)

In the blanks provided, indicate whether the italicized phrase is a preposition, infinitive, participle, or gerund.

Example: The car, *having been sold for $550,* was worth at least $2,000.

_____*participle*_____

1. *Growing up in a big city* made Jack street-smart.

   _____

2. Meredith decided *to cast her fate to the wind.*

   _____

3. Eunice enjoys *working with computers.*

   _____

4. Gladys earns her living by *selling real estate.*

   _____

5. Do not park *near a fire hydrant.*

   _____

6. *Selected for the field assignment,* Terry felt honored and challenged.

   _____

7. The poor man can be seen every day, *standing at the street corner.*

   _____

8. *Parking in a no parking zone* can be hazardous to your health.

   _____

9. Margaret is looking forward to the new carpet *to be installed this morning.*

   _____

10. The woman *appointed chairperson of the organization* knew there was much work to be done.

    _____

Review Exercise 3-C   *Using Prepositional and Verbal Phrases*

Make up sentences that contain the phrases indicated.

Example: participial phrase at the beginning of a sentence

Having studied until 4:00 a.m. the night before, Jenny was exhausted when she took the test.

1. gerund phrase used as a direct object

   _____

   _____

2. infinitive phrase in present perfect tense

   _____

   _____

3. participial phrase following the noun it modifies

   _____

   _____

4. infinitive phrase used as direct object

   _____

   _____

5. gerund phrase used as subject

   _____

   _____

6. prepositional phrase functioning as an adjective

   _____

   _____

7. infinitive phrase used as subject

_____

_____

8. gerund phrase used as object of a preposition

_____

_____

9. prepositional phrase functioning as an adverb

_____

_____

10. infinitive phrase functioning as an adjective

_____

_____

4

Clauses

In Chapter 2 you learned that conjunctions are connecting words; they connect words and word groups. The two main word groups conjunctions connect are phrases and clauses. Remember that a phrase is a group of related words that does not contain a subject and a verb. *At the man's home* is a phrase, a prepositional phrase. **A clause is a group of related words that does contain a subject and a verb.** *Until the checkered flag was waved* is a clause. The subject is *flag* and the verb is *was waved*. Phrases and clauses can be quite similar, the main difference being that a clause contains a subject and a verb whereas a phrase does not contain either a subject or a verb. Look at the following examples.

Before the dance my date took me out to dinner.

Before the dance began, my date took me out to dinner.

In the first example, *before the dance* is a phrase; it does not contain a subject and a verb. In the second example, *before the dance began* is a clause; it contains the subject *dance* and the verb *began*. The two sentences are similar in meaning, but the structure of the word groups is quite different.

Main Clauses and
Subordinate Clauses

There are two types of clauses: main clauses and subordinate clauses. Of course, because they are clauses, both types contain subjects and verbs. A *main clause* expresses a complete thought.

I received an A on my theme.
> The sentence contains a subject and a verb and expresses a complete thought. The main clause *I received an A on my theme* can stand alone. It does not need anything else to complete its meaning.

Sometimes the subject of a main clause may be a pronoun. Because the noun for which the pronoun stands will be clear in the context of the other sentences, such a main clause still expresses a complete thought. For example, in the sentence *She is perhaps the best American poet of the nineteenth century,* the pronoun *she* would be clearly understandable to a reader who has been reading about Emily Dickinson. In determining whether a clause expresses a complete thought, do not let pronouns confuse you.

The other type of clause is a *subordinate clause.* A subordinate clause does not express a complete thought. It depends on a main clause to complete its meaning.

> If I were taller, I could play center on the basketball team.
> > *If I were taller* is a subordinate clause. It does not express a complete thought; it cannot stand alone. It depends on the main clause *I could play center on the basketball team* to complete its meaning.

Coordinate conjunctions (*and, or, nor, but, for, yet, so*) can connect only words or word groups of equal rank. Therefore, they can connect two main clauses or two subordinate clauses. They cannot connect a main clause to a subordinate clause because main clauses and subordinate clauses are not of equal rank.

> John hid the ring in the attic, but Mary found it.
> > The conjunction *but* connects the main clauses *John hid the ring in the attic* and *Mary found it.*

> Whoever is the most dependable and whoever finishes first will receive a bonus.
> > The conjunction *and* connects the two subordinate clauses *whoever is the most dependable* and *whoever finishes first.*

> Whoever finishes first and he will receive a bonus.
> > Clearly the sentence is incorrect. A coordinate conjunction cannot connect a subordinate clause (*whoever finishes first*) and a main clause (*he will receive a bonus*).

Practice Sentences 4-1

Underline the main clauses in the sentences below.

Example: Although the game was close during the first half, <u>Indiana University won 94 to 76</u>.

1. Cliff Davis ran the offense for the Hoosiers.

2. He had fifteen assists, but he only scored eight points.

3. Mark Hammonds, Indiana's center, scored thirty-two points, although he only had five rebounds.

4. Although he is not usually a starter, Carlyle Rankin was Indiana's most valuable player.

5. He had twenty-three points, thirteen rebounds, and eleven assists.

6. Carlyle was up for the game because his high school buddy played for Iowa.

7. Carlyle's jump shots in the lane turned the tide in the second half.

8. When the two teams play later in the season, Indiana will need another strong performance by Rankin.

9. Indiana's coach praised Rankin, of course, but he also complimented the team play of Iowa.

10. If Carlyle is healthy next Wednesday, he will start against the University of Illinois.

Subordinate conjunctions, on the other hand, can connect only word groups of unequal rank. In other words, they connect main clauses and subordinate clauses.

> Until the project is completed, Barbara will not leave the laboratory. The word *until* subordinates the clause *until the project is completed* and connects it to the main clause *Barbara will not leave the laboratory. Until* is a subordinate conjunction.

> Randy made a donation because he felt the money would help. *Because* is a subordinate conjunction connecting the subordinate clause *because he felt the money would help* to the main clause *Randy made a donation.*

The following list of words often used as subordinating conjunctions may help you recognize both the conjunctions themselves and the subordinate clauses they introduce:

after	as though	since	until
although	because	so that	when
as	before	than	whenever
as if	if	though	whereas
as much as	in order that	unless	wherever
as long as			while

Good writers often use subordinate clauses to include specific details that qualify or explain a main clause. The most important point is usually stated in the main clause. It is sometimes difficult to tell what a writer's main point is when main clauses and subordinate clauses are used carelessly. Look at the following main clauses.

> June wants a lucrative career.
> June goes to law school.

If your main point is that June goes to law school, you might say

Since June wants a lucrative career, she is going to law school.

On the other hand, if your main point is that June wants a lucrative career, you might say

June wants a lucrative career when she finishes law school.

Be aware that different subordinate conjunctions can serve different purposes. The subordinate conjunction *because* generally explains *why*.

Why?

Scott walked three miles in a blizzard *because his car broke down*.

The subordinate conjunctions *if* and *unless* answer the question: On what condition?

On what condition?

If you do your homework on Tuesday, you can go to the carnival Wednesday night.

You will not obtain your realtor's license

On what condition?

unless you study for the state licensing examination.

Some subordinate conjunctions tell when an event will occur.

When?

The annual Snow Bowl will be held *when the first snowflakes fall*.

Clearly, subordinate clauses are useful tools for writers.

Practice Sentences 4-2

Underline the subordinate clauses in the following sentences.

Example: Tommy wanted to go to the top of the Washington Monument <u>before he went home</u>.

1. Naturally, I hoped that he would change his mind.

2. There was a line of people that wrapped around the base of the Monument twice.

3. If the line had been a lot shorter, we would have gone to the top of the Monument then.

4. Instead, Tommy decided that he wanted to go to the Lincoln Memorial.

5. We saw the Reflecting Pool which leads up to the Memorial.

6. When we were in the Memorial, the seated figure of Lincoln looked enormous.

7. That all Americans will always be free was Lincoln's dream.

8. Because he was only seven, however, Tommy wasn't greatly impressed by such noble sentiments.

9. When we returned to the Washington Monument, the line was much shorter.

10. Tommy was happy as he looked out of the windows atop the Monument.

More About Subordinate Clauses

Subordinate clauses are sometimes introduced by *relative pronouns* rather than by subordinate conjunctions. A relative pronoun is a pronoun that can connect a subordinate clause to a main clause. A few of the most common relative pronouns are *who, whom, whose, which*, and *that*. Relative pronouns serve much the same function in subordinate clauses as subordinate conjunctions; however, since pronouns can be subjects and objects of verbs whereas conjunctions cannot be, a distinction must be made between the two.

> Do the job while you are feeling well.
>> *While* is a subordinate conjunction connecting the subordinate clause *while you are feeling well* to the main clause *do the job*.

> The man who will win the race must practice constantly.
>> *Who* connects the subordinate clause *who will win the race* to the main clause *the man must practice constantly*. However, *who* cannot be considered a subordinate conjunction. A subordinate conjunction cannot be the subject of a verb, but *who* is the subject of the verb *will win*. Thus, *who* is given the special name relative pronoun. The word *who* is a pronoun taking the place of the noun *man*. The sentence literally means *The man (the man will win the race) must practice constantly*.

Relative pronouns eliminate repetition. Look at the following examples.

Without a relative pronoun: Ms. Carr works sixty hours a week. Ms. Carr wants a more responsible position with the company.

With a relative pronoun: Ms. Carr, *who* works sixty hours a week, wants a more responsible position with the company.

Notice that the sentence with the relative pronoun combines two sentences into one and names Ms. Carr only once. As we mentioned, relative pronouns connect subordinate clauses to main clauses. Here, *who works sixty hours a week* is a subordinate clause. Without the main clause, *Ms.*

Carr wants a more responsible position with the company, the subordinate clause is incomplete.

Adjective Clauses

Subordinate clauses are like phrases in that they function as either adjectives, adverbs, or nouns. Adjective clauses modify nouns or pronouns and generally follow the words they modify. Adjective clauses are frequently introduced by relative pronouns. Just like one-word adjectives, adjective clauses answer the questions Which one? What kind? How many?

> The man <u>who repaired my car</u> graduated from MIT.
> *Who repaired my car* is an adjective clause introduced by the relative pronoun *who,* modifying the noun *man,* and answering the question Which man?

> Jackel and Swaim Company has an antique chest <u>that I want</u>.
> *That I want* is an adjective clause introduced by the relative pronoun *that,* modifying the noun *chest,* and answering the question Which chest?

It is not unusual, however, to find adjective clauses introduced by subordinate conjunctions.

> Meet me at the bar <u>where we first met</u>.
> *Where we first met* is an adjective clause modifying the noun *bar,* introduced by the subordinate conjunction *where,* and answering the question Which bar?

> Now is the time <u>when a decision must be made</u>.
> *When a decision must be made* is an adjective clause modifying the noun *time,* introduced by the subordinate conjunction *when,* and answering the question Which time?

Practice Sentences 4-3

In the following sentences, underline the adjective clauses.

> **Example:** The airplane <u>that Slim bought</u> was a disaster.

1. The wings, which were barely attached, were badly rusted.

2. The engine that he thought was sound needed an overhaul.

3. The instrument panel, which looked good to Slim, needed to be replaced.

4. Even the seats that were made of leather fell apart when Slim sat in them.

5. The tail section, which had recently been painted, was hanging on by a prayer.

6. The previous owner, whom Slim had trusted, was no longer in the state.

7. When Slim asked the man who works in the body shop for a repair estimate, the man laughed.

8. The insurance agent that Slim had worked with for years told him to forget it.

9. Slim was beginning to question the wisdom of the purchase that he had made.

10. Slim's wife, who had been with him for twelve years, suggested he sleep in the plane.

Adverb Clauses

Adverb clauses modify adjectives, verbs, or other adverbs and are introduced by subordinate conjunctions such as *where, if, when, because, although, before,* etc. Like one-word adverbs, adverb clauses answer the questions How? When? Where? Why? To what extent? and On what condition?

If I clean the house today, I can play golf this weekend.
> *If I clean the house today* is an adverb clause introduced by the subordinate conjunction *if* and answering the question On what condition?

I could not work the problem because my mind was on the game.
> *Because my mind was on the game* is an adverb clause beginning with the subordinate conjunction *because* and answering the question Why?

Mow the lawn after you go to the grocery store.
> *After you go to the grocery store* is an adverb clause beginning with the subordinate conjunction *after* and answering the question When?

Practice Sentences 4-4

Underline the adverb clauses in the following sentences.

Example: Nathan bought a truck because he hauled a lot of equipment to his land on the river.

1. When the weather was nice, he carried a gas stove, an inflatable boat, inner tubes, and several friends.

2. Nathan and his friends usually stayed until it got dark.

3. The truck was easy to pack up since it didn't have a camper top.

4. Sometimes Nathan went camping by himself because he liked time alone by the river.

5. Once when he was there by himself, a violent thunderstorm came up.

6. Even though the road was muddy, the truck came through fine.

7. On another occasion, Nathan went to the river while there was snow on the ground.

8. Although snow was up to the axle, the truck kept going.

9. Nathan returned home because he got cold.

10. We got stuck in his driveway because he could not see the ice under the snow.

Remember that adjective clauses and adverb clauses are modifying clauses. That is, they add extra information to clarify something else. Sentences that contain adjective and adverb clauses must also contain main clauses. If they did not, the sentences would not express complete thoughts.

If I clean the house today is a subordinate clause; it does not express a complete thought. On the other hand, *The man graduated from MIT, Jackel and Swaim Company has an antique chest,* and *I can play golf this weekend* are all sentences, expressing complete thoughts. Notice that modifying clauses can be omitted from sentences and the sentences still express complete thoughts. Another thing to remember in studying subordinate clauses is that the whole clause works as one word.

The <u>black</u> car needs a good coating of wax.
    Black is a one-word adjective describing *car.*

The car <u>that is painted black</u> needs a good coating of wax.
    That is painted black is an adjective clause modifying the noun *car.*

In analyzing the subordinate clause, though, you cannot say Which car? *black* car. You must say Which car? the one *that is painted black.* The words in a subordinate clause are a unit. You cannot separate the words and have the separated words modify the main clause. Again, you must consider the group of related words in the subordinate clause as one word.

Also, in studying clauses, do not be surprised to find phrases and clauses that seem to do the same thing.

The man <u>reading the road map</u> is lost.
The man <u>who is reading the road map</u> is lost.

The first sentence contains the participial phrase *reading the road map* which modifies the noun *man*. The second sentence contains the adjective clause *who is reading the road map* which modifies the noun *man*. Both the phrase and the clause do the same thing. The difference between them is grammatical. The phrase does not contain a subject and a verb, and the clause does. Sometimes different grammatical constructions can communicate the same meaning. This choice of different ways to say the same thing gives language flexibility and variety. If you have a good understanding of what phrases are and what clauses are, you will not have trouble distinguishing between them.

Noun Clauses

Noun clauses are usually introduced by relative pronouns.

John knows <u>who will win the race this year</u>.
> *Who will win the race this year* is a noun clause. It is the direct object of the verb *knows* and is introduced by the relative pronoun *who*.

Nouns, unlike adjectives and adverbs, are not modifiers. They are naming words. Nouns commonly function as subjects, direct objects, objects of prepositions, and predicate nominatives, though they can have other functions too. The point that you must remember, however, is that nouns are more important in sentences than adjectives and adverbs. If you take a noun clause out of a sentence, the sentence will no longer stand on its own.

<u>Whoever completes the assignment first</u> wins the cheesecake.
> *Whoever completes the assignment first* cannot be left out of the sentence without destroying the meaning. *Wins the cheesecake* cannot stand on its own. It is not a main clause because it does not contain a subject and therefore cannot express a complete thought.

Adjectives and adverbs can be removed from a sentence just as your tonsils and your appendix can be removed from your body. Without adjectives and adverbs the sentence can still function, although the meaning of the sentence may be altered. For example, *The boys who wear white socks are spurned by the girls* implies a different meaning than *The boys are spurned by the girls*. *Who wear white socks* is an essential adjective clause because it is essential to the meaning of the sentence. The girls do not spurn all the boys, only those who wear white socks. The sentence without the adjective clause, however, indicates that the girls spurn all the boys. Nevertheless, whether the sentence contains the adjective clause or not, it still functions and still makes sense. On the other hand, if a noun clause is removed from a sentence, the sentence can no longer function, just as your car could no longer function if the engine were removed.

Remember the importance of a noun clause to a sentence, or you will not always be able to recognize a complex sentence. A complex sentence contains one main clause and at least one subordinate clause. (See Chapter 5 for more on complex sentences.) When the subordinate clause is an adjective clause, the main clause still makes sense without it:

> **Adjective:** Anna gave Phil, who is her neighbor's husband, a gold ring.
>> With the adjective clause *who is her neighbor's husband* omitted, the main clause still expresses a complete thought, *Anna gave Phil a gold ring.*

When an adverb clause is omitted from a sentence, the main clause that is left can stand alone.

> **Adverb:** I would like to finish the novel before I mow the lawn.
>> With *before I mow the lawn* omitted, the main clause still expresses a complete thought, *I would like to finish the novel.*

The sentences containing the adjective clause and the adverb clause are complex sentences. Each sentence contains one main clause and one subordinate clause.

The sentence you read earlier containing a noun clause is also a complex sentence.

> Whoever completes the assignment first wins the cheesecake.

In this sentence the subordinate clause is the noun clause *whoever completes the assignment first*, which functions as the subject. The main clause is the whole sentence. Thus the sentence is a complex sentence containing one main clause and one subordinate clause. When the subordinate clause is a noun clause, it is so important to the main clause that it is inherently part of the main clause itself. If you put the subordinate clause in brackets and underline the main clause, the example sentence looks like this:

> [Whoever completes the assignment first] wins the cheesecake.

Notice what happens if the subordinate clause is a noun clause functioning as the object of a preposition.

Give the lab report to [whoever is on duty.]

The main clause would be left hanging at the word *to* without an object for the preposition if the subordinate noun clause were omitted. Notice again that the subordinate clause is a group of related words functioning as one word. If the sentence had read, *Give the lab report to Dr. Smith*, then *Dr. Smith* would have been the object of the preposition *to*. Now, however, instead of just one person's name you have a clause (*whoever is on duty*) functioning as the object of the preposition. The principle is the same.

Since noun clauses generally function as subjects, direct objects, objects of prepositions, or predicate nominatives, you may find it helpful to study examples of each before you start identifying noun clauses in practice sentences.

Subject: Whoever shoots an arrow through the axe handles will win Penelope's hand.

Direct object: I think that Sam Brame is the best-dressed man in town.

Object of preposition: The boss is saving the gold drafting set for whoever produces the best design.

Predicate nominative: The job is what Greg needs.

Practice Sentences 4-5

Underline the noun clauses in the following sentences, and in the blanks provided indicate whether each is used as a subject, direct object, object of preposition, or predicate nominative.

Example: Jane only sees what she wants to see.

direct object

1. Whoever writes the best poem will win the prize.

_____

2. The contract will be awarded to whoever submits the lowest bid.

_____

3. I believe Einstein's general theory of relativity is valid.

_____

4. The company will pay double time to whoever works on Saturday.

_____

5. A leisurely trip to Bermuda is what I need.

_____

6. Fred said he was quitting the job in two weeks.

_____

7. The trained bear could be what the circus needs.

_____

8. Whomever the astronauts select will be the captain on the next mission.

_____

9. The teacher talked about whatever the students wanted to learn.

_____

10. Carlyle told his supervisor whatever he wanted to hear.

_____

Misplaced Subordinate Clauses

Effectively using subordinate clauses can improve your writing. But an improper use of subordinate clauses can confuse, if not amuse, your reader. You must make sure that adjective clauses are placed near the words they modify.

The book belongs to the young student that contains 300 pages of color reproductions.
As stated, the student contains 300 pages of color reproductions.

The sentence should have been written so that the adjective clause *that contains 300 pages of color reproductions* was placed nearer the word it modifies:

The book that contains 300 pages of color reproductions belongs to the young student.

John Fergusson bought a tractor from a local farmer that runs on diesel fuel.

A sentence like this would amuse your reader—at your expense. The adjective clause should be placed nearer the word *tractor*:

John Fergusson bought a tractor that runs on diesel fuel from a local farmer.

Review Exercise 4-A   Identifying Types of Subordinate Clauses (I)

In the blanks provided, indicate whether the clauses (in italics) are adjective (adj.), adverb (adv.), or noun (n.) clauses.

Example: Brian told a woman in his class *that she was too old for him.*

_____ *n.* _____

1. To say *that Sandy was offended* would be an understatement.

_____

2. *When she had calmed down enough to speak*, she asked Brian his age.

_____

3. He said *that he would be twenty-two in September.*

_____

4. Brian asked Sandy *what her age was.*

_____

5. She said *that she was thirty-five.*

_____

6. Brian said people don't even think the same *when they get over thirty.*

_____

7. She asked about these differences *which he thought were so great.*

_____

8. *After he thought about it a little while*, Brian explained that people over thirty don't seem to enjoy life anymore.

_____

9. Sandy told him *that she found life more fulfilling after thirty.*

_____

10. *Because this didn't make any sense to him*, he asked her to have dinner with him Saturday night to explain what she meant.

_____

Review Exercise 4-B   Identifying Types of Subordinate Clauses (II)

In the blanks provided, indicate whether the clauses in italics are adjective (adj.), adverb (adv.), or noun (n.) clauses.

Example: The belt *that Van decided to make* was simple.

_____ *adj.* _____

1. *When he had everything together,* he began work.

   _____

2. The first thing *that he had to do* was cut the belt to the right length.

   _____

3. *After the length of the belt was determined,* he beveled the edges.

   _____

4. Next, he cut the border with a special tool *that he had.*

   _____

5. Now he had to decide *which tools to use for the pattern.*

   _____

6. *What pattern to make* is the most important decision in making a belt.

   _____

7. *After Van thought about it,* he settled on a basketweave pattern.

   _____

8. He decided to dye the belt black *since he needed a black dress belt.*

   _____

9. He put on two coatings of a water-repellent finish *that he bought at the leather shop.*

   _____

10. Van attached the buckle and showed the belt to *whoever came near him.*

_____

Review Exercise 4-C   Using Subordinate Clauses

Make up sentences containing the following specified clauses, and underline the clause.

Example: an adjective clause beginning with *that*

The tall brick building that is located on South Campus is not adequately lighted at night.

1. an adjective clause beginning with *who*

   _____

   _____

2. a noun clause used as the object of a preposition

   _____

   _____

3. an adverb clause beginning with *since*

   _____

   _____

4. a noun clause used as a predicate nominative

   _____

   _____

5. an adverb clause beginning with *unless*

   _____

   _____

6. a noun clause used as a subject

   _____

   _____

7. an adverb clause beginning with *if*

8. a noun clause used as a direct object

9. an adjective clause beginning with *which*

10. an adverb clause beginning with *because*

Review Exercise 4-D   Correcting Misplaced Subordinate Clauses

In the space provided, rewrite each of the following sentences by placing the modifying subordinate clauses nearer the words they modify.

Example: Mr. DeCinzio is the tall man using the snow shovel who is our mayor.

Mr. De Cinzio, who is our mayor, is the tall man using the snow shovel.

1. Becky used her new blender to make a carrot cake for her friend that she got for Christmas.

_____

_____

2. Margaret has a dead skunk in her driveway that needs to be removed.

_____

_____

3. Darren shot the deer with his rifle that was eating all his corn.

_____

_____

4. Because he was caught smoking in the men's room, the principal sent Robert home.

_____

_____

5. The doctor gave Brian medicine for his sick stomach who had already missed four days of work.

_____

_____

6. Alice told her husband to be home promptly for dinner who had been arriving later and later.

_____

_____

7. The young man broke several pieces of equipment in the chemistry lab that was not doing well in the course.

_____

_____

8. The employees were ignored during the merger who had worked there for thirty years.

_____

_____

9. The piece of metal struck Herman in the head that had to be removed.

_____

_____

10. Nancy dropped the iron on her foot which was set for 130 degrees.

_____

_____

5

Sentence Types and Sentence Variety

In order to give your writing variety, you will need to use the four types of sentences: simple, compound, complex, and compound-complex. These sentence types are summarized in the following chart.

Sentence Types	Main Clauses	Subordinate Clauses
Simple	1	0
Compound	2 or more	0
Complex	1	1 or more
Compound-Complex	2 or more	1 or more

Later in this chapter, you will learn how to use your knowledge of sentence types to write more effective sentences through the use of sentence variety, parallelism, and the control of excessive main clauses and subordination.

Sentence Types

Simple Sentences

A simple sentence contains one main clause. That is, it contains one subject and one verb and expresses a complete thought.

> s.   v.
> *Jake loves* Ruth.

> s.   v.
> *Anne has become* a successful lawyer.

Both sentences are simple sentences. An imperative command can also be a simple sentence.

> Stop!
> Hush!

Stop! and *Hush!* are simple sentences. The subject *you* is understood, and the individual words express a complete thought. Simple sentences can also have compound subjects.

John, Ted, Bob, Alice, and Sheila went to the country fair.
> The subject is compounded five times. Grammatically, however, it still has only one subject and one verb, and thus is a simple sentence. Similarly, the verb can be compounded.

Shirley cleaned the house, washed her dress, and went to dinner at Delmonico's.
> The verb is compounded three times, but the sentence is still a simple sentence. It contains several verbs, which all have the same subject.

And, of course, a simple sentence can contain a compound subject and a compound verb.

John, Mary, Ted, Susan, Greg, and Peggy went to dinner, danced until 8:00, and saw a play at the local theater.
> This sentence is still just a simple sentence. It contains only one verb and one subject. The same group of nouns is the subject of the same group of verbs.

Remember when studying sentence types that you are counting only clauses. All you have to do is learn the four types of sentences and then count the number of main and subordinate clauses in a sentence to see which type of sentence you have. But only clauses count.

By hanging on to the window ledge, Barbara was able to escape the fire in her room.
> *Hanging on to the window ledge* is a participial phrase and *to escape the fire in her room* is an infinitive phrase, but the sentence is a simple sentence because it contains only one verb *was* and one subject *Barbara*. The whole sentence, of course, expresses a complete thought. Do not be misled by considering verbal phrases as subordinate clauses. Remember, phrases do not contain subjects and verbs.

Practice Sentences 5-1

Underline the subject(s) and circle the verb(s) in each of the following simple sentences.

Example: Priscilla (had) a difficult summer.

1. In June she was ill with a temperature of 102°.

2. After this, she injured her eye and had to wear a patch.

3. She had difficulty wearing the patch under her glasses.

4. Finally, she and the doctor decided to remove the patch.

5. About that time she developed an irritating skin rash.

6. On the way to the dermatologist, she was struck by a hit-and-run driver.

7. The police and the sheriff's department investigated the accident and found witnesses.

8. Priscilla was angry in court and testified against the man.

9. In the courtroom parking lot, Priscilla looked and looked but found no car.

10. It had been ticketed and towed.

Compound Sentences

A compound sentence contains two or more main clauses and no subordinate clauses. You might think of a compound sentence as two or more simple sentences put into one sentence. The main clauses of a compound sentence can be joined in two ways. They may be joined by a semicolon:

> In some ways transformational grammar is easier than traditional grammar; transformational grammar uses fewer terms.

They may be joined by a comma and a coordinate conjunction (*and, or, nor, for, but, yet, so*).

> In some ways transformational grammar is easier than traditional grammar, but most students prefer the traditional approach.

Remember that a compound sentence can be composed of more than two main clauses. It can have as many main clauses as you can think up, as long as it contains no subordinate clauses.

> In some ways transformational grammar is easier than traditional grammar, but most students prefer the traditional method; they are more comfortable with the vocabulary of traditional grammar, and they are hesitant to face a new way of studying the language.

That compound sentence contains four main clauses and no subordinate clauses.

First main clause:	In some ways transformational grammar is easier than traditional grammar,
Second main clause:	but most students prefer the traditional method;

Third main clause:	they are more comfortable with the vocabulary of traditional grammar,
Fourth main clause:	and they are hesitant to face a new way of studying the language.

The first and second main clauses are joined by a comma and the coordinate conjunction *but*. The second and third main clauses are joined by a semicolon. The third and fourth main clauses are joined by a comma and the coordinate conjunction *and*.

As you have seen, compound sentences connect main clauses. However, the main clauses they connect should relate to each other logically. For example, a sentence such as *James Comer is a strong Democrat, and Lassie has fleas* is ridiculous. Though grammatically correct, the sentence contains two main clauses that are not logically related.

Practice Sentences 5-2

Indicate the break(s) between the main clauses in the following compound sentences by putting a circle at the break(s) between main clauses.

Example: Professor Hutchins was teaching a class in political science⊙ but his students were not paying attention.

1. He discussed the political theories of Thomas Jefferson, and then he contrasted them with the theories of Alexander Hamilton.

2. Professor Hutchins was really getting into the subject, but he was interrupted by a student's snoring.

3. Professor Hutchins liked the republican form of government advocated by Jefferson, yet he had a totalitarian reaction toward the student.

4. Either explain why you are sleeping in class, or get out immediately.

5. The student said the theory was boring; he explained that he wanted to learn practical politics.

6. Professor Hutchins discussed the matter with his student after class, and they agreed to try an experiment.

7. Two weeks would be spent in class on political theory; then two weeks would be spent on practical applications.

8. Professor Hutchins insisted that some knowledge of theory was necessary to understand what actually occurred in practice, and eventually the student agreed.

9. The student stayed awake and studied much harder, but he was still a little skeptical.

10. At a political rally during the second two-week period, the student was fascinated, but Professor Hutchins was arrested for disorderly conduct.

Complex Sentences

A complex sentence has one main clause and one or more subordinate clauses.

[After I read the article], I disagreed with the author even more than before.

> *After I read the article* is an introductory adverb clause. *I disagreed with the author even more than before* is a main clause. The sentence is complex.

The man [who wins the most primaries] will receive the nomination in Philadelphia [where the convention is to be held].

> The above sentence has one main clause (underlined) and two subordinate clauses (bracketed), so it is a complex sentence. (See pp. 272–273)

Remember from the preceding chapter, however, that noun clauses are different from modifying clauses. With noun clauses the subordinate clause will be an integral part of the main clause.

[Whoever wins the primaries] will go to Philadelphia.

> *Whoever wins the primaries* is a noun clause, subject of the verb *will go*. The main clause is the whole sentence *Whoever wins the primaries will go to Philadelphia.* You must consider the noun clause subject to be an integral part of the main clause; obviously *will go to Philadelphia* could not be a main clause since it neither contains a subject nor expresses a complete thought. The whole sentence is a complex sentence.

Practice Sentences 5-3

In the following sentences, underline the main clauses and bracket the subordinate clauses.

Example: The Student Government Association decided to have a meeting [because they were upset about the new policy].

1. The college president had said that students could no longer smoke in the cafeteria.

2. The policy, which was instituted for health reasons, seemed dictatorial to the students.

3. After the president of the SGA opened the meeting, chaos erupted because everyone wanted to speak at once.

4. The president established order and recognized a young woman that was sitting in the front row.

5. She said that she had a right to smoke if she wanted to do so.

6. She was angry because she felt her constitutional rights were being threatened.

7. Suddenly another student shouted that he didn't want to get lung cancer from her smoke.

8. She said that was as ridiculous as fluorocarbons from deodorant cans destroying the ozone layer.

9. The meeting nearly turned into a riot until the president suggested a compromise.

10. Now the cafeteria where the students eat is divided into Smoking and No Smoking sections.

You should realize that some subordinate clauses functioning as adjectives and nouns may omit the relative pronouns ordinarily used to connect the subordinate clause to the main clause.

A 1956 Thunderbird is the car I want.
> *I want* is an adjective clause modifying the noun *car*. The sentence could be written with the relative pronoun included: A 1956 Thunderbird is the car *that I want.*

The same situation occurs with noun clauses.

The man at the nursery knows I want the pink azalea.
> *I want the pink azalea* is a noun clause that functions as the direct object of the verb *knows*.

The sentence could be written this way:

The man at the nursery knows *that I want the pink azalea.*

Both sentences are complex sentences whether the relative pronoun is present or not.

Remember, a clause is a group of related words that contains a subject and a verb. Every time you find a different verb that takes its own subject, you have another clause. In the sentence *The man at the nursery knows I want the pink azalea,* you should recognize that *man* is the subject of the verb *knows* and that *I* is the subject of the verb *want*.

Compound-Complex Sentences

A compound-complex sentence contains two or more main clauses and one or more subordinate clauses.

> I wanted to go to the outdoor concert, but I had to change my plans since my lab report is due by 5:00 P.M.
>
> > *I wanted to go to the outdoor concert* is a main clause; *but I had to change my plans* is a main clause; *since my lab report is due by 5:00 P.M.* is a subordinate adverb clause telling why or on what condition.

Here the main clauses are underlined and the subordinate clauses are in brackets:

> <u>I wanted to go to the outdoor concert</u>, but <u>I had to change my plans</u> [since my lab report is due by 5:00 P.M.]

Look at the following sentence:

> [When the plants started producing,] <u>we noticed a problem</u> [because many of the tomatoes had rotten spots on the bottom;] <u>we called a botanist</u>, and <u>he told us the solution</u>.

Notice that the sentence contains three main clauses and two subordinate clauses. The sentence is compound-complex.

Do not forget that some of your subordinate clauses in compound-complex sentences may be noun clauses.

> noun clause
> <u>I know [what you want to hear], so you are not going to be disappointed</u>.

Also, you must remember that some of the relative pronouns may be omitted in compound-complex sentences just as they were in complex sentences.

> <u>Dr. Smith said [you performed well]</u>, but <u>he told me [you had some trouble with a chapter]</u> [you had worked on the week before].
>
> > *You performed well* is a noun clause direct object; the relative pronoun *that* is omitted. *You had some trouble with a chapter* is a noun clause direct object; again the relative pronoun *that* is omitted. *You worked on the week before* is a subordinate adjective clause modifying *chapter;* the relative pronoun *(that)* is omitted.

Practice Sentences 5-4

Underline the main clauses in the following compound-complex sentences and bracket the subordinate clauses.

Example: <u>Ramona wants to get a job</u> [that will pay her well,] <u>but</u>
<u>she doesn't have a college degree</u>.

1. Mort bought a new car, but he was dissatisfied with it since it could only go 120 miles an hour on a race track.

2. Sue got her pepperoni pizza, but she sent it back when she saw anchovies on it.

3. Because he was not a very good dancer, Alfred was uncomfortable at parties; in fact, he was even uncomfortable around girls.

4. Look before you leap, or you may regret your move for a long time.

5. The jury members entered the courtroom when the judge called them, but they still had not reached a decision.

6. The man said that he did not agree with the new law; furthermore, he intended to change it.

7. Arlene looked at houses for days, but she bought the one on Lowe Street because she liked the floor plan and the location.

8. William thought his watch was broken, but it only needed a battery.

9. Fred purchased a scientific calculator since he was not good in math, and his grades improved significantly.

10. Lamont saw the most beautiful girl he had ever seen, but she was just a picture in a magazine.

Sentence Variety and Improvement

Sentence Variety

Good writing contains a variety of sentence structures and types. It will have introductory phrases and clauses sometimes, short simple sentences sometimes, and long, involved compound-complex sentences sometimes; occasionally good writing will have a compound sentence or two, though compound sentences are perhaps the least used of the four types.

Denise wanted to buy a 1978 Volkswagen convertible. She knew it was a classic. She was not sure she could afford the price the owner asked. Seven thousand dollars seemed like too much. She considered offering $6,000. She really thought $5,000 or $5,500 was more reasonable. She knew the car had to be hers. She test drove it and offered $5,300. There was some negotiating. Denise and the owner settled on a price of $6,000. The owner wanted more. Denise felt it was too much. But now Denise is the proud owner.

The paragraph is rather dull and choppy. It lacks variety and a smooth flow. Now read the revised version of the paragraph and see the difference:

Although Denise knew the 1978 Volkswagen convertible was a classic, she was not sure she could afford the price asked by the owner. Thinking $7,000 was too much, she considered offering $6,000. In her mind she felt $5,000 or $5,500 was a more reasonable price, but in her heart she knew the car had to be hers. She test drove it and offered $5,300. After some negotiation, Denise and the owner settled on a purchase price of $6,000. The owner felt she should have gotten more, and Denise felt she paid too much. However, Denise is the proud owner of a classic automobile.

The revised version has more complex sentences. If used skillfully, complex sentences and compound-complex sentences can communicate more information in fewer sentences and with a smoother flow than simple sentences and compound sentences. If you are conscious of varying your sentence patterns when you write, you can greatly improve your writing. There are, however, other techniques besides varying sentence types.

1. Beginning sentences with participial phrases is an excellent way to alter the potentially monotonous subject-verb-object pattern.

Bob loves Cheryl deeply, and he proposed to her last Friday night.

The sentence is grammatically correct. But look what happens when the sentence is rewritten with an introductory participial phrase:

Loving Cheryl deeply, Bob proposed to her last Friday night.

The verbal quality of *loving* immediately gets the reader's attention. Also, the sentence has a little more suspense since the reader has to wait longer before coming to the main part of the sentence.

2. Another useful technique for getting variety in your sentence structures is to begin some sentences with introductory adverb clauses.

The championship game was canceled due to rain. Everyone stayed in the dorm.

The two sentences do not even seem to belong together. But by using an introductory adverb clause, the two sentences become one sentence.

> Since the championship game was canceled due to rain, everyone stayed in the dorm.

Sentence variety can be improved somewhat just by using an adverb or adverbs at the beginning of the sentence.

> Interestingly enough, everyone stayed in the dorm.

Interestingly enough is an adverbial expression. Since it does not modify any particular word in the sentence, it is known as an absolute construction. The expression just used is called an adverb absolute. Be sure not to overuse the adverb absolute construction; it is merely a technique for achieving variety and is not necessarily beneficial or detrimental. Some readers do not like adverb absolutes like *interestingly* and *hopefully*. Author and commentator Edwin Newman has a sign over his office door that reads, "Abandon *hopefully*, all ye that enter here."

Practice Sentences 5-5

The following sentences begin with the subject; rewrite them using either introductory participial phrases, introductory adverb clauses, adverb absolutes, or elliptical clauses to vary the sentence patterns.

> **Example:** Sonya worked all summer, and she earned the money for her college tuition.

> *Working all summer, Sonya earned the money for her college tuition.*

1. Susan's car was badly damaged in an accident, and she had to start taking a taxi to work.

_____

_____

2. Nicole was planning to get married, and she had a lawyer prepare a prenuptial agreement.

_____

_____

3. Lewis dropped his lunch tray in the cafeteria. He was extremely embarrassed.

   _____

   _____

4. Emily already has plans for her tax refund. She wants a 10-speed bicycle, some 6–7 ounces of leather for her projects, and a new SLR camera.

   _____

   _____

5. Sara finally got her car started, and then went on to work.

   _____

   _____

6. Sheila gave a fine performance on opening night even though she had never acted before.

   _____

   _____

7. It is interesting that the town's new zoning limits do not include the mayor's house.

   _____

   _____

8. Lee wants to be a professional dancer, but his father says he can't make a living at it.

   _____

   _____

9. Libby, although she is only fifteen, is the soloist at her church.

   _____

   _____

10. Byron is depressed now, but he will feel better on payday.

_____

_____

Parallelism

Another way to improve your sentence structure is by the effective use of parallelism. Parallelism is the similarity of grammatical form between two or more elements that serve the same function. The underlying principle of parallelism is that in a series nouns should be balanced with nouns, verbs with verbs, adjectives with adjectives, infinitive phrases with infinitive phrases, etc. In the sentence *I have an apple, an orange, and a tomato,* the words *an* before *apple, an* before *orange,* and *a* before *tomato* illustrate the correct parallel use of words. The sentence *I bought an apple, orange, and a tomato* is not parallel. The word *an* appears before the word *apple* and *a* appears before *tomato;* but since there is no adjective before the word *orange,* the series is not parallel. Errors of this kind are known as faulty parallelism. Such errors can be distracting to readers. Notice the faulty parallelism in the following sentence: *This summer I want to get plenty of rest, to attend summer school, and play golf.* As is often the case, the faulty parallelism can be corrected in more than one way. The sign of the infinitive *(to)* can be added before *play golf: This summer I want to get plenty of rest, to attend summer school, and to play golf.* Or the sign of the infinitive may be given just once, making the other two phrases parallel with the word *to: This summer I want to get plenty of rest, attend summer school, and play golf.* The second way is preferable because fewer words are used to achieve equal clarity.

Phrases are parallel when infinitives are paired with infinitives and gerunds are paired with gerunds.

Parallel: Jack wants to be elected chairman and to set up a new finance committee.
The infinitive phrases *to be elected chairman* and *to set up a new finance committee* are parallel.

Parallel: Dawn likes riding horses and playing tennis.
The two gerund phrases *riding horses* and *playing tennis* are parallel.

Faulty parallelism arises when phrases are not in the same grammatical form.

Not parallel: Dawn likes riding horses and to play tennis.
The gerund phrase *riding horses* is not grammatically equal to the infinitive phrase *to play tennis.*

Parallel subordinate clauses repeat the relative pronouns that introduce them.

Parallel: Kurt knows that he will get the job and that he will be good at it.
> The subordinate clauses *that he will get the job* and *that he will be good at it* are parallel because both are introduced by the relative pronoun *that* and both are objects of the verb *knows*.

When one of the relative pronouns is omitted, the sentence is confusing.

Not parallel: Kurt knows that he will get the job and he will be good at it.

Sometimes entire sentences are parallel (or balanced).

Parallel: The country will move ahead with the administration's new programs. The citizens will move ahead with the country.

Parallel sentences are often used in speeches because they are dramatic and effective. However, too many parallel sentences in writing may seem repetitious.

In your writing be sure the elements you connect are parallel.

Not parallel: Joan runs to lose weight, for exercise, and because she enjoys running.
> The sentence connects an infinitive phrase (to lose weight), a prepositional phrase (for exercise), and an adverb clause (because she enjoys running). The sentence can be made parallel by making all the elements grammatically equal.

Parallel: Joan runs because she loses weight, gets exercise, and enjoys running.

Not parallel: We can improve ourselves by setting goals and determination.

Parallel: We can improve ourselves by setting goals and having determination.

Not parallel: Whether in a crowd or when he was alone, Conrad was always the same.

Parallel: Whether alone or in a crowd, Conrad was always the same.

Not parallel: Irving Smith is a man with a muscular build and who attends a health spa every week.

Parallel: Irving Smith is a man who has a muscular build and (or *who*) attends a health spa every week.

Avoiding Excessive Main Clauses

Too many main clauses in a row result in choppy and distracting writing. The Tom, Dick, and Jane books students once learned to read in elementary school are an example of how too many simple sentences cause choppiness.

> Tom has a sister. His sister is Jane. Tom and Jane have a neighbor. The neighbor is Dick. Dick has a dog. The dog is Spot.

If it were not for the excitement of learning to read, children would have a difficult time enduring many such sentences. Compound sentences can be equally choppy when you merely string together a lot of main clauses in one sentence.

> I really like to go bowling on Friday nights, and I am pretty good, and I might make the all-star team, but I don't know many people at the bowling lanes, and I need to know the judges selecting the all-stars.

You can avoid such strung-out compound sentences by subordinating some of the clauses, by using compound verbs, by using phrases, and by rewriting the one sentence into two or more sentences.

> I enjoy my Friday night bowling and bowl pretty well. By getting to know more people at the bowling lanes, I would have a good chance of making the all-star team. A prospect must know the judges.

The long, stringy sentence has now become three sentences. There is greater variety, the paragraph is easier to read, and the essential information is not altered.

Avoiding Excessive Subordination

Mark Twain once wrote a story about an old man who tried to tell a story about a ram. Unfortunately, the narrator got so bogged down in details that the story never got told. Whenever the narrator thought of another character, he gave so much of the character's genealogy that he forgot the character's significance to the story. The reader never does learn anything about the ram; the narrator went to sleep before completing his tale. Your writing can get bogged down in details, too, if you subordinate excessively.

Look at the following sentence:

> The man who is now my next-door neighbor recently bought himself a new car that is so big it won't fit into his garage that was built by the previous owner of the house who owned a Volkswagen.

The sentence is grammatically correct, but it sounds as though it is continually running downhill. The only cure for a sentence like this is to rewrite it, rearranging the details and perhaps leaving some of them out.

> The garage, having been built for the previous owner's Volkswagen, could not accommodate my neighbor's new car.

The sentence is even more effective if shorter still.

> The garage built for the previous owner's Volkswagen could not accommodate my neighbor's new car.

Review Exercise 5-A   Identifying Sentence Types (I)

In the blanks provided, indicate whether the sentences are simple, compound, complex, or compound-complex.

Example: Give the cigar to the woman that had a baby at 12:14 A.M. on January 1.

_____*Complex*_____

1. The woman who gave birth to the first baby of the year in Madison County actually gave birth to the first five babies.

_____

2. The first child born was a girl.

_____

3. The next three children were boys; the last child born was a girl.

_____

4. The entire county was excited because no quintuplets had ever been born in Madison County; the newspapers devoted many columns to the story.

_____

5. The two girls were named Shauna and Cheryl, and the boys were named Chip, Donnie, and Sidney.

_____

6. The mother, who is a twenty-six-year-old bookkeeper, cannot believe what happened.

_____

7. The doctors told her that it would probably be a multiple birth, but she was thinking twins or triplets.

_____

8. The father, who is a welder, went into shock when he realized what had happened.

_____

9. In fact, he is still in shock.

   _____

10. The townspeople hope that the whole family will be healthy, and they have even opened a scholarship fund for the children.

   _____

Review Exercise 5-B Identifying Sentence Types (II)

In the blanks provided, indicate whether the sentences are simple, compound, complex, or compound-complex.

Example: Mary, who is a full-time student, tries to do well in her courses.

_____*Complex*_____

1. She takes good notes and reads all the material assigned.

_____

2. Maintaining an A average for two years, she doesn't want to mar her record now.

_____

3. She prefers English and history, but she wants to be a physics major.

_____

4. Since Mary has always been good in mathematics, physics is easy for her, but she likes the more abstract thinking in the humanities also.

_____

5. Most of her fellow physics majors do not understand this at all.

_____

6. They like the exactness of mathematics and science; many of them say that they feel lost in humanities courses.

_____

7. Mary feels that being able to appreciate abstract thinking has been an advantage in studying theoretical mathematics.

_____

8. Her writing ability has enabled her to achieve good grades on laboratory reports and other papers for science courses.

_____

9. After a great deal of thought, Mary decided what she would do.

_____

10. She would choose theoretical physics as a vocation and read novels and poetry as an avocation.

_____

Review Exercise 5-C   Using Sentence Variety (I)

If the following simple sentences were put in paragraph form, the paragraph would be choppy and dull. Use phrases and subordinate clauses to improve the paragraph, rewriting the sentences in any way you can to improve the monotonous subject-verb pattern. After you have rewritten the paragraph by using phrases and varying the sentence structure, rewrite the paragraph in two more ways. Combine the sentences any way you wish.

Blaine is a painter.
He prefers to paint landscapes.
He generally paints with oils.
Today he is going to paint a river scene.
He must have his materials.
He gets out his easel.
Next comes the box of paints.
He also needs his brushes.
He has five different palette knives.
Naturally there is a palette for mixing colors.
He has a canvas.
He puts the canvas on the easel.
He looks at the river.
The river is in front of him.
He decides which colors to use.
He puts paint on the palette.
He mixes the colors.
He begins painting.

_____

_____

_____

_____

_____

_____

_____

Review Exercise 5-D   Using Sentence Variety (II)

If the following simple sentences were put in paragraph form, the paragraph would be choppy and dull. Use phrases and subordinate clauses to improve the paragraph, rewriting the sentences in any way you can to improve the monotonous subject-verb pattern. After you have rewritten the paragraph by using phrases and varying the sentence structure, rewrite the paragraph in two ways. Combine the sentences any way you wish.

Antonio likes many different sports.
He prefers soccer.
Soccer is the national sport in his country.
His native country is Colombia in South America.
Colombians play soccer from the time they can walk.
Just about every Colombian boy has a soccer ball.
As a child Antonio practiced keeping the ball in the air without using his hands.
He was very good at it by the time he was ten years old.
Antonio was surprised to find most men in the United States knew little about soccer.
Antonio was much more skilled than his friends from the United States.
These friends challenged Antonio to a basketball game.
Antonio beat them at their own game.
Antonio is 6'7" tall and a good athlete.

_____

_____

_____

_____

_____

_____

_____

_____

_____

_____

Review Exercise 5-E   Correcting Faulty Parallelism

Each of the following sentences contains errors in parallel structure. Rewrite each sentence and correct the faulty parallelism.

Example: The waiter was a man with a pleasant smile and who had good manners.

The waiter was a man who had a pleasant smile and who had good manners.

or

The waiter was a man with a pleasant smile and good manners.

1. Participants in the bike-a-thon could ride bicycles, tricycles, or they could even ride unicycles.

2. Your goals in a typing class are to increase speed and reducing errors.

3. Olivia is an excellent student who studies hard, does her work on time, and she always makes good grades.

4. Our front lawn needs mowing and to be trimmed.

5. Charles doesn't know whether he is to drive or if Claude will.

_____

_____

6. Sheila enjoys painting portraits and likes to paint landscapes.

_____

_____

7. Ms. Barnes asked that her employees refrain from excessive noise during break and if they would avoid smoking on the elevator.

_____

_____

8. Carol always takes her son to school, to work, and church.

_____

_____

9. Joan's father gave her orders to deposit her paycheck and then she is to come straight home.

_____

_____

10. Whether Jack eats a sandwich for lunch or if he has a full-course meal, he is always hungry by mid-afternoon.

_____

_____

Review Exercise 5-F   Improving Sentence Structure

Indicate whether the following sentences contain excessive main clauses or excessive subordination. *Then rewrite each sentence to correct the problem.*

Example: After the softball game was over, I bought a new bat that was longer and heavier than the ones which the manager, who was in his first year, provided because he got them at a good price from his brother-in-law, who was in the sporting goods business.

excessive subordination

_____

_____

_____

_____

1.   I bought an electronic organ that was on sale at a local department store which was going out of business because the owner had recently died and his son, who is a friend of mine, did not want to take over the business.

_____

_____

_____

_____

2.   Willona wanted to make her own dress for the dance, but she did not know much about either sewing or sewing machines, and her first attempt was not very successful; and the third looked like pajamas for Big Bird, but the fourth attempt was a success; it came from Macy's.

_____

_____

_____

_____

3. Aaron went to the library to check out a book for his English class, but when he got there he saw the girl of his dreams, and she saw him, but Aaron was not the man of her dreams, and she tried to avoid contact; poor Aaron checked out his book and went back to the dorm.

_____

_____

_____

_____

4. Ronnell, who works part-time at the laundry, is an expert who knows exactly how to remove any kind of stain which a customer might have who comes to the laundry where he works.

_____

_____

_____

_____

5. Bernice, who is twenty-three years old, bought herself a gun because she wanted some protection from what she called "nuts" if one were ever to accost her on the street because he thought she looked like a tempting target.

_____

_____

_____

_____

6. Shawn canceled a date with Lisa, and he made an emergency appointment with the dentist; his false tooth had come out, and he was too vain to let her see him without it.

_____

_____

_____

_____

_____

7. Hilary is the best student in her class, and she wants to attend medical school, but she knows it is very expensive, and she is not sure about receiving a full scholarship.

_____

_____

_____

_____

_____

8. Quinn bought a car from a friend who lives in Billings, Montana, which is a nice place to live if you don't mind snow in the winter that comes up to your doorknob.

_____

_____

_____

_____

_____

9. Vance is an unemployed young man who likes to spend money on whatever happens to be his hobby at the time even though some of his hobbies are so expensive that his employed friends cannot afford them.

_____

_____

_____

_____

_____

10. Kayla did well on her college entrance tests, and she decided she wanted to go to college, but she couldn't decide which college to attend, and she sent applications to twenty-three schools, but she was still undecided after receiving twenty letters of acceptance.

_____

_____

_____

_____

_____

6

Agreement

Subject-Verb Agreement

The main thing to remember about subject-verb agreement is that the subject must agree with the verb in number. If the subject is singular, the verb should be singular; if the subject is plural, the verb should be plural. You do not want to commit errors in agreement. Though agreement errors are not serious barriers to communication, they often create social barriers.

Errors in agreement are easy to correct. By careful proofreading, you could probably identify all such errors. Nevertheless, it is not surprising that many people make careless slips. Children just learning the language know that the plural of *boy* is formed by adding an *-s*. They consider it only logical that the verb should also have an *-s*, so they say *The boys shows their rocks*. Unfortunately, the English language is not so conveniently logical. In English most nouns do form their plurals by adding an *-s*.

Singular	add *-s*	*Plural*
house		houses
chair		chairs
desk		desks
car		cars
book		books
sofa		sofas
phone		phones
girl		girl

But verbs do not form their plurals in the same way. Look at the following conjugation:

Singular	*Plural*
I look	we look
you look	you look
he, she, it looks	they look

Notice that the form of the verb that ends in *-s* is singular, not plural. It is the third person singular form of the verb that ends in *-s*.

Singular	remove *-s*	*Plural*
comes		come
runs		run
sees		see
throws		throw
jumps		jump

Notice, also, that only the present tense presents a problem. If a verb is in the past tense, for example, there is no *-s* form.

I looked	we looked
you looked	you looked
he, she, it looked	they looked

Remember the basic rule of subject-verb agreement: the subject must agree with the verb in number.

The boy looks.
> The word *boy* is a singular noun, so it takes the singular form of the verb *(looks)*.

The boys look.
> The word *boys* is plural, so the verb *(look)* is plural.

Practice Sentences 6-1

In each of the following sentences, underline the correct verb choice.

Example: I (<u>read</u>, reads) to my child every night.

1. The baseball pitching machine (throw, throws) balls with great accuracy.

2. My grass (grow, grows) faster than my desire to mow it.

3. The glasses on the bar (is, are) attractive, but cheap.

4. The test questions (is, are) difficult.

5. The Frost twins (pick, picks) apples for their uncle every year.

6. The car dealer (claim, claims) to be honest.

7. The cassette recorder (eat, eats) up all my tape.

8. The coins (is, are) for my soft drink.

9. Roulette (is, are) a more interesting game than many people think.

10. Arnold's son (break, breaks) every toy given to him.

Beware of the following situations concerning subject-verb agreement, so you can avoid awkward choices in your writing.

1.   Words having an *s* in the last syllable can be misleading.

The scientist studies the problem every day.
Scientist is singular because it does not end in *-s*. The verb correctly takes the singular form. If you are not careful, however, you will hear the *s* in *scientist* and consider it plural and commit the following error:

The scientist study the problem every day.
   Scientist is singular, but the verb *study* is plural; the subject and verb do not agree in number.

The verb can also have an *s* sound.

Quarterbacks risk their careers every time they are tackled.
   Risk is a verb with an *s* sound. You must realize that the verb is plural as it is and thus is correctly used with the plural *quarterbacks*. The following error is easy to make.

The quarterback risk his career every time he is tackled.
   Now the verb *risk* has an *s* sound, and it almost sounds correctly used. However, the third person *quarterback* is a singular noun and should have a third person singular verb, which is the verb form ending in *-s*.

The quarterback risks his career every time he is tackled.

Sometimes both the subject and the verb end in *s* sounds.

The scientist exists to work and to learn.
   Now both the subject *scientist* and the verb *exists* end in *-s* sounds. But since the subject is singular and does not end in *-s* and since the verb is singular and does end in *-s*, the subject and verb agree in number. Avoid the following error:

The scientist exist to work and to learn.
   The subject is singular, but the verb is plural; thus the sentence contains an agreement error.

2.   Some people tend to reverse the basic rule that subject and verb should agree in number.

Nonstandard: Bob do very well when given enough time.
Standard: Bob does very well when given enough time.

In the first sentence *Bob* is the singular subject, but the verb is the plural *do;* the subject and verb do not agree in number.

In the second sentence *Bob* is the singular subject and *does* is the singular verb; the subject and verb agree in number. Try to avoid writing sentences like the first example.

Nonstandard: The girls goes to a square dance every Saturday night.
Standard: The girls go to a square dance every Saturday night.

The subject and verb do not agree in the first sentence because the subject *girls* is plural but the verb *goes* is singular.

There is agreement between the subject and verb of the second example, however. The subject *girls* and the verb *go* are both plural.

Practice Sentences 6-2

Underline the correct verb in each of the following sentences.

Example: Elise (study, <u>studies</u>) her course notes every evening.

1. Cass (appraise, appraises) diamonds for his father's jewelry store.

2. Psychologists (say, says) everyone has some mental hangups.

3. Mrs. Williams (celebrate, celebrates) the anniversary of her gall bladder surgery every year.

4. Statisticians (say, says) Americans are getting taller.

5. Iris (go, goes) to her aerobics class every Tuesday.

6. Scientists (tell, tells) us not to smoke.

7. Criminologists (attend, attends) all the meetings they can.

8. Bernice (see, sees) her father at least once a week.

9. Mr. and Mrs. Stevens (send, sends) their daughter off to school each morning.

10. Ernest (play, plays) the title role in *The Importance of Being Earnest.*

3. Words and phrases coming between the subject and the verb can be misleading.

The statues in the park on Main Street are beautiful.
> *Statues* is the subject, and since it is plural, it takes the plural form of the verb *are*. *Park* and *street* are singular, but they are objects of prepositions, not part of the subject.

John, as well as several other men, loves Mary.
> Even though the word *men* comes between the subject *John* and the verb *loves*, the sentence still must have a singular verb agreeing with the singular subject.

Similarly, if the subject were plural, the verb would be plural:

Several men, including John, love Mary.
> The plural subject *men* is not affected by the expression *including John* and therefore the verb is correctly plural, *love*.

Practice Sentences 6-3

Underline the correct verb in each of the following sentences.

Example: The statues in the park (<u>make</u>, makes) good bird rests.

1. The dog with all the ticks and fleas (need, needs) a bath.
2. The boy with the sad blue eyes (is, are) not really sad at all.
3. Barbara, as well as her friends Alice and Sue, (is, are) going to the meeting in Los Angeles.
4. The Adams Antique Store on the corner of Main and Crutchfield Streets (has, have) old items, but no real antiques.
5. The students in the library (is, are) generally quiet and studious.
6. The chalk purchased by the public schools (come, comes) in six different colors.
7. Many sports fans, including Lorna, (prefer, prefers) basketball to football.
8. Any car with dual headlights (blind, blinds) me at night.
9. Swanson, along with Dale and Henry, (is, are) going to the World 600.
10. A computer with two disk drives (is, are) more versatile than a one-drive machine.

4. Subjects connected by *and* are generally plural. That two subjects joined by *and* are plural should be obvious: one plus one equals two.

Bud and Roscoe are fine men.
> *Bud* is singular; *Roscoe* is singular—but together they are two men, and thus the subject is plural and needs a plural verb, *are*.

Of course, there may be more than two singular subjects joined by *and:*

> Mark Twain, Henry James, Nathaniel Hawthorne, Herman Melville, and William Faulkner are just a few of America's well-known authors.
>> Though each author is an individual, together the five authors make up the plural subject that needs the plural verb, *are.*

Sometimes the two "subjects" joined by *and* may relate to the same person.

> My best friend and adviser is my wife.
>> *Friend* and *adviser* both mean the same person and thus the verb is singular, *is.* Such sentences do not cause much confusion because the meaning is normally clear.

> Ham and eggs is a good dish.
>> Though there are two separate nouns joined by *and,* the verb is singular *(is)* because *ham and eggs* refers to one particular dish.

Practice Sentences 6-4

Underline the correct verb in each of the following sentences.

Example: Mel and Sue (<u>spend</u>, spends) money freely.

1. My wife, who is also my best friend, (is, are) very reliable.

2. Paige and Angie (is, are) inseparable.

3. Ellen, Kathy, Jack, and Darryll (attend, attends) movies every Saturday.

4. His best friend and companion (is, are) his dog.

5. The goalie on our soccer team and catcher on our baseball team (perform, performs) admirably in both sports.

6. Chicken pox, measles, and mumps (is, are) all common childhood illnesses.

7. Scott and Cheryl (has, have) a good relationship.

8. Mrs. Durallis, who is my neighbor, (sends, send) $50 a week to her son in college.

9. Mr. Rogers and Big Bird (entertains, entertain) children.

10. Alcohol and automobiles (is, are) not a good combination.

   5.   Indefinite pronouns are sometimes treated as singular and sometimes as plural. Indefinite pronouns such as *another, anyone, anybody, anything, each, either, everyone, everybody, everything, neither, no one, nobody, nothing, one, someone, somebody, something* are grammatically considered to be singular in formal English.

Everyone on the team performs well.
> Though the word *everyone* seems to indicate more than one person, the word is an indefinite pronoun that is considered to be grammatically singular, and thus *everyone* takes the singular form of the verb, *performs*.

Remember, grammar organizes the way language is used; grammar is not necessarily logical because language is not necessarily logical. You say, "The trousers are hanging on the line," even though the noun *trousers* indicates only one (singular) garment.

Each of the women puts in as much time as she can on the project.
> *Each* is an indefinite pronoun considered to be singular, so it takes the singular verb *puts*.

Indefinite pronouns such as *several, both,* and *many* are plural when used as subjects.

Both of the men are in the race.
> *Both* is clearly plural, and therefore the verb is plural.

Several of the runners have as many as five pairs of track shoes.
> *Several* is plural and takes the plural verb *have*.

Indefinite pronouns such as *none* and *some* can be either singular or plural depending on meaning.

Some of the gold was pure.
> The word *some* is used in a singular sense to indicate one particular portion and takes the singular verb.

Some of the men were exhausted after the workday ended.
> *Some* is used as an indefinite pronoun like *several, both,* and *many*. It clearly means more than one of the men and therefore takes the plural verb.

None of that money is mine.

None of the applicants were hired.

Practice Sentences 6-5

Underline the correct verb in the following sentences.

Example: Someone (is, are) going to have to take responsibility.

1. Both of the men (does, do) well when the pressure is on.

2. Somebody on the staff (wants, want) a new editor.

3. Everyone (is, are) convinced that an annual is worthwhile.

4. Some of the women (goes, go) to the track every morning.

5. Anything (goes, go) in the sport of rugby.

6. No one (likes, like) the aluminum bats used in college baseball.

7. Anyone who knows the rules (thinks, think) chess is a challenging game.

8. Some of the stolen bonds (was, were) recovered.

9. The coach said that anyone who hustles (makes, make) the team.

10. No one (wants, want) to do well more than Harvey.

6.   Singular subjects connected by *or, nor, either . . . or,* or *neither . . . nor* need a singular verb because either choice would be singular. For example,

> Either Blanca or Larry is going to be appointed to the position.
> If Blanca is chosen, the subject is singular. If Larry is chosen, the subject is singular. Therefore, the verb in either case would be singular, *is going.*

The same situation would exist with *neither . . . nor:*

> Neither Blanca nor Larry is going to be appointed to the position.

Be careful, however, when one of the subjects is singular and one is plural. The verb must agree with the subject nearer the verb.

> Neither the employees nor the owner has control over the strike.
> The singular subject *owner* is nearer the verb, and thus the singular form of the verb *(has)* is used.

> Neither the owner nor the employees have control over the strike.
> Now the plural subject *employees* is nearer the verb, so the correct verb form is the plural *have.*

Practice Sentences 6-6

Underline the correct verb in the following sentences.

Example: Neither the cars nor the garage (<u>is</u>, are) in good shape.

1. Either Ralph Sheen or Sally Bolts (is, are) going to be the new IBM employee.

2. Neither the Nelsons nor the Cleavers (is, are) on television anymore.

3. Neither the coach nor the players (want, wants) to go back home after the loss.

4. Either the players or the owners (is, are) going to have to back off.

5. Neither the basketball nor the football (is, are) properly inflated.

6. Neither the students nor the professor (is, are) handling the situation well.

7. Either the boss or the employees (is, are) going to be very pleased.

8. Either the postmaster or his son (is, are) to be arraigned on criminal charges.

9. Neither Sally nor her mother (is, are) responsible for the damage.

10. Either the doctor or the nurses (open, opens) the doors every day.

7. Sentences that have the verb preceding the subject require special attention. Many sentences beginning with prepositional phrases can be confusing.

> Off the northwest coast of Scotland are the Western Isles.
> The subject is the plural *Western Isles.* Don't let the singular *coast* or the singular *Scotland* confuse you; both are objects of prepositions. Since the subject is the plural *Western Isles,* the verb is the plural *are.*

Sentences beginning with *there is* or *there are* alter the ordinary subject-verb order.

> There is only one man working on the pump.
> The subject is *man,* and that is why the verb is singular.

> There are three hundred men working on the reactor.
> This time the subject is the plural *men,* so the verb is the plural *are.*

In speech, especially, you have to be careful with *there is* or *there are* sentences since you have to choose your verb before you state your subject. In writing, you should avoid sentences beginning with *there is* and *there are.*

Practice Sentences 6-7

Underline the correct verb in the following sentences.

> **Example:** There (is, <u>are</u>) three women and two men on the debating team.

1. Near the drainpipe in the backyard (is, are) the six kittens.

2. Behind the cabinet doors (is, are) a roach the size of your fist.

3. There (is, are) to be a meeting of the minds at the Pentagon this afternoon.

4. Outside in the snow (play, plays) the happy children.

5. There (is, are) a man hard at work in his backyard chopping wood.

6. In a tunnel under the ground (is, are) the men working on the power lines.

7. There (is, are) only one person I feel comfortable with for hours at a time.

8. Behind the hedge (stands, stand) a man with a parabolic reflector.

9. There (was, were) enough tension in the room to coil a spring.

10. Behind the door of the research laboratory (stands, stand) a woman hard at work.

8.   Nouns such as *family, jury, council, group, committee, board, faculty,* and the like may be considered either singular or plural depending on meaning.

A word such as *family* is known as a collective noun. It can represent either one collective unit or the plural components of the unit.

A family is not as close a social unit as it used to be.
> The noun *family* refers to a collective unit (one group), and therefore the singular verb *is* must be used with the singular subject.

The family have to plan their activities for the week.
> In this sentence *family* is a plural word because it refers to the members of the group as several individuals, thus the plural verb, *have.*

The jury is returning to the courtroom.
> The subject *jury* is a collective unit and therefore singular.

The jury are arguing among themselves.
> The word *jury* is referring to twelve people as individuals and is therefore plural.

In general usage *the number* (meaning one particular number) is considered singular whereas *a number* (meaning some) is considered plural. The difference between *a number* and *the number* stems from the difference between the general article *a* and the definite article *the*, a difference most people never notice. If you say *a monkey*, you are referring to any monkey; whereas if you say *the monkey*, you are referring to a particular one.

The number of Phi Beta Kappa students is small.

A number of students are going to the game.

The number of select grapes is increasing every year.

A number of grapes are needed to make one bottle of wine.

Practice Sentences 6-8

Underline the correct verb in the following sentences.

Example: A number of people (is, <u>are</u>) expected to be absent.

1. The class (is, are) deciding on its senior gift to the school.
2. The faculty (is, are) concerned about the shortage of time in its new exam schedule.
3. The number of freshmen elected at the last induction ceremony (is, are) small.
4. The board (has, have) to complete its budget by next Thursday.
5. The family always (studies, study) its vacation plans carefully.
6. A number of athletes on the team (was, were) suspended because of the drug test results.
7. The committee (is, are) thinking about reconsidering its findings.
8. The number of applicants for the scholarship (was, were) small.
9. The jury (orders, order) its meals at the same time each day.
10. The number of Hispanics attending medical school in Florida (increases, increase) each year.

9.   A relative pronoun used as a subject may take either a singular verb or a plural verb depending on the pronoun's antecedent. (Relative pronouns are words such as *who, whom, whose, which,* and *that* that serve as both pronouns and subordinators—as in the sentence *The man who receives the trophy must win the race by at least one lap.*)

Remember that an antecedent is the noun a pronoun takes the place of. If the antecedent of a relative pronoun is singular, the pronoun must take a singular verb.

         sing.   sing.

One problem ←(that)→ arises in nuclear reactors is excessive heat.
    That is a relative pronoun; its antecedent is the singular noun *problem.* Therefore, the verb *arises* must be singular to agree with its singular subject *that.*

pl.
The problems ←(that)→ arise in nuclear reactors are many and
complex.
> The plural word *problems* is the antecedent of the relative
> pronoun *that*, making the word *that* plural. Thus, the plural
> form of the verb *(arise)* must be used to agree with its relative
> pronoun subject.

pl.
People ←(who)→ go down into the mines have courage.
> *People* is plural, *who* is plural; the verb *go* must be plural to
> agree with the word *who*.

sing.
A dog ←(that)→ is constantly scratching probably has fleas.
> *That* must be singular since its antecedent *dog* is singular. The
> verb *is* must then be singular to agree with its subject *that*.

He is one of those workers who want the best possible product.
> In this sentence the antecedent of *who* is the plural noun
> *workers;* thus the plural form of the verb *(want)* is used.

Practice Sentences 6-9

Underline the correct verb in the following sentences.

Example: The firewood that (<u>was</u>, were) delivered yesterday was
rotten.

1. The students usually prefer the professors who (prepares, prepare)
   their lectures thoroughly.

2. Most people trust whoever (inspires, inspire) them the most.

3. Ambrose Bierce is the man that (defines, define) *positive* as "mistaken at the top of one's lungs."

4. The equipment that (was, were) purchased for the camping trip
   never arrived.

5. The students who (contributes, contribute) the most to the paper
   this year will receive the best staff positions next year.

6. The clothes on display at the yard sale are not the ones that (is, are)
   for sale.

7. The animal that wins the prizes at the dog shows is not necessarily
   the one that (makes, make) the best pet.

8. An electrical appliance that (has, have) a damaged cord should be
   repaired.

9. Putting a lot of money into a lawn that is not properly maintained (makes, make) little sense.

10. The conference recognizes the athletes that (does, do) the most for their schools.

10.   Gerund subjects take singular verbs. A gerund is a verbal that ends in *-ing* and functions as a noun. When the subject of a sentence is a gerund, use a singular verb.

Seeing all of Shakespeare's history plays performed was his goal.
   Seeing is the gerund subject so the singular form of the verb *(was)* is used.

Playing tennis once a week is a good way to get the exercise your body needs.
   Playing is the singular gerund subject of the singular verb *is*.

Practice Sentences 6-10

Underline the correct verb in the following sentences.

Example: Pumping gas (is, are) how Rhonda earned her spending money this summer.

1. Seeing *Gone with the Wind* and *Forever Amber* back to back at an all-night drive-in movie (has, have) been a dream of mine for years.

2. Watching too much TV every day (become, becomes) a habit if you aren't careful.

3. Scrubbing toilets and bathtubs (is, are) not my favorite household task.

4. Planning the trip carefully ahead of time (make, makes) for a more enjoyable vacation.

5. Drinking too much alcohol (upset, upsets) your equilibrium.

11.   Some nouns are grammatically singular though they end in *-s*. Quite a few nouns are plural in form (end in *-s*) but singular in meaning. Words such as *news, physics, economics, aeronautics, athletics, aesthetics,* and *measles* are all singular nouns. These nouns should cause you little if any confusion because you never hear them in any other form.

sing. sing.
The news is all bad this evening.

sing. sing.
Measles is a disease potentially dangerous to some people.

        sing.   sing.
Aesthetics is very difficult to teach.

Many book, magazine, and newspaper titles end in -*s* but take singular verbs. Such a title is singular because it indicates the name of only one book, magazine, or newspaper.

> *The Complete Grimm's Fairy Tales* is a fascinating collection of stories for young and old.
>> Though the last word in the title is a noun ending in -*s (Tales)*, the verb must be singular *(is)*. After all, *The Complete Grimm's Fairy Tales* is only one title of one book.

           sing.   sing.
The New York Times leads all American newspapers in sales.

           sing.   sing.
Changing Times comes out every month.

Practice Sentences 6-11

Underline the correct verb in the following sentences.

> **Example:** *U.S. News & World Report* (<u>covers</u>, cover) international events.

1. Physics (does, do) not interest everyone.

2. Aeronautics (is, are) a specialized branch of physics.

3. *Gardening News* (is, are) published quarterly.

4. Mumps generally (spreads, spread) very rapidly in a community.

5. Toast and jelly (is, are) not quite enough breakfast for Mike.

6. Economics (is, are) a class I had to study hard in.

7. Joe thinks molasses (is, are) delicious.

8. Measles (is, are) very contagious.

9. News (seems, seem) to be discouraging these days.

10. Aesthetics (is, are) the subject of most interest to artists.

Pronoun-Antecedent Agreement

Pronouns and their antecedents must agree in number just as subjects and verbs do. Many of the same principles apply because the situations are similar. When an antecedent is singular, the pronoun referring to it should be singular; when an antecedent is plural, the pronoun referring to it should be plural.

1. A singular pronoun is used to refer to such words as *another, anyone, anybody, each, either, everyone, everybody, kind, man, woman, neither, no one, nobody, one, person, someone, somebody, sort,* and *type.*

> A person must do her work on time.
>> *Person* is the singular antecedent of the singular pronoun *her.* The pronoun and its antecedent are both singular and therefore agree in number.

> The woman worked all Friday night preparing for the yard sale she was to have on Saturday.
>> *Woman* is the singular antecedent of the singular pronoun *she.* The pronoun and its antecedent are in agreement.

> Anyone can learn English grammar if he studies hard enough.
>> *Anyone* is an indefinite pronoun considered to be singular. The singular pronoun *he* refers to the singular *anyone,* so pronouns and antecedent agree.

Even though many television commercials say things like "Everyone in today's chaotic world feels free to do their own thing," traditional usage requires a singular pronoun in place of the plural *their.* When the gender is in doubt, some writers prefer to use the *he or she* form:

> Any student may do the extra credit project if he or she feels it will be beneficial.

Since it is distracting to have a proliferation of *he or she's* in a paper (as in the sentence *Every man or woman should do his or her own thing as he or she sees fit*), the problem can be avoided by using a plural subject and the pronoun *their:*

> Today's students feel free to pursue their own interests.

Words such as *kind, type,* and *sort* require special attention when they are used with the adjectival pronouns *this* and *these, that* and *those.*

> These kind are generally preferred.
>> *These* is plural, and *kind* is singular. The sentence should read:

> This kind is generally preferred.
>> or
> These kinds are generally preferred.

> Those type of inventions never work efficiently.
>> *Those* is plural, and *type* is singular. The sentence should read:

> This type of invention never works efficiently.
>> or
> Those types of inventions never work efficiently.

Practice Sentences 6-12

Underline the correct pronoun in the following sentences.

Example: Anyone can do that trick if (<u>he/she practices</u>, they practice).

1. (That, Those) types of tomatoes are the best.

2. Each man is expected to keep up with (his, their) own equipment.

3. Everyone can keep (his/her, their) weight down if necessary.

4. The article said (this, those) aluminum baseball bats hit the ball fifteen to twenty feet farther than the wooden ones.

5. Each of the women had (her, their) own views about marriage.

6. Someone forgot to turn off (his/her, their) bath water.

7. Each person contributed what (he/she, they) could afford.

8. (These, This) kind of rose produces a small flower.

9. Every member of the faculty expressed (his/her, their) opinion concerning the new attendance policy.

10. It should be easy for either of the two women to prove (her, their) qualifications for the job.

2. Two or more antecedents joined by *and* are referred to by a plural pronoun.

Hugh and Jimmy do all they can to maintain the building.
Hugh and *Jimmy* become plural by being connected with the conjunction *and;* therefore, the plural *they* is needed so the antecedents and pronoun will agree.

The buildings to be destroyed were the Kingsmore Building, the Avondale Tower, and the Madison Mart; they are all important buildings in the city's history.
They is a plural pronoun referring to the antecedents *Kingsmore Building, Avondale Tower,* and *Madison Mart*—which are plural because they are connected by *and.*

Practice Sentences 6-13

Underline the correct pronoun in the following sentences.

Example: Charles and Jerry were taken to (his, <u>their</u>) job site in a helicopter.

1. The men from the fraternities and the women from the sororities are planning to work at (her, their) Save the Children Festival all day.

2. The president and the students agree that no speed bumps are needed at (his, their) campus.

3. Darlene and her parents go to Shatley Springs every year on (her, their) vacation.

4. Judy and her sister Tina are successful physical therapists in (her, their) hometown.

5. Tim and Todd are having difficulty in (his, their) engineering courses.

3. Two or more singular antecedents joined by *or* or *nor* are referred to by a singular pronoun.

Either Jack or Tom will be ready when he is called.

No matter which of the two antecedents *(Jack, Tom)* is selected, the result will be a singular masculine antecedent; therefore, the pronoun *he* is singular and agrees with the antecedent in number.

Neither Sue nor Marie has advanced in the firm as rapidly as she expected.

She is the correct singular pronoun choice because the two singular antecedents joined by *nor* are both female.

When one of the choices is singular and the other is plural, however, the pronoun should agree with the nearer antecedent. This situation, of course, is similar to that of singular subjects joined by *or* or *nor,* which we discussed under Subject-Verb Agreement.

Neither the doctor nor the nurses will be well received when they announce the decision.

Doctor is singular, and *nurses* is plural; since the plural *nurses* is nearer the pronoun, the plural pronoun *they* is the correct choice.

On the other hand, if the two antecedents were reversed, the pronoun would have to change.

pl.   sing.
Neither the nurses nor the doctor will be well received
sing.
when he announces the decision.

Practice Sentences 6-14

Underline the correct pronoun in the following sentences.

Example: Neither Nichole nor Christine thought (she, they) would get to go to the beach.

1. Either Marie or her two sisters can wear (her, their) mother's clothes.

2. Neither the nurses nor the doctor liked (his/her, their) own suggestions.

3. Neither Ronnell nor Neal felt (he, they) had a chance at the job.

4. Neither the teacher nor the students (was, were) fond of the new administrator.

5. Either Amanda or Margaret will go if (she, they) can.

6. Neither Quinn nor Roman doubted (his, their) ability to do the assignment.

7. Neither the manager nor the players liked (his/her, their) new ballpark.

8. Either the students or the college president will have to alter (his/her, their) stand.

9. Either Stuart or Victor will have to contact (his, their) insurance company about the tree that fell on the fence.

10. Neither the mother nor her children showed up for (her, their) physical examinations.

4. Collective nouns will be referred to by either singular or plural pronouns depending on meaning.

The team follows its coach's orders.
The team discuss their differences at every meeting.

Both sentences are correct. In the first, *team* is considered a unit (singular) and is referred to by the singular pronoun *its*. Pronoun and antecedent agree in number. In the second sentence, *team* is considered as separate individual members (plural) and is referred to by the plural pronoun *their*. Pronoun and antecedent agree. Notice in both cases that due to the verb only one pronoun can be correct. As soon as you say *The team follows*, the *-s* on the verb makes *team* singular. To say *The team follows their coach's orders* would be inconsistent and therefore incorrect. Similarly, when you say *The team discuss* you have made the collective noun plural, and it requires a plural pronoun.

Practice Sentences 6-15

Underline the correct pronoun in the following sentences.

Example: The group agree that (its, their) meetings are too long.

1. The committee feels it has too many responsibilities on (its, their) shoulders.

2. The clergy proposes to abolish (its, their) former ruling.

3. The mob have (its, their) own spokesperson.

4. The association has established (itself, themselves) a budget.

5. The class know (it, they) must keep quiet.

6. The herd is grazing leisurely in (its, their) pasture.

7. The assembly have repeatedly broken (its, their) rules.

8. That council has decided to extend (its, their) membership policies.

9. That class is very happy with (its, their) new teacher.

10. The jury is presenting (its, their) verdict.

5.   The pronoun *who* is usually used in referring to people; the pronoun *which* in referring to animals and things; and the pronoun *that* in referring to either persons, places, animals, or things.

Person: There is the contestant (who) is most likely to win the pageant.

Animal: The dog (that) steals Mr. Brown's newspaper is an Irish setter.

Thing: My aunt's hand-carved bed, (which) she bought last year, is a beautiful piece of furniture.

Place: It is New York (that) I like most of all.

Practice Sentences 6-16

Underline the correct pronoun in the following sentences.

> **Example:** Lassie is the famous dog (that, who) was in the movies and on television.

1. The gangster (which, that) lost his gun was in trouble.

2. The tiger (who, which) performed best was very old.

3. She lent her books to the man (who, which) was doing poorly in the course.

4. The woman (that, which) lost her purse was frantic.

5. Anyone (who, which) wants to be well rounded should read as well as exercise.

Review Exercise 6-A   Making Subjects and Verbs Agree (I)

Underline the correct verb in the following sentences.

Example: The trustees (is, <u>are</u>) proud of the school they have established.

1. Becky's company (donate, donates) $5,000 to the United Way each year.

2. The team's members (is, are) encouraged to work with nonprofit charity organizations.

3. Either the chairman or one of his department members (preside, presides) at a national conference every year.

4. Lynette Tompson, as well as her employees, (try, tries) to keep up with changes in the tax laws.

5. Since the import market (is, are) constantly expanding, Ralph must stay well informed.

6. Rodney is one of many professional athletes who (find, finds) that frequent travel strains a marriage.

7. Pauline's stocks and bonds (supplement, supplements) her income.

8. Sometimes the Lions Club and the Kiwanis Club (compete, competes) with each other to serve the public.

9. The Chief Executive Officer, as well as all the other employees, (was, were) at a loss when the computer was knocked out by lightning.

10. Doris (manage, manages) her own insurance agency in Albany, New York.

Review Exercise 6-B Making Subjects and Verbs Agree (II)

Underline the correct verb in the following sentences.

Example: In the creek behind the house (stands, <u>stand</u>) three blue herons.

1. There (is, are) nine members of the Eureka Community College Drama Club.

2. Dwight, Bubba, and Lynn (works, work) as stagehands.

3. Either Nell or Juanita (plays, play) the female lead.

4. Tony and Rojas usually (performs, perform) the leading male roles.

5. There (is, are) one member of the club that prefers the comic roles.

6. If there is any humor in a character's part, Woodrow (wants, want) to play him.

7. Teresa is shy and (takes, take) any role assigned.

8. In a locked room behind the stage (is, are) all of the club's costumes.

9. *Macbeth* and *She Stoops to Conquer* (was, were) performed last year.

10. There (was, were) no costumes for *Macbeth* because no one could find the key to the locked room.

Review Exercise 6-C   Correcting Agreement Errors

Correct the agreement errors in the following sentences.

work
Example: The men ~~works~~ hard laying the track every day.

1. A careful evaluation of the specifications are necessary.

2. The musician at the church play both the organ and the piano.

3. *The Canterbury Tales* are Chaucer's best-known work.

4. Becky, as well as Jason and Nikki, are planning a surprise party for Nanny.

5. Judd does not want to work for the Three Mile Island Company, but his bosses pays him too much to quit.

6. Ham and eggs are Colleen's favorite breakfast dish.

7. Guns and knives is both dangerous weapons.

8. Far back in the jungle lives Tarzan and Jane.

9. Mary Beth don't want to get married, but her friends says she should.

10. All previous editions of the book is outdated.

Review Exercise 6-D   Making Pronouns and Antecedents Agree (I)

Underline the correct pronoun in the following sentences.

Example: Betty and Regina decided to take (her, <u>their</u>) vacation together.

1. Josi and Katherine decided to open (her, their) own suntan parlor.

2. The equipment was more expensive than anticipated, and (it, they) arrived late.

3. Neither of the women knew what (she, they) were in for.

4. All of the customers insisted that (his, their) tanning booths were too hot.

5. Sure enough, the electrician had not done (his, their) job correctly.

6. The booths were set entirely too high for any customer to remain in for the full thirty minutes (she, they) paid for.

7. The thermostats were set to burn the customers, not to tan (him, them).

8. Josi and Katherine corrected all of the booths in (her, their) parlor.

9. Eventually the customers started coming back to improve (his, their) tan.

10. Josi and Katherine are building (her, their) bank accounts on the vanity of others.

Review Exercise 6-E   Making Pronouns and Antecedents Agree (II)

Underline the correct pronoun in the following sentences.

Example: The Shaw family members will meet at the lake house next month for (its, <u>their</u>) fifteenth consecutive reunion.

1. Sis and her family will be there with (its, their) snack food and toys.

2. Brother Bill will bring (his, their) special allergy pillow.

3. Fortunately Bill's wife Libby and daughters Susan and Ellen do not have (his, their) allergy.

4. Mother will furnish (her, their) car for the trip.

5. Nathan will bring his son Terry, and (he, they) will share the bedroom nearest the den.

6. Sis, Libby, and Bill will most likely be the ones (who, which) will plan the reunion.

7. The girls were disappointed when (she, they) woke up to hear rain falling.

8. The mothers were also disappointed by the weather on (her, their) vacation.

9. Since it wasn't an electrical storm, the children were permitted to do what (he, they) had come for—go swimming.

10. It was another successful reunion, and parents and children alike were glad (he, they) came.

Review Exercise 6-F   Correcting Pronoun-Antecedent Agreement Errors

In the following sentences correct all the errors in pronoun-antecedent agreement.

Example: Each of the women wanted to look ~~their~~ *her* best for the interview.

1. Dressed in his blue jeans and tennis shoes, Charles and Raymond set out on a fishing trip.

2. If a person weighs less than 110 pounds, they are not permitted to donate blood.

3. I prefer those kind of tomatoes to these kind.

4. The seminar was extremely interesting, but a couple of attendees acted as if he was bored.

5. Mr. Harold is the kind of neighbor which is always there when needed.

6. The staff feel its company is using them.

7. All students are eligible to try out for the play if he or she wants to have a part.

8. Either Nan or Jill will deliver their campaign speech next.

9. Measles are an annoying disease which is potentially dangerous to some people.

10. Neither the bank manager nor the employees could tell the police he actually saw the robber's face.

Review Exercise 6-G   Changing the Number (I)

The following paragraph is written in the singular number (child is). *Rewrite the paragraph in the plural number* (children are).

Example: The tree is green.

The trees are green.

1. The child is thinking about her future. *2*. How much education will she need? *3*. She knows that professional careers will be open to her. *4*. She could be a truck driver, a beautician, a housewife, or whatever she set her mind to be. *5*. She doesn't think she will be a housewife. *6*. She wants to get out of the house. *7*. She also wants to be financially independent. *8*. She does think she probably will want to get married. *9*. She wants to share her life. *10*. Fortunately, she has plenty of time before she has to make these decisions.

_____

_____

_____

_____

_____

_____

_____

_____

_____

NAME _____ CLASS _____

Review Exercise 6-H   Changing the Number (II)

The following paragraph is written in the plural number (men are). *Rewrite the paragraph in the singular number* (man is).

Example: The houses are expensive.

The house is expensive. _____

1. The men go to the gym to work out. *2.* They lift weights for thirty minutes. *3.* They work on strengthening different parts of their bodies. *4.* When no one is looking, they flex their muscles in front of a mirror. *5.* They picture themselves as Mr. Universe. *6.* Then they jog for twenty minutes. *7.* They imagine themselves setting a new world record for the mile. *8.* After jogging, they swim a few laps in the pool. *9.* They see themselves going for a new Olympic record. *10.* Then they go home and watch TV for the rest of the evening.

_____

_____

_____

_____

_____

_____

_____

_____

_____

7

Identifying and Correcting Sentence Fragments

A sentence fragment is part of a sentence. But what is a sentence? Some people consider a sentence to be a word or group of words that expresses a complete thought. This definition, however, brings up another question: "What is a complete thought?" Just as the part of speech of a word in a particular sentence can be determined only by how the word is used in context, what may be considered a complete thought in one context may not make sense in another. For example, if someone you did not know and had not spoken with came up to you and said, "flying," you might think the person was crazy. On the other hand, if you asked someone, "Are you flying or driving to the conference in Chicago?" the one-word answer *flying* would express a complete thought. Similarly, if you ask someone, "Will you go to the dance with me Saturday night?" the one-word answer *yes* or *no* is a complete thought. Clearly, whether an expression is considered a complete thought or not depends on the context.

Some writers, however, unintentionally treat incomplete thoughts as correct sentences. Such "sentences" can be very distracting to readers. Therefore, you should learn what a grammatically complete sentence is in order to avoid unintentional fragments. **A grammatically complete sentence is a word or group of words that contains a subject and verb (either stated or implied) and expresses a complete thought.**

John Victor owns over 1,000 books.

The sentence contains the verb *owns* and the subject *John Victor*, and the statement is a complete thought.

Jump!

The sentence contains the verb *jump*, and it has the implied subject *you*. The sentence is grammatically complete and expresses a complete thought. A sentence fragment, then, is a word or group of words beginning with a capital letter and ending with a period, exclamation point, or question mark that is not grammatically complete or that does not express a complete thought.

And was rowing hard to reach the lighthouse.

The group of words is a fragment. It does not contain a subject, and it does not express a complete thought.

You should strive to make your sentences grammatically complete. Although some writers occasionally construct intentional fragments, papers that are written primarily to inform the reader should avoid fragments. In informative writing, your main goal is clarity. Fragments do not help you attain this goal. Most sentence fragments are unintentional and are usually a result of rapid writing and poor proofreading. The first part of this chapter will help you learn to identify sentence fragments; the second part will give you guidance on how to eliminate fragments in your writing.

Types of Sentence Fragments

Knowing the most common types of sentence fragments can help you avoid using them. In general, four types of word groups are mistaken for sentences: (1) phrases, (2) subordinate clauses, (3) nouns followed by modifiers, and (4) sentences beginning with *and* or *but*.

Phrases as Fragments

One of the most common sentence fragment errors is mistaking phrases for grammatically complete sentences. Remember, a phrase is a group of related words that does not contain a subject and verb. Since a phrase contains no subject and verb, it cannot be a grammatically complete sentence. Also, a phrase does not express a complete thought. Even if a prepositional, infinitive, participial, or gerund phrase begins with a capital letter and ends with a period, it is still a fragment.

In that gigantic swamp in Harlow County.
　　The two prepositional phrases constitute a fragment.

To do the job adequately and proficiently.
　　The infinitive phrase is a fragment.

Having eaten thirteen bowls of oyster soup.
　　The participial phrase is a fragment.

Generating fifty kilowatts per day.
　　The verbal phrase (potentially either participle or gerund) is a fragment.

Proofread your writing to see that you have not carelessly treated a phrase as a complete sentence.

Practice Sentences 7-1

In the blanks provided, indicate whether the following word groups are complete sentences or phrases.

Example: Purchasing enough leather supplies for a pocketbook.

phrase
_____

1. Rosa began making her mother's birthday present.

    _____

2. Cutting out the pattern very carefully.

    _____

3. Being sure not to waste any leather.

    _____

4. One piece of leather having cost her $25.

    _____

5. She was now ready to begin tooling the leather.

    _____

6. The design was already drawn on tracing paper.

    _____

7. Carefully centering the design on the leather.

    _____

8. She dampened the leather and transferred the design onto it.

    _____

9. The stitching being the next step.

    _____

10. Finally, putting on the straps and the hardware.

    _____

Subordinate Clauses as Fragments

Another type of sentence fragment error is mistaking subordinate clauses for complete sentences. Remember, a subordinate clause is a group of related words that contains a subject and a verb but that does not express a complete thought.

Note: A group of related words that contains a subject and a verb is not necessarily a grammatically complete sentence.

Since a subordinate clause depends on the main clause to complete its meaning, it cannot stand alone as a sentence.

Until the stadium is cleaned of all debris.
Whoever is elected to the student government association.
Which is a fine stream for trout fishing.

All the previous word groups are fragments. You must be careful in your writing to avoid such fragments.

Practice Sentences 7-2

In the blanks provided, indicate which of the following word groups are complete sentences and which are subordinate clauses.

Example: Because Scott had been working on his car for over three years.

subordinate clause

1. He was excited about the upcoming car show.

   _____

2. Which was to be held in May at the fairgrounds.

   _____

3. He had built the car from the chassis up.

   _____

4. Although a few finishing touches were needed on the body work.

   _____

5. The car was just about ready to be shown.

   _____

6. When he drove his "new" 1957 Ford Fairlane 500 on the grounds.

———————————————

7. He was positive heads would turn.

———————————————

8. Even though he did not plan to sell the car.

———————————————

9. He was curious how much he might be offered.

———————————————

10. Nothing could compensate him for the time and memories he had in the show-winning car.

———————————————

Noun Followed by Modifier as Fragment

Though phrases and subordinate clauses mistakenly treated as complete sentences are the main causes of fragments, there are others. Often a noun will be followed by an adjective clause that modifies it:

The pilot who shot down the Red Baron in World War I.

Who shot down the Red Baron in World War I is an adjective clause modifying the noun *pilot*. The entire group of words beginning with *The* and ending with the period is a fragment because it does not express a complete thought. The noun *pilot* appears to be a subject, but there is no verb for it to be the subject of. The fragment can be made into a complete sentence simply by supplying a verb:

The pilot who shot down the Red Baron in World War I was not Eddie Rickenbacker.

Now the noun *pilot* is the subject of the verb *was* and the group of words is a complete sentence.

Fragments Caused by Beginning Sentences with *And* or *But*

Another way writers mistakenly create fragments is by beginning sentences with the word *and* or *but*.

And was forced to find an alternative procedure.

The group of words is a fragment because there is no subject for the verb *was forced*. Because the mistake with *and* is so easy to commit, many teachers tell students not to begin sentences with the words *and* or *but*. Actually, there is nothing grammatically wrong with beginning a sentence with the words *and* or *but* as long as what follows is a grammatically complete sentence. If the preceding sentence had been written *And the astronaut was forced to find an alternative procedure,* the sentence would have been grammatically complete. In fact, words like *and* and *but* can sometimes be effective in making sentences flow together smoothly.

> Bob wants to ask Carol Downs to the class picnic. But he is afraid to ask her.

By setting the second sentence off with a period and a capital letter, the writer has emphasized Bob's lack of courage. Of course, such sentences beginning with coordinate conjunctions are generally used for either transition or emphasis; therefore, as with most effective writing techniques, they should be used sparingly. It is important to be sure that sentences beginning with coordinate conjunctions are grammatically complete.

Practice Sentences 7-3

Indicate whether the subject or the verb is missing in the following fragments.

Example: Mike at the defensive back position for Brevard College.

<u>   *verb*   </u>

1. And being only 5′6″ tall was too short for the position.

            _____

2. But, nevertheless, was aggressive and hit hard.

            _____

3. Mike, being outstanding at his position as a high school player.

            _____

4. Had wanted to play for one of the major football schools.

            _____

5. The coaches of these schools, however, expressing little interest in him as a prospect.

_____

6. So, therefore, could only do his best with the opportunities available.

_____

7. At Brevard College, having earned a reputation as a hard hitter.

_____

8. Won the conference trophy as Best Defensive Player.

_____

9. Mike, accidentally injuring a player on another team rather seriously.

_____

10. Then and there decided to give up football.

_____

Correcting Sentence Fragments

Now that you have an understanding of sentence fragments, you should be able to proofread your own papers and remove any fragments you may have accidentally written. The two main things to check for in proofreading are (1) that each group of words treated as a sentence does contain a subject and a verb and (2) that each group of words treated as a sentence containing a subject and a verb does not begin with either a subordinate conjunction or a relative pronoun. If the group of words does not contain a subject and a verb, it is probably a phrase. If the word group contains a subject and a verb but is introduced by a relative pronoun or a subordinate conjunction, it is probably a subordinate clause.

In the event your proofreading does turn up a sentence fragment, you should not have much trouble correcting the error. If you can detect that a group of words is a fragment, you should have a good enough understanding of fragments and sentences by now to repair the fragment yourself. Fragments can be corrected in several ways. One of the easiest ways is to attach the fragment to another sentence.

Fragment: I really like to go swimming. In the pond near Ms. Johnson's apiary.

Correct the fragment by attaching it to the complete sentence:

Full Sentence: I really like to go swimming in the pond near Ms. Johnson's apiary.

Fragment: After I finished the novel. I went to bed.

Correct the fragment by attaching it to the complete sentence:

Full Sentence: After I finished the novel, I went to bed.

Fragments can also be corrected by supplying the missing subjects or verbs.

Fragment: The antique that I purchased in Williamsburg, Virginia.

Correct the fragment by providing the noun *antique* with a verb:

Full Sentence: The antique that I purchased in Williamsburg, Virginia, disintegrated.

Now *antique* is the subject of the verb *disintegrated* and the sentence is complete.

Fragment: But was not completed by the July 15 deadline.

Correct the fragment by providing the verb *was completed* with a subject:

Full Sentence: But the project was not completed by the July 15 deadline.

Now *project* is the subject of the verb *was completed* and the sentence is complete.

Occasionally a fragment is so fragmentary or so confused that it must be completely rewritten.

Fragment: The botanical gardens in Chapel Hill, North Carolina, being the place.

The group of words should be completely rewritten:

Full Sentence: Only plants native to North Carolina can be found in the botanical gardens in Chapel Hill, North Carolina.

Be sure not to confuse verbals and verbs. The *-ing* form of a verb cannot be a main verb without an auxiliary.

Fragment: The bridge being over two thousand feet long.

Being is a verbal, not a verb. The verbal should be converted into a main verb.

Full Sentence: The bridge *is* over two thousand feet long.

Practice Sentences 7-4

In the space provided, rewrite each fragment so that it becomes a complete sentence.

Example: Being extremely quiet and rather shy.

James is extremely quiet and rather

shy.

1. Aunt May, having gained forty pounds since her retirement.

_____

_____

2. A habit which can lead to lung cancer and heart problems.

_____

_____

3. His glasses being so thick they looked like telescopes.

_____

_____

4. Her beautiful size 5 shoes on her size 7 feet.

_____

_____

5. Having become more and more fond of vacations since his wife's death.

_____

_____

_____

6. John's wife being fond of his red hair and freckles.

_____

_____

7. And pulled a muscle in his back playing tennis with his daughter.

_____

_____

8. An unexpected October sunburn that was extremely painful.

_____

_____

9. But provided the automobile accident victim all the assistance her medical training had prepared her to give.

_____

_____

10. A beautiful dress with gold filigree in the bodice.

_____

_____

Review Exercise 7-A Identifying Sentence Fragments (I)

In the blanks provided, indicate whether the following word groups are complete sentences or fragments.

Example: The volleyball game that was scheduled to begin at 2:00 P.M.

fragment

1. Featured two-year college teams from across the state.

   _____

2. Naturally, the teams from California were favored.

   _____

3. Being able to play twelve months a year on the beaches.

   _____

4. But when the matches actually got under way.

   _____

5. Everyone was surprised to find the teams so evenly balanced.

   _____

6. Another surprise was that many smaller schools fared well against larger schools.

   _____

7. The tournament that included both men and women's teams.

   _____

8. Being a good opportunity for coaches to look at Olympic hopefuls.

   _____

9. The men's teams had more spikes, but the women's teams had better volleys.

   _____

10. Eventually, however, the tournament being won by a school in southern California.

_____

Review Exercise 7-B   Identifying Sentence Fragments (II)

In the blanks provided, indicate whether the following word groups are complete sentences or fragments.

Example: Ralph, planning to head for the beach just as soon as he finished the exam.

_____*fragment*_____

1. He had the cooler all packed and a paper bag full of clothes.

_____

2. The car having a full tank of gas, waiting for him in the school parking lot.

_____

3. Now for the test that he really didn't have the time or the patience to take.

_____

4. But he faced his academic responsibility bravely.

_____

5. Sitting down at the desk trying to psych himself up for the test.

_____

6. He could barely sit still.

_____

7. Trying desperately to answer questions for which he was sure he knew the answers.

_____

8. His legs were shaking and his heart was pounding while he tried to force himself to concentrate.

_____

9. Getting the best of both worlds with a great time at the beach and a 94 on the exam.

   _____

10. Though successful, Ralph decided he did not want to take a test under that much pressure again.

    _____

Review Exercise 7-C Correcting Sentence Fragments (I)

In the following paragraphs, circle the number of every word group that is a fragment. Correct all sentence fragments.

Example: *(1).* Being good in both drawing and math. *2.* Elyse decided to study architecture.

1. Lionell decided to take up golf. *2.* A sport that he had never tried before. *3.* Borrowing a set of clubs from a friend. *4.* He headed for the golf course. *5.* He teed the ball up for the first hole. *6.* Swinging with great power and confidence. *7.* He missed the ball completely. *8.* After his friends finally quit laughing. *9.* He tried again. *10.* This time the ball went over 200 yards straight down the middle of the fairway. *11.* His next shot landing on the green only fifteen feet from the flag. *12.* Was the best shot in the foursome. *13.* Unfortunately, he three putted the hole. *14.* By the time he completed the first five holes. *15.* Lionell decided he liked the game. *16.* He enjoyed hitting the ball off the tee. *17.* And hitting iron shots onto the green. *18.* Putting, however, wasn't his strong point. *19.* Nevertheless, he enjoyed his first outing. *20.* And shot a score of 112.

21. Now he was hooked on the game. *22.* Even though he didn't have any clubs of his own. *23.* His determination being strong, however. *24.* He went to a local pro shop and bought a complete set. *25.* He also bought a golf wardrobe. *26.* After he had purchased everything he needed. *27.* He couldn't wait to play golf at every opportunity. *28.* But after playing six more times, new clubs, new clothes and all. *29.* He was unable to break 120. *30.* Lionell has an ad in the classified section for a set of golf clubs "like new."

Review Exercise 7-D   Correcting Sentence Fragments (II)

In the following paragraphs, circle the number of every word group that is a fragment. Correct all sentence fragments.

Example: *1.* Martha cannot drive with young children in the car.
the
② Yelling and screaming ~~getting~~ *get* on her nerves and ~~affect~~ *affect*
~~ing~~ her concentration.

1. Andy signed up for a one-semester course in electronics. *2.* Though he had never studied the subject before. *3.* Having taken the general physics prerequisite. *4.* He thought he should do well in the courses. *5.* The professor spent four days introducing material. *6.* That most electronics professors spend an entire semester on.

7. Things didn't get any better at the end of the course. *8.* When the course was nearly over and it was time to take the exam. *9.* Andy was in for quite a shock. *10.* He was expected to design an amplifier to certain specifications. *11.* Although he didn't have the vaguest idea how. *12.* Somehow—through study, tutoring, and prayer—he passed the course. *13.* Never intending, however, to take another course in electronics.

8

Identifying and Correcting Fused Sentences and Comma Splices

When studying comma splices and fused sentences, you are learning as much about punctuation as you are about grammar. In this chapter, you will first learn to recognize these types of sentence errors; then you will see the four ways in which fused or comma-spliced sentences can be corrected.

Fused Sentences

A *fused sentence* is the result of combining main clauses without putting any punctuation between them.

> I saw Shakespeare's *Henry IV, Part One*, last night this evening I am going to see *Henry IV, Part Two*.

The break between main clauses is between the words *night* and *this*. Because no punctuation is present, the sentence is fused.

> I saw *Henry IV, Part One*, last night this evening I am going to see *Henry IV, Part Two*, next week I will attend *Henry V* I look forward to seeing every play.

Now the sentence is fused in three places—between *night* and *this*, between *Two* and *next*, between *V* and *I*.

Practice Sentences 8-1

Circle the break between main clauses in each of the following fused sentences.

> **Example:** Joan has worked at a nursing home for several years ◯ she finds the work challenging.

1. She always felt close to her grandparents the job is an extension of that relationship.

2. Some of the residents are by no means senile Joan enjoys talking with them.

3. The nursing home residents genuinely love their children and grandchildren unfortunately, some of the children are unkind to their parents.

4. The children never come by to see them this, of course, hurts the residents deeply.

5. Sometimes the children will even try to take control of their parents' estates they say the parents are incompetent.

6. Joan thinks such treatment is awful she tries to help her patients stand up for their legal rights.

7. Many local judges help her they don't like the thought of themselves or their parents being treated that way.

8. There is a brighter side, Joan gets to see some of the residents fall in love.

9. Some of the patients feel love at this age is even better than in youth there is a much deeper interest in companionship and in the other person's individuality.

10. Never underestimate the power of love snow on the roof doesn't mean there's no fire in the furnace.

There are two correct ways to join the main clauses of a compound sentence: use (1) a semicolon or (2) a comma and one of the coordinate conjunctions (and, or, nor, but, yet, so).

John Davis spent over thirty hours preparing the report for his boss; it was never read.
The sentence is correct because a semicolon joins the break between the main clauses.

John Davis spent over thirty hours preparing the report for his boss, but it was never read.
The sentence is correct because the comma and the coordinate conjunction but join the break between main clauses.

Notice that the sentence with the semicolon packs a punch. It is more direct and forceful. Although the sentence with the comma and the coordinating conjunction gives the same information, the fact that John Davis' report was not read has been de-emphasized by the inclusion of the comma and coordinating conjunction. Thus, in your writing the punctuation you use can determine the emphasis you wish to place on an idea. Naturally, the main clauses being joined must be logically related.

> I bought a Panasonic radio, and *Ulysses* was banned in this country until 1933.

Though the sentence is correctly punctuated, it is an extremely bad sentence. No amount of punctuation can improve such an illogical sentence.

Practice Sentences 8-2

Correct each of the following fused sentences by putting a semicolon where it is needed.

Example: Lamarre is a good student; his favorite class is chemistry.

1. When he was in high school, he scored higher than anyone else in the state on a standardized test he is, of course, very proud of this accomplishment.

2. Quite frankly, he has not found the competition in college that he expected many of his peers have difficulty with the abstract concepts.

3. He hopes that things will be different when he is an upperclassman fellow chemistry majors should be more knowledgeable and more motivated.

4. Lamarre enjoys his afternoons in the laboratory he can see the practical application of the theory discussed in class and in the text.

5. Lamarre's chemistry professor says Lamarre has the most potential of any student he has had in years he believes Lamarre has a good background and a good attitude.

6. Upon graduation Lamarre plans to do graduate work at MIT this school was suggested by his professors.

7. Meanwhile, he is studying halogens he already knows more than most air conditioner repairmen that work with halogens every day.

8. Next week he will be studying the nitrogen family he has heard the professor brings a container of liquid nitrogen to class.

9. This should be interesting a rubber ball can be frozen solid by dipping it in liquid nitrogen.

10. The professor let Lamarre dip a rubber ball into the liquid nitrogen he threw it just over his roommate's head.

Practice Sentences 8-3

Correct each of the following sentences by providing an appropriate co-ordinate conjunction to accompany the comma.

Example: Ghost stories and legends abound in North Carolina, *and* many books relating these stories have been written.

1. Many of the stories are said to be based on fact, there are people who have witnessed the events.

2. The Devil's Tramping Ground is a huge, bare circle in which no vegetation will grow, it is located in the central part of the state.

3. In the legend of the Devil's Tramping Ground, it is said the Devil removes any objects placed in the bare spot, no one has ever proved that it is actually the Devil who removes them.

4. Another story, the legend of the Brown Mountain Light, has many explanations, each one differs in its interpretation of the meaning of the mysterious light.

5. In the mountains of North Carolina, a mysterious light appears, there is no apparent reason for the light.

6. Some people say an old slave has come back from his grave carrying a lantern and looking for his master, a song called "The Brown Mountain Light" relates that version, although that is not the most popular explanation.

7. Another popular legend is of a young girl who hitches a ride with strangers and disappears from their car, she always appears on dark, foggy nights and wears a white gown.

8. Apparently, a young girl was killed on a bridge near Chapel Hill many years ago, ever since that foggy night, she has been trying to get someone to take her home.

9. Many people say they have stopped to pick her up and take her home, she always disappears without a trace before they reach her home.

10. You should never tell a North Carolinian that these stories are not true, you may be speaking to someone who has witnessed one of these mysteries.

Comma Splices

Now that you know how the main clauses of a sentence can be correctly joined by a comma, look at how they are often incorrectly joined by a comma. The *comma splice* error is the result of combining main clauses with a comma where the comma is insufficient punctuation.

> Mary is a dedicated homemaker on the weekends, she vacuums the floors and puts everything in its proper place.
>> The break between main clauses occurs between *weekends* and *she*. The sentence is comma spliced since a comma is not sufficient punctuation to join the main clauses.

> Mary is a dedicated homemaker on the weekends, she vacuums the floors and puts everything in its proper place, then on Monday she ignores the house, she will not perform any domestic chores until Friday.
>> Now the sentence is comma spliced three times: between *homemaker* and *she*, between *place* and *then*, and between *house* and *she*. Remember, a sentence that is comma spliced always contains a comma.

Practice Sentences 8-4

Circle the comma-spliced breaks between main clauses in the following sentences.

Example: Joe bought a brand new umbrella this afternoon, it was expensive and monogrammed with his initials.

1. Two days after he bought it there was a heavy downpour, naturally, this was just what Joe had been waiting for.

2. Joe took the umbrella with him to the school cafeteria, he hung it on a peg away from all the other umbrellas.

3. Proud of his fine umbrella, Joe ate an expensive meal, he felt like a real gentleman.

4. After the meal Joe went to get his umbrella, it was gone.

5. Someone had stolen it, the thief now owned an umbrella with Joe's initials on it.

6. Joe was extremely angry, he stole the first expensive umbrella he saw.

7. This was an unusual thing for him to do, Joe isn't a thief.

8. He tried to find the owner in order to return the umbrella, he was unable to do so.

9. He took the umbrella with him to the cafeteria the next time it rained, it was gone when he went to get it after his meal.

10. Joe went to the store the very next day, he bought the cheapest umbrella he could find.

Practice Sentences 8-5

Circle the comma-spliced breaks between main clauses in the following sentences.

Example: The Jeffersons recently purchased a puppy, the dog is a Labrador Retriever named Blackie.

1. Julio ordered a chain saw from a mail-order company, he thought he got a good deal.

2. The saw was supposed to arrive in about ten days, instead it was five weeks before the saw came.

3. Julio went to pick the saw up at the post office, he was surprised to find three packages rather than just one.

4. Julio figured he was going to have to put the saw together, this thought didn't please him.

5. At home he opened all the boxes, each box contained a complete chain saw.

6. He called the company to explain the mistake, the company representative told him to ship two of them back.

7. Julio found out that it would cost him $87 for the return shipment, he also learned that his credit card had been billed for three saws.

8. The company representative told Julio he would be reimbursed for return freight, the two saws were then returned to the company.

9. The saws did not arrive at the company, the representative told Julio to put a tracer on the return shipment.

10. Eventually Julio's account was straightened out, he has not ordered anything else by mail.

Conjunctive Adverbs and Transitional Phrases

Words such as *however* and expressions such as *on the other hand* often occur at the break between main clauses. Such words and expressions are modifiers that are used to connect clauses. The individual words are called *conjunctive adverbs;* the multiword expressions are called *transitional phrases.* Conjunctive adverbs and transitional phrases are not coordinate conjunctions and cannot connect main clauses with just a comma.

> My professor likes the novelist John Gardner, however, she believes John Updike is a better craftsman.
>> The sentence is comma spliced between *Gardner* and *however.* To keep the sentence compound, you would need to use a semicolon.

> My professor likes the novelist John Gardner; however, she believes John Updike is a better craftsman.

Many of the following words and phrases appear at the break between main clauses.

Conjunctive Adverbs	*Transitional Phrases*
accordingly	as a result
also	at the same time
besides	for example
consequently	in addition
furthermore	in fact
hence	in other words
henceforth	on the contrary
however	on the other hand
indeed	that is
likewise	
meanwhile	
moreover	
nevertheless	
otherwise	
still	
then	
therefore	
thus	

It may be easier for you to understand the difference between pure coordinate conjunctions and the words and phrases on the list above if you realize that conjunctions are used to connect, whereas the listed words and phrases just help the sentence flow smoothly.

In the following sentence, *but* can be only where it is; it does not fit or make sense in any other position:

Correct: Ralph likes his secretary a great deal, but he likes his wife even more.

Incorrect: Ralph likes his secretary a great deal; he but likes his wife even more.

Incorrect: Ralph likes his secretary a great deal; he likes his wife even more but.

Notice that versions 2 and 3 are awkward and nonsensical. The reason is that *but* is a pure conjunction and can only be used to connect.

On the other hand, a word such as *however* can fit in several positions in the sentence and still make sense:

Ralph likes his secretary a great deal; however, he likes his wife even more.

1. Ralph likes his secretary a great deal; he likes his wife, however, even more.

2. Ralph likes his secretary a great deal; he likes his wife even more, however.

The word *however* (and the other words and phrases listed) can be moved around in the sentence because it is not a pure connector.

Remember, only coordinate conjunctions can connect main clauses with just a comma before them; the other words and phrases cannot. Avoid sentences such as the following:

Jane thought she wanted to go to dental school she decided, however, to major in drama instead.

   Though the sentence contains the word *however* with a comma before it, the sentence is fused between *school* and *she* and not comma spliced, since *however* is not at the break between clauses.

Most important, you should remember that a sentence can be neither comma spliced nor fused if it does not contain at least two main clauses.

Short Fiction of the Masters is a good anthology.

   The sentence is just a simple sentence containing one main clause.

Ways to Correct Comma Splices and Fused Sentences

There are four ways to correct comma splices and fused sentences.

Fused: Jane thought she wanted to go to dental school she decided to major in drama instead.

Comma splice: Jane thought she wanted to go to dental school, she decided to major in drama instead.

1. The main clauses can be rewritten as separate sentences:

    Jane thought she wanted to go to dental school. She decided to major in drama instead.

2. One of the main clauses can be rewritten as a subordinate clause:

    Although Jane thought she wanted to go to dental school, she decided to major in drama instead.

3. A semicolon can be put between the main clauses:

    Jane thought she wanted to go to dental school; she decided to major in drama instead.

4. A comma and a coordinate conjunction can be put at the break between clauses:

    Jane thought she wanted to go to dental school, but she decided to major in drama instead.

The way you choose to correct a comma splice will depend on your personal preferences and on the meaning you wish to convey. For example, the coordinate conjunction *and* balances two main clauses, whereas the coordinate conjunctions *but* and *yet* contrast them.

Balancing: Robert wanted to buy Janice an expensive winter coat, <u>and</u> he went to the nicest store in town to find one.

Robert wanted to buy Janice an expensive winter coat, <u>but</u> he could not afford to get the one he really liked.

Subordinating one of the clauses de-emphasizes it.

De-emphasizing: Although Robert wanted to buy Janice an expensive winter coat, he couldn't afford to get the one he really liked.

Combining two main clauses in one sentence with a semicolon between them gives each clause equal emphasis and indicates the close relationship in meaning between the two.

Equalizing: Robert wanted to buy Janice an expensive winter coat; he went to the nicest store in town to find one.

Putting the main clauses in two separate sentences emphasizes each one more.

Emphasizing: Robert wanted to buy Janice an expensive winter coat. He could not afford to get the one he really liked.

No one method of correcting comma splices and fused sentences is more correct than another. Just strive for variety in your writing and avoid overworking any one technique.

Review Exercise 8-A   Identifying Fused Sentences and Comma Splices (I)

In the blanks provided, indicate whether the following sentences are correct, comma spliced, or fused.

Example: Nearly everyone on campus got involved in Sheffield Community College's softball program even the faculty fielded a team.

_____ *fused* _____

1. Each team had at least two women on it, some of the female athletes were very good.

_____

2. Most of these women had honed their skills by playing on commercial league teams for several summers.

_____

3. Some of the men thought the women batters would be easy outs they changed their minds when the ball went over their heads.

_____

4. Few of the early-round games were close, the better teams often won by ten or fifteen runs.

_____

5. Although no one expected it, the faculty team made a good showing.

_____

6. They won their first game 14–6, they did even better in their second game.

_____

7. All of the student teams wanted to play "the old folks" they thought it was fun to play their teachers.

_____

8. The student umpire was accused of calling the game in favor of the faculty the members of the student teams said the umpire was trying to get a better grade.

                                        _____

9. At any rate, the championship game came down to a student team against the faculty, there were many spectators.

                                        _____

10. Although the faculty played well, their team lost 9–6.

                                        _____

Review Exercise 8-B Identifying Fused Sentences and Comma Splices (II)

In the blanks provided, indicate whether the following sentences are correct, comma spliced, or fused.

Example: Joann decided to take a college course in English literature she had enjoyed the subject in high school.

fused

1. She found she wasn't interested in some of the material, *Beowulf* and *The Vision of Piers Plowman* left her cold.

   _____

2. Chaucer was a different matter, however; she thoroughly enjoyed *The Canterbury Tales.*

   _____

3. She thought the Pardoner was an interesting character he told the Canterbury pilgrims exactly how he parted people from their money.

   _____

4. After telling the pilgrims this, he used the ploy on them.

   _____

5. It didn't work the Host was far too smart to be tricked so easily.

   _____

6. Joann also liked the Wife of Bath, perhaps the best-known figure in *The Canterbury Tales.*

   _____

7. Joann liked the Wife's forthright honesty the character liked sex and said so.

   _____

8. Joann also liked the Wife's frank assessment of marriage, Chaucer's character felt the woman should be dominant in a marriage.

   _____

9. Joann was not offended by the Wife's indelicate language, in fact, Joann felt the work seemed more modern because of such frankness.

                                        _____

10. Joann's favorite story, however, was "The Nun's Priest's Tale" she cackled over the adventures of Chantecleer and Pertelote.

                                        _____

Review Exercise 8-C   Identifying Fused Sentences and Comma Splices (III)

In the blanks provided, indicate whether the following sentences are correct, comma spliced, or fused.

Example: Joan has a 350 Kawasaki motorcycle her husband worries about her safety.

_____*fused*_____

1. Dr. Robinson is a physician in Tempe, Arizona; he has practiced medicine there for twenty-five years.

   _____

2. One night he drove to a patient's home to examine her, he parked his car in front of her house.

   _____

3. After the examination he returned to his car, and he headed back home.

   _____

4. About three miles down the road, he heard a noise in the back.

   _____

5. There was a man hiding in the back he said he wanted all the narcotics in the medical bag.

   _____

6. On another occasion, the safe was stolen from his office, thieves took the entire safe, not just the contents.

   _____

7. The work, of course, is not generally so dangerous, but it is hard work with long hours.

   _____

8. On several occasions he has been so tired that he failed to put the telephone receiver back on the cradle properly the operator couldn't get through with emergency calls.

_____

9. In the middle of the night Dr. Robinson and his family have been awakened by the police, the officers have come to notify Dr. Robinson of an emergency.

_____

10. Dr. Robinson continues to practice despite the "inconveniences," he enjoys the practice of medicine.

_____

Review Exercise 8-D   Correcting Fused Sentences and Comma Splices

In the spaces provided, rewrite the following comma splices and fused sentences, correcting the sentence faults by one of the four methods explained in this chapter.

Example: Blair has an appointment to get a permanent this afternoon she hopes the chemicals don't have a strong odor.

Blair has an appointment to get a permanent this afternoon, but she hopes the chemicals don't have a strong odor.

1. Corbin prefers pizza with nothing on it but cheese and tomato sauce however, he will eat a pizza with all the toppings if someone else is buying.

2. Josh bought a boat for $250 he fixed it up by himself and was offered $3,000 for it.

3. Melanie plays the banjo very well she has won several contests.

4. James finally agreed to paint his grandmother's house as she wanted it, her house is the only purple one in the neighborhood with maroon trim.

5. Stephanie had an accident on her four-wheeler, she broke her arm in two places.

_____

_____

6. Dr. Gorriaran burned his tie in lab last week he got it too close to a Bunsen burner.

_____

_____

7. Rebecca dropped her English class after having missed several sessions in a row the class interfered with her job.

_____

_____

8. Juanita had no difficulty in her Spanish class it came to her naturally.

_____

_____

9. Ginger is a professional photographer who enjoys her work, she especially likes doing portraits of children.

_____

_____

10. Darryl's mother refuses to let him watch any R-rated movies he told her that all the best movies were R-rated.

_____

_____

9

Pronoun Case and Reference

Case

Pronouns are naming words that are used to take the place of nouns. Just like nouns, pronouns usually function as subjects, direct objects, indirect objects, objects of prepositions, and predicate nominatives. The case of a pronoun shows its function in a sentence. There are three cases in English: nominative, objective, and possessive. Here is a list of pronouns classified by case:

Nominative	Objective	Possessive
I	me	my (mine)
you	you	your (yours)
it	it	its
we	us	our (ours)
he, she	him, her	his, her (hers)
they	them	their (theirs)
who	whom	whose
whoever	whomever	

Nominative Case

1. Pronouns used as subjects require the nominative case.

    I am going to get a loan today.
    > *I* is in the nominative case because it is the subject of the verb *am going.*

    They will complete the float in time for the parade.
    > *They* is in the nominative case because it is the subject of the verb *will complete.*

2. Pronouns used as predicate nominatives require the nominative case.

> The winner was he who spoke first.
> > *He* is in the nominative case because it is a predicate nominative.

> It is I.
> > *I* functions as a predicate nominative and is therefore in the nominative case.

3. An appositive is a noun or pronoun that renames or explains another noun or pronoun. When an appositive renames a word in the nominative case, it too is in the nominative case.

> Two men, John and Bob, attended the special dinner.
> > *Men* is the subject of the verb *attended* and is therefore in the nominative case. The words *John* and *Bob* rename the noun *men* and are therefore appositives.

> Two men, Bob and I, attended the special dinner.
> > Now *I* is a pronoun in the nominative case. It is in apposition with the subject *men*, which is a noun in the nominative case.

> The girls, Judy and she, built a model of the Globe Theatre.
> > *She* is in the nominative case because it is in apposition with a word in the nominative case, the subject *girls*.

Practice Sentences 9-1

Underline the pronouns in the nominative case.

> **Example:** I think Lisa would make a good sales manager.

> 1. She is familiar with the computers.

> 2. Lisa is the only salesperson who has experience on all models.

> 3. Whoever has a question goes to Lisa.

> 4. Furthermore, Lisa is a person who is comfortable with all kinds of people.

> 5. She is definitely my choice.

Objective Case

1. Pronouns used as objects require the objective case. The most common types of objects are direct objects, indirect objects, and objects of prepositions.

> Do you really love her?
> > *Her* is in the objective case because it is the direct object of the verb *do love*.

Judy gave him a sweater for his birthday.
> *Him* is in the objective case because it is the indirect object of the verb *gave*.

Give the free pass to me.
> *Me* is in the objective case because it is the object of the preposition *to*.

2. The objective case is also used for a pronoun that functions as the object of a verbal.

To arrest him is the FBI's goal.
> *Him* is in the objective case because it is the object of the infinitive *to arrest*.

Getting him to the podium at last, Judy sat down.
> *Him* is in the objective case because it is the object of the participle *getting*.

3. And a pronoun in apposition with a word in the objective case goes in the objective case.

The committee elected two representatives—Susan and me.
> *Me* is in the objective case because it is in apposition with the direct object *representatives*.

Save the biggest applause for the finalists—the Cardinals and us.
> *Us* is in apposition with the word *finalists*, which is the object of the preposition *for*.

Remember that a pronoun appositive can be in either the objective or nominative case, depending on the case of the word the pronoun is in apposition with. You should also realize that the pronoun itself may take an appositive.

We runners were breathing hard during the race.
> *Runners* is in apposition with the pronoun *we*. *We* is used correctly in the nominative case because it is the subject of the verb *were breathing*.

The coach gave the trophy to us winners.
> *Us* is used correctly in the objective case because it is the object of the preposition *to*. *Winners* is an appositive and does not affect the pronoun choice.

Practice Sentences 9-2

Underline the pronouns in the objective case.

Example: Mary gave <u>him</u> a brass spittoon.

1. The vice president promoted her to the position of sales manager.

2. The coach told us to hustle.

3. Mother told us girls to get quiet.

4. The man whom he most admired died in an accident.

5. Mrs. Terrill gave me a nice Christmas bonus.

Who / Whom

You need to be careful when *who* and *whom* appear in subordinate clauses. *Who* and *whoever* are nominative case forms that will ordinarily function as subjects. But *who* and *whoever* will often be the subjects of the subordinate clauses in which they appear, not necessarily the subject of the whole sentence.

Who will win the British Open this year?
> In this sentence *who* is the subject of the whole sentence since *will win* is the only verb.

Whoever picks the most cucumbers will win a bushel of corn.
> In this sentence *whoever* is the subject of the verb *picks*, but the whole noun clause *whoever picks the most cucumbers* is the subject of the whole sentence. *Whoever* is just the subject of the verb in its clause.

John likes whoever travels to the games with him.
> *Whoever* is the subject of the verb *travels*. The whole noun clause *whoever travels to the games with him* is the direct object of the verb *likes*.

A subordinate who/whom clause may function as an object of a preposition.

He worked with whoever needed him most.
> *Whoever needed him most* is the object of the preposition *with*. *Whoever* is the subject of the verb *needed* in the subordinate clause.

The subordinate who/whom clauses may have other functions.

Knowing (who, whom) would win the election, the mayor withdrew from the race.
> *Who* is the subject of the verb *would win*. The whole noun clause *who would win the election* is the object of the participle *knowing*.

Give (whoever, whomever) eats the most an Alka-Seltzer tablet.
> *Whoever* is the subject of the verb *eats*. The whole noun clause *whoever eats the most* is an indirect object of the verb *give*.

Arthur Hall is a man (who, whom) greatly admires the films of W. C. Fields.

> This time the subordinate clause is an adjective clause. *Who greatly admires the films of W. C. Fields* modifies the noun *man*. *Who* is the correct choice because it is the subject of the verb *admires*.

When the verb in a subordinate who/whom clause already has a subject, the correct choice is usually *whom*, functioning as a direct object of the verb in the subordinate clause.

Whomever she prefers will be appointed.

Whomever she prefers is the noun clause subject of the verb *will be appointed*. Within the noun clause *she* is the subject of the verb *prefers*; she prefers whom? the answer is *whomever*. Once you realize that the verb *prefers* already has a subject, you should realize that *whomever* is the direct object.

The woman (who, whom) John loves is a truck driver.

> *Whom* is the correct choice because it is the direct object of the verb *loves* in the subordinate clause.

You should be careful with who/whom clauses in sentences that contain expressions such as *I think, I feel, I believe, you may recall,* etc. Such expressions are merely parenthetical interrupters that are not grammatically relevant. The expressions have to be mentally ignored.

Janet is the girl who I think deserves the award.

> *Janet* is the subject of the verb *is*, and *who* is the subject of the verb *deserves*.

If you are careful in your writing to make sure each verb has a subject, you will avoid sentences such as *Janet is the girl whom I think deserves the award*. If *whom* were considered the object of the verb *think*, the verb *deserves* would not have a subject.

Practice Sentences 9-3

Identify the correct sentences by placing a C by the number; correct the errors in all others.

Example: Ms. Martin is a woman ~~who~~ *whom* most people respect.

1. Rebecca Martin is the candidate whom I feel is the best qualified.

2. If Ms. Martin is elected to the Senate, she will be a senator who will always vote in the best interest of the nation.

3. She will not be easily persuaded by lobbyists whom are seeking to serve their own selfish interests.

4. In the past Ms. Martin has publicly supported those whom advocated equal rights for all people.

5. As a state senator, she was one of very few who people thought was honest.

6. She is also a diplomat, one who knows how to sell an idea but also how to compromise in case of stalemate.

7. She is the person whom you may recall did most for the state in upgrading education.

8. Ms. Martin knows she cannot please everyone who votes for her.

9. She promises to vote her conscience and best judgment, and in so doing she may at times anger those whom she feels helped her get elected.

10. Let's hope that the voters who turn out on November 2 recognize good character and integrity and vote for Ms. Martin.

Pronouns are sometimes used following such words as *than* and *as*. Often such uses only imply a subject and/or verb. You must recognize what is omitted.

Fred likes Kathy better than I.
Fred likes Kathy better than me.

Both sentences are correct, but they mean quite different things. The first sentence has an implied verb:

Fred likes Kathy better than I [do].
I is the subject of the understood verb *do* (or *like*).

The second has an implied subject and verb.

Fred likes Kathy better than [he likes] me.
Me is the object of the understood expression *he* likes.

In your own writing you want to communicate the right message to the reader. The sentence ending with *I* means something very different indeed from the one ending with *me*. As Mark Twain said, "The difference between the right word and the almost right word is the difference between lightning and the lightning bug."

Possessive Case

The possessive case is generally used before a gerund.

Mr. Jones does not like Susan's staying out past midnight.
The proper noun *Susan* is possessive because it precedes the gerund *staying*.

His practicing four hours each day won him the prize.
> *His* is in the possessive case. It precedes the gerund *practicing,* which is the subject of the verb *won.*

He soon tired of our complaining.
> *Our* is in the possessive case because it precedes the gerund *complaining,* the object of the preposition *of.*

Practice Sentences 9-4

Identify the correct sentences by placing a C by the number; correct the errors in all others.

Example: ~~Him~~ *His* mowing the lawn before breakfast surprised everyone.

1. We were surprised at them doing so well.

2. My anger was evident by my arguing with the other driver.

3. Him driving the ball 300 yards impressed us all.

4. Lloyd paying his rent on time was a first.

5. Your lending me the notes was a big help.

Reference

As a writer you need to be certain your pronouns are in the right case. You must also be sure the noun the pronoun stands for (the antecedent) is obvious to the reader. When the reader cannot tell what noun the pronoun refers to, the writer has put up a barrier to communication known as faulty pronoun reference. There is more than one type of faulty pronoun reference to avoid.

1. Avoid sentences that have two possible antecedents for a pronoun.

Incorrect: Susan told Jane that she had an attractive coiffure.

The pronoun is *she,* but is the antecedent *Susan* or *Jane?*

Correct: Susan told Jane, "You have an attractive coiffure."

Now the reader knows that Jane has the attractive coiffure.

Incorrect: Bob told Ralph that he had stolen three dollars.

Is the antecedent of *he* supposed to be *Bob* or *Ralph?*

Correct: Bob confessed to Ralph that he had stolen three dollars.

Now the reader knows that the antecedent of *he* is Bob.

Practice Sentences 9-5

In the space provided, rewrite the following sentences by eliminating the faulty pronoun reference.

Example: David drove his father to his house.

David drove his father to David's house.

1. Jim told his father he had mowed and trimmed the lawn very nicely.

_____

_____

2. Randy told Lewis his car had been stolen.

_____

_____

3. Steve told Sandra's brother his shoe was untied.

_____

_____

4. The teacher told the substitute she had to go home.

_____

_____

5. Ellen told Darlene she would be waiting a long time for her first paycheck.

_____

_____

2. Avoid sentences that have antecedents remote from the pronoun. An antecedent is said to be remote if it is too far from the pronoun.

> The noise was disturbing to everyone in the class. The teacher felt the rusty machine was to blame. It reached a level of 180 decibels.

Does *it* refer to *noise* or *machine*?

> The noise, which reached a level of 180 decibels, was disturbing to everyone in the class. The teacher felt the rusty machine was to blame.

Now there is no remote pronoun reference. The unclear *it* has been removed.

> The amateur radio operators installed their equipment in the shopping center. The shoppers were very interested. They stayed through the lunch hour.

Does the *they* mean the operators or the shoppers?

> The amateur radio operators installed their equipment in the shopping center; they stayed through the lunch hour. The shoppers were very interested.

Since the pronoun *they* comes in the same sentence as its antecedent *operators* and before the word *shoppers*, the reference is no longer remote.

A special type of obscure reference occurs when the antecedent is in the possessive case.

> While John's car was being repaired, he played nine holes of golf.

The antecedent of *he* is *John's*. Good writers avoid placing the antecedent in the possessive case. One reason is *John's* is an adjective modifying *car*, telling which car. The antecedent of a pronoun should not be an adjective.

> While John was having his car repaired, he played nine holes of golf.

Now the antecedent of both *his* and *he* is the nonpossessive word *John*.

Practice Sentences 9-6

In the space provided, revise each of the following sentences so that the remote reference is eliminated.

Example: When it rained, it dampened our spirits.

The rain dampened our spirits).

1. The employees' cars have broken windshields and dented fenders; they were beaten with the club of a vandal.

_____

_____

2. Denise put a sash on her new dress; it was very attractive.

_____

_____

3. When Mary's idea was enthusiastically applauded, she was very happy.

_____

_____

4. The children all brought their radios to the birthday party; they played noisily all afternoon.

_____

_____

5. The apartment on the second floor has a window with a bright red shade; it is quite attractive.

_____

_____

3. Avoid sentences that have *this, that,* or *which* referring to the general idea of a preceding clause or sentence. Though some writers allow *this, that,* or *which* to refer to general ideas, more precise writers employ a particular word as the antecedent of *this, that,* or *which.*

Careless: Democrats should support the party's candidates. This is what party members are told.

Precise: Party members are told to support the Democratic candidates.

Careless: Everyone wanted the man to stand up for his rights. That is what they came to see.
    What is the antecedent of *that?*

Precise: Everyone came to see the man stand up for his rights.

Practice Sentences 9-7

In the space provided, revise each of the following sentences so that the vague references caused by this, that, *and* which *are eliminated.*

Example: The Ronald Haney Company did not give any Christmas bonuses last year. That is unusual.

It was unusual for the Ronald Haney Company not to give any Christmas bonuses last year.

1. John's becoming an engineer, which was a surprise to those familiar with his weakness in mathematics, is proving to be profitable for him.

   _____

   _____

2. Alice stayed up all night studying for the CPA examination. That is why she is so sleepy today.

   _____

   _____

3. The fine professor who never published any articles did not receive tenure, which is exactly what the students had predicted.

   _____

   _____

4. Keith cooked a nice Chinese dinner for Sue. That is unusual for him.

   _____

   _____

5. The car ran perfectly for Joe Wood during the test drive but then broke down on the way home, which is his usual bad luck.

   _____

   _____

4. Avoid implied antecedents. Antecedents should be stated rather than merely implied.

Implied: Although the test was easy, they had a lot of trouble.

Stated: Although the test was easy, the students had a lot of trouble.

Implied: Joseph Gluck delivered a good sermon. They told him so as they left the church.

Stated: Joseph Gluck delivered a good sermon. The members of the congregation told him so as they left the church.

Practice Sentences 9-8

In the space provided, revise the following sentences so that the pronouns have stated antecedents.

Example: The man ate so voraciously he finished it in five minutes.

The man ate so voraciously he finished the steak in five minutes.

1. My father put a heavy chain on the dog's collar; he cannot escape.

   _____

   _____

2. The garden was surrounded by a garage and a barn; it did not need work.

   _____

   _____

3. After you finish sanding, I will take it to Ms. Jones.

   _____

   _____

4. When he photocopied the last page, he took it to be bound.

   _____

   _____

5. Because she had been writing all day, it was not a task she wanted to start again.

   _____

   _____

5. Avoid awkward use of the indefinite *it, you,* or *they.* The awkwardness results from the pronoun's lack of a specific antecedent.

Awkward: It says to jog three miles every day.

Improved: The article says to jog three miles every day.

Awkward: Many states require you to burn the headlight day or night when riding a motorcycle.

Improved: Many states require motorcyclists to burn the headlight day or night.

Awkward: At one revival they said watching television was a sin.

Improved: At one revival the preacher said watching television was a sin.

Practice Sentences 9-9

In the space provided, revise the following sentences to eliminate the indefinite use of it, you, *and* they.

> **Example:** Most of the summer jobs have been filled; they have hired only college graduates so far.

Most of the summer jobs have been filled; the employers have hired only college graduates so far.

1. Diane recently read a book in which it tells the importance of physical fitness.

_____

_____

2. Mark, they say, has a lot of little eccentricities.

_____

_____

3. They say you should never swim after eating, but it has never bothered me.

_____

_____

4. It says the speed limit is 55 m.p.h.

_____

_____

5. They say money can't buy happiness, but I wonder if it is true.

_____

_____

6. Avoid using both the definite and the indefinite *it* in a sentence.

Awkward: Although it is a good day to clean the pool, it is not extremely dirty.
    The first *it* is indefinite; the second *it* refers to the noun *pool*.

Improved: Although it is a good day for cleaning, the pool is not extremely dirty.

Awkward: We intended to plant a peach tree this fall. It is too late to plant it now.
    The first *it* is indefinite; the second *it* refers to the noun *tree*.

Improved: We intended to plant a peach tree this fall. It is too late now.

Practice Sentences 9-10

In the space provided, revise each of the following sentences so that both the definite and indefinite it *are not present.*

Example: Since it is my desire to teach, I hope I will be able to do it well.

Since I want to teach, I hope I will be a good teacher.

1. Although it is a good topic for a research paper, it cannot have so controversial a thesis.

_____

_____

2. It is a good time to wax the floor since the children are not at home to mar it.

_____

_____

3. It is a good time for playing tennis on the school court since it will not be in use.

_____

_____

4. Even though it rained on the day of our picnic, it was a great success.

_____

_____

5. Shirley passed the test even though it was hard. It is good she did.

_____

_____

Review Exercise 9-A Using Pronoun Case Correctly (I)

In the following sentences, underline the correct choice.

Example: Give the gold wrench to (<u>whoever</u>, whomever) is the best mechanic.

1. It was (she, her) that designed most of the dresses.

2. (Whoever, Whomever) the president selects will chair the new committee.

3. (We, Us) girls did not want Jerry to come with us on our coffee break.

4. Claudine loves (whoever, whomever) is with her at the time.

5. Ada knows (she, her) is next in line for a promotion.

6. Richard asked Rachel to go to the dance with (he, him).

7. The student was upset with the grade (she, her) received.

8. (Our, Us) planning the landscape saved a lot of money.

9. (Whoever, Whomever) writes the best essay will receive a Cross pen.

10. The two joggers, Jake and (he, him), keep daily jogging charts.

Review Exercise 9-B Using Pronoun Case Correctly (II)

In the following sentences, underline the correct choice.

Example: I did not allow the man's anger to get to (I, <u>me</u>).

1. The family picked strawberries for (whoever, whomever) was willing to pay $2.50 per gallon.

2. (She, Her) climbing the twelve flights of steps was an unwanted exercise.

3. (We, Us) members of the club must stand together.

4. It must have been (she, her) that finished the project last night.

5. A local garden club will present the Community Award to (whoever, whomever) has the best-landscaped and best-maintained lawn.

6. All of the people on the team—Bill, Susan, Howard, and (I, me)—worked very hard.

7. Justin doesn't seem to be as intelligent as (she, her).

8. (Us, Our) coming home early surprised Mom.

9. (Whoever, Whomever) the president nominates is questioned by the council.

10. It must have been (he, him) who took the daily work schedule from the bulletin board.

Review Exercise 9-C   Using Pronoun Case Correctly (III)

Correct the case errors in the following sentences.

Example: Betty and ~~her~~ *she* refused to help their mother in the garden.

1. Ariel plays the piano better than him.

2. Us girls should help them with expenses if we can.

3. Whoever the teachers select will have the lead in the play.

4. He plays better golf than her.

5. Whom do you think can hit the ball the farthest?

6. Everyone but he was ready on time.

7. Dad gave Bill and I enough money to buy the new lawnmower.

8. It must have been her who borrowed his car.

9. I do not like him using my comb.

10. Whom is most qualified for his former job?

Review Exercise 9-D   Correcting Faulty Pronoun Reference (I)

In the space provided, revise each of the following sentences to eliminate faulty pronoun reference.

Example: They say never to volunteer for anything.

Army veterans say never to volunteer for
anything.

1. Bob told Herbert he should be going.

_____

_____

2. Gary's attending a university is expensive for his parents; he is being supported totally by them.

_____

_____

3. They say one should never swim alone.

_____

_____

4. Children should unquestionably obey all adults. This is what some children are taught.

_____

_____

5. Although it is not always necessary to have a physical exam, it could save some people a lot of suffering.

_____

_____

6. The ceiling with a hole in it presents a problem when it is full of people.

_____

_____

7. Although it was bad weather for a wedding, it went smoothly.

_____

_____

8. Jane told Ruth her hair needed trimming.

_____

_____

9. The store manager put an antique doll on the marble pedestal; a stranger wrote a bad check and took it.

_____

_____

10. They say Mr. Kelly is losing his mind.

_____

_____

Review Exercise 9-E *Correcting Faulty Pronoun Reference (II)*

In the space provided, revise each of the following sentences to eliminate faulty pronoun reference.

Example: The wardens patrol the river, which makes it difficult to fish illegally.

The wardens' patrolling the river prevents

illegal fishing.

1. After assigning the homework, Mr. Jones told them it was not necessary to turn it in.

_____

_____

2. They tell me that dependability in an employee is a desirable trait.

_____

_____

3. My high school English teacher taught grammar well. That is one thing I will never forget.

_____

_____

4. On a crisp and windy day, it is nice to feel it blowing through your hair.

_____

_____

5. Mr. Waters told Mr. Williams he would not be attending the convention.

_____

_____

6. It is one thing to be rich, but it is quite another to flaunt it.

_____

_____

7. They say a penny saved is a penny earned.

_____

_____

8. The textbook had a mistake in it, which confused the students.

_____

_____

9. The smell of smoke from burning wood in a fireplace gives me a feeling of security. This is one of my favorite memories.

_____

_____

10. When children trick-or-treat Ms. Lawson at Halloween, she always gives cookies and kisses them good-bye.

_____

_____

10

Adjectives and Adverbs

Adjectives and adverbs are modifiers. Adjectives modify nouns and pronouns, and they answer the questions Which one? What kind? and How many? Adverbs modify verbs, adjectives, and other adverbs, and they answer the questions How? When? Why? Where? To what extent? and On what condition?

Forming Adjectives and Adverbs

Some adjectives are formed by adding the endings *-al, -able, -ful, -ish, -ive, -less,* and *-y* to the noun or verb form.

Noun or Verb	Adjective
mayor	mayoral
credit	creditable
fruit	fruitful
self	selfish
progress	progressive
use	useless
sleep	sleepy

Many adverbs are formed by adding the ending *-ly* to adjectives.

Adjective	Adverb
brave	bravely
courageous	courageously
careful	carefully
religious	religiously

However, not all words ending in *-ly* are adverbs. The adjective *lonely* is a good example of this. Furthermore, not all adverbs end in *-ly;* for instance, *very, soon, now,* and *not* are all frequently used adverbs. Though most words ending in *-ly* function as adverbs, the only sure way to tell is to see how the word is used in the sentence. If the word modifies a noun or a pronoun, it is an adjective. If the word modifies a verb, an adjective, or another adverb, it is an adverb.

Using Adjectives and Adverbs Correctly

Some writers use adjectives where they should use adverbs and vice versa. Though such usage is not often a serious barrier to communication, it can distract the reader. A useful rule to remember is that adverbs generally follow action verbs and adjectives generally follow linking verbs.

> J.P. Wright dances gracefully to any kind of music.
> The action verb *dances* takes the adverb *gracefully*. *Gracefully* modifies the verb *dances* and answers the question Dances how?

> Mario Andretti drives all racing cars expertly.
> *Expertly* is an adverb modifying the verb *drives* and answers the question Drives how?

> The coffee tastes bitter.
> The adjective *bitter* follows the linking verb *tastes*.

> The flowers smell sweet.
> The adjective *sweet* follows the linking verb *smell*.

Practice Sentences 10-1

In the following sentences, underline the adverb that modifies the action verb.

Example: Perry won Qwyn's hand <u>easily</u>.

1. My brother reviews his financial affairs carefully.

2. Adrian always takes the same route to school.

3. Gayle sang the hymn beautifully.

4. Wayne took the garbage out quickly before his father returned.

5. Tommy readily admitted that the broken window was his fault.

6. Allison performed the entire ballet gracefully.

7. Gloria confessed quickly to her role in the prank.

8. The teacher returns papers promptly.

9. Ron swiftly grabbed the book when he realized its value.

10. Ronna wanted the problem resolved immediately.

Linking verbs, which generally take adjectives, do not express any action; they express a state of existence, being, or emotion. The adjective following a linking verb usually modifies the subject.

Pat Johnson is lazy.
Lazy is an adjective modifying the subject *Pat Johnson*.
Lazy is a predicate adjective.

A list of commonly used linking verbs includes:

is		appear
am		become
was	forms of the	seem
were	verb *to be*	taste
been		feel
being		smell
		look
		sound

Practice Sentences 10-2

In the following sentences, underline the adjectives that follow the linking verbs.

Example: The golf course is <u>beautiful</u> this time of the year.

1. Grady's electric sander was expensive.
2. Ralph's dog is ready for the dog show this weekend.
3. The coffee in the cafeteria was bitter this morning.
4. Geraldo's hair looks nice.
5. Beatrice appeared confident after her interview.
6. The project has been ready for nearly two weeks.
7. Benny's new woodcarving was different.
8. The flowers on the table smelled fresh.
9. Sidney seems happy at this college.
10. Mia became enthusiastic about her new job after the first paycheck.

In your writing, you must be aware of whether the verb is an action verb or a linking verb. Some of the linking verbs in our list can also be action verbs, depending on how they are used in the sentence.

The bottle selling for $1,250 looks fragile.
>*Looks* is a linking verb. The bottle has no eyes with which to look; it is not looking. Therefore, the adjective *fragile* is used to modify the subject *bottle*.

Dick Allen looks carefully at every item on sale.
>In this sentence *looks* is an action verb. Dick Allen has eyes, and he is looking. Therefore, the adverb *carefully* is used to modify the verb *looks*.

Look at these two sentences:

The unblended Scotch tastes bitter.
The man tastes the rare Scotch admiringly.

In the first sentence, the Scotch has no tongue with which to taste, so *tastes* is a linking verb. The subject *Scotch* is modified by the predicate adjective *bitter*. In the second sentence, the man can taste and is doing so. Therefore, the adverb *admiringly* modifies the action verb *tastes*. Do not carelessly use an adjective where an adverb should be used.

Faulty: Sing the song forceful.
Correct: Sing the song forcefully.
>*Forcefully* is an adverb modifying the action verb *sing*.

Faulty: The carpenter is a real fine man.
Correct: The carpenter is a really fine man.
>*Really* is an adverb modifying the adjective *fine*.

Faulty: Jane sure won that event.
Correct: Jane surely won that event.
>*Surely* is an adverb modifying the verb *won*.

Faulty: John plays his position good.
Correct: John plays his position well.
>*Well* is an adverb modifying the verb *plays*.

Practice Sentences 10-3

In the following sentences, underline the correct word.

Example: Becky glared (anger, <u>angrily</u>) at the officer.

1. Blaine can take notes very (quick, quickly).
2. The lemonade tastes (bitter, bitterly).
3. The table saw cuts (smooth, smoothly).
4. The band saw does not cut metal (good, well).
5. Tony sipped his drink (slow, slowly).

6. The flowers on Margaret's desk smell (fresh, freshly).

7. Percy became (confident, confidently) after the first lap.

8. The professor lectured very (rapid, rapidly).

9. My son looks (careful, carefully) before crossing the street.

10. Your hair looks (attractive, attractively) today.

Degrees of Adjectives and Adverbs

Adjectives and adverbs are said to have degrees. The positive degree does not compare; the comparative degree compares two persons or things; and the superlative degree compares three or more persons or things.

Positive degree: Inez is tall.
Comparative degree: Sharon is taller than Carletta.
Superlative degree: Mary is the tallest girl in the dorm.

Look at the following chart:

Number of Syllables in Word	Positive Degree	Comparative Degree	Superlative Degree
1	rich	richer	richest
1	brave	braver	bravest
2	fancy	fancier	fanciest
2	handsome	more handsome	most handsome
3	beautiful	more beautiful	most beautiful
4	mysterious	more mysterious	most mysterious

Notice that adjectives of one syllable form the comparative degree by adding *-er* to the positive degree and form the superlative degree by adding *-est* to the positive degree. (*Brave, braver, bravest* is an exception only because the *e* is already on the word.) Notice that adjectives of three syllables or more form the comparative degree by adding the word *more* before the positive degree and the superlative degree by adding the word *most*. The words *more* and *most* in the comparative and superlative degrees indicate an ascending comparison.

Bob is more intelligent than Ralph.
Albert is the most intelligent of all.

To indicate a descending comparison, use the words *less* and *least*:

Bob is less intelligent than Ralph.
Albert is the least intelligent of all.

The chart indicates that words of two syllables may use either the *-er, -est* forms or the *more, most* forms. The main thing to remember, however, is that the two different forms should never be mixed. If you use *-er*, do not use *more*. It is poor usage to say *Bob is more richer than Ralph.*

Some comparative forms are irregular. These irregular forms must be memorized.

Positive	Comparative	Superlative
bad, badly	worse	worst
far	farther, further	farthest, furthest
good, well	better	best
little	less	least
many, much	more	most
several, some		

Make sure your comparisons are logical. Some words are absolute in meaning and cannot be compared. *Unique, empty, dead, perfect, entirely, round* are all absolutes. If a snowflake is unique, it is unique. It makes no sense to say one snowflake is more unique than another. The word *unique* means *one of a kind*, and thus by definition the word allows no comparison.

Practice Sentences 10-4

In the following sentences, underline the correct word.

Example: Chad is the (better, <u>best</u>) golfer on the team.

1. He drives the ball (more accurately, most accurately) than Stuart.

2. He also putts the ball (better, best) than Neal.

3. He is the (more intent, most intent) member of the team.

4. He always listens to instructions (good, well).

5. Furthermore, he is the (better, best) team player.

6. He works (good, well) with his teammates to get the best team score.

7. He is (more serious, most serious) about his game than Michael.

8. Chad has (less, least) trouble with shots from sand traps than anyone in the conference.

9. For one thing, he hits (few, fewest) shots into sand traps.

10. The coach says Chad is the (better, best) golfer he has ever coached.

Using Nouns as Modifiers

Some writers awkwardly use nouns as adjectives. In a sentence such as *Marlene Draughn is interested in theater history,* the noun *theater* is used as an adjective modifying *history.* The sentence is effective. However, in a sentence like *Jack Nelson is a mayor candidate,* the use of the noun *mayor* as an adjective modifying *candidate* is ineffective. The correct word is the adjective *mayoral,* a mayoral candidate.

Practice Sentences 10-5

In the space provided, rewrite each of the following sentences using the proper adjective form of the word incorrectly used as a noun.

Example: Sandra applied for a job as a dentist assistant.

Sandra applied for a job as a dental assistant.

1. The incumbent hopes to win the president election.

2. The Canada Mounties are known all over the world.

3. The judiciary decision was vague and inconclusive.

4. The governor race was won by the newcomer.

5. The idiot policy of forcing everyone to wear ties was enforced.

6. You can easily recognize Fred by his child pranks.

_____

_____

7. For movies rated PG, parent guidance is suggested.

_____

_____

8. His company contributed to the Senate campaign.

_____

_____

9. Mr. Borden's company is being sued for practicing race discrimination in hiring.

_____

_____

10. This new promotion technique should add millions of dollars to our annual gross sales figure.

_____

_____

Review Exercise 10-A   Using Adjectives and Adverbs Correctly (I)

Underline the correct word in the following sentences.

Example: Jeremy and Christine decided to have the (better, <u>best</u>) picnic ever.

1. They planned (good, well) for their outing.

2. They listened to the weather forecast (careful, carefully).

3. They would feel (awful, awfully) bad if it rained.

4. They even bought the (more expensive, most expensive) picnic basket they could find.

5. Jeremy even had his car (professional, professionally) cleaned.

6. He knew Christine couldn't stand a (real, really) dirty car.

7. Christine selected the food for the picnic (careful, carefully).

8. She examined the chicken (close, closely).

9. She bought a (better, best) bottle of wine than usual.

10. But on the day of the picnic Jeremy's car would not crank (proper, properly).

Review Exercise 10-B Using Adjectives and Adverbs Correctly (II)

Underline the correct choice in the following sentences.

Example: Mary Bunker runs the 5,000 meter race very (good, <u>well</u>).

1. She is the (better, best) runner on her team.

2. She has practiced (diligent, diligently) for years to achieve her level of success.

3. On top of this, however, she has learned how to run a (strategic, strategically) race.

4. She studies previous races of her opponents (intent, intently).

5. She looks (close, closely) at opponents' tactics.

6. Mary knows which opponent is the (better, best) pacesetter.

7. She knows which one has the (stronger, strongest) kick at the end.

8. Mary runs near the front of the pack but does not get too (close, closely) to the front-runner.

9. She (careful, carefully) conserves some energy to ward off the fastest sprinter down the stretch.

10. Her strategy is (real, really) successful most of the time.

Review Exercise 10-C   Using Adjectives and Adverbs
Correctly (III)

In the space provided, rewrite each of the following sentences correctly.

Example: Cheryl is the better beautician in the freshman class.

Cheryl is the best beautician in the freshman class.

1. She treats all her customers polite.

2. She is most patient with her customers than the other students.

3. Cheryl washes each customer's hair thorough.

4. Each customer's hairdo is the most unique.

5. Cheryl wants the customer to feel beautifuller than when she came in.

6. She works real hard with each customer.

7. She sure sets ambitious goals for herself.

_____

_____

8. She plans to complete operate her own shop upon graduation.

_____

_____

9. The other students think she is definite crazy.

_____

_____

10. Her teachers, however, are confidently that she will succeed.

_____

_____

PUNCTUATION AND MECHANICS

11

Commas

The comma is the most frequently used mark of punctuation. It is also the most frequently misused. Any punctuation mark that is used for as many different purposes as the comma is bound to create problems. The comma separates, introduces, and shows omission.

Though a comma indicates only a brief pause, its presence or absence can have a strong effect on the clarity of a sentence. If a writer fails to put a comma in where it is needed, the reader might misinterpret the sentence.

> The government supplied guns, tanks, bulletproof cars and trucks. Were the trucks also bulletproof? They would seem to be, judging by the punctuation.

As always, though, language and punctuation are changing. The trend in recent years has been, "when in doubt, don't." In other words, if you cannot think of a specific reason why the comma should be used, leave it out. In this chapter we will explain the specific instances where commas should be used. If you master these rules, you should have little trouble with the comma. In order to help you group the numerous rules under a few general headings, the uses of the comma have been subdivided as follows:

Main clauses
Introductory elements
Items in a series and coordinate adjectives
Nonrestrictive, parenthetical, and contrasting elements
Dates, degrees, place names, and long numbers
Unnecessary commas

Main Clauses

Use commas to separate main clauses when they are joined by *and, or, nor, but, yet,* and *so.*

> I find the study of the English language interesting, but I do not understand the confusing spelling rules.

> Mr. James Fincaster is a lawyer in New York City, and his son is an accountant there.

Note: Some writers do not use a comma before a coordinate conjunction connecting two short main clauses, especially if the subject is the same in both clauses.

Mary washed her hair and then she blow-dried it.

Practice Sentences 11-1

In the following sentences, insert commas where they are needed.

Example: Christy gave a speech today on how to make lemonade pie,but she forgot to bring a pie shell.

1. Marty installed a new phone jack and it worked perfectly.

2. Dale's parents do not want him to write a book about his childhood yet he is determined.

3. Yvonne decorated a cake for a neighbor's wedding but her family ate it.

4. Gus's father is a highway patrolman yet Gus was clocked at 160 miles an hour.

5. Allen was a paratrooper in the military but he won't have anything to do with skydiving.

6. Dana must get the batter out or the coach will send in a new pitcher.

7. Jerri did not want to go on the fishing trip yet she went to keep peace in the family.

8. Joanna got soaked in the storm and she even had her umbrella with her.

9. The child felt sad during the morning recess but he seemed happier after lunch.

10. Benny thought the medication was too expensive but it was effective.

Introductory Elements

1. Use commas to set off long (one-half line or more) introductory adverb clauses.

Although the weather was ideal, Jane wouldn't leave the house.

If the aldermen would only act, the problem would be resolved.

Notice that adverb clauses tacked on to the end of a sentence do not have to be set off with commas:

Jane wouldn't leave the house although the weather was ideal.

2.   Use commas to set off introductory verbal phrases.

Plying his trade expertly, the salesman sold the woman a car she couldn't afford.

To be perfectly honest, Gerald Smitherman cannot handle that job.

3.   Use commas to set off long (one-half line or more) introductory prepositional phrases.

In the dugout after the second game of a doubleheader, the catcher looked as if he couldn't even stand up.

After eating three sixteen-inch pizzas in twenty minutes, Bob was still hungry.

4.   Use commas to set off absolute constructions that come at the beginning of a sentence. **An absolute construction is a word or group of words that relates to the thought of the sentence in which it is found, but is not grammatically related to any particular word in the sentence.**

Adverb absolute: Interestingly enough, no one had any desire to lead the new club.

Nominative absolute: The gate not yet being open to the public, Dale and Yvonne had to park three blocks away.

5.   Use commas to set off nouns of direct address.

John, did you go to the Kiwanis Club meeting last night?

Barbara, please pick me up two king-size sheets if they are on sale.

6.   Use commas to set off mild interjections and *yes* or *no* answers followed by more explanation.

Well, I guess I could have done a better job if I had prepared more thoroughly.

Yes, I believe Bob does intend to go to the district meeting.

7.   Use commas to set off introductory conjunctive adverbs and transitional phrases. (See Chapter 8.)

Nevertheless, Jane is still the best person for the job even though she does work slowly.

On the other hand, the commissioners could just rezone the whole area.

8. Use commas to introduce short quotations.

Mary said, "Nellie Forbush has to wash her hair in every perform-ance of *South Pacific*."

The young quarterback whispered to the coach, "Some of the starters broke the team rules last night."

9. Use commas to set off some introductory expressions in order to pre-vent misreading.

A few days before Bob set out on a trip and wrecked his car.
The sentence needs a comma after *before* to prevent misreading.

A few days before, Bob set out on a trip and wrecked his car.

In 1979 273 people were killed in a DC-10 crash.
The sentence needs a comma between the numbers.

In 1979, 273 people were killed in a DC-10 crash.
Better yet, rewrite it.

The crash of a DC-10 in 1979 killed 273 people.

Practice Sentences 11-2

In the following sentences, insert commas where they are needed.

Example: The bedrooms not being furnished yet, the couple had to sleep in the den.

1. Since you have a broken finger I will start the lawnmower for you.

2. Yogi Berra supposedly once told a young ball player "Your future is all ahead of you."

3. Surprisingly enough I finished preparing my income taxes in January.

4. Near the car attendants were estimating the damage.

5. The grass seed not having taken root the violent thunderstorm washed all the topsoil away.

6. After you go to the bank and deposit your paycheck why don't you take me out to dinner?

7. In the beautiful green pasture near my neighbor's new barn his horses are grazing contentedly.

8. Gen. Douglas McArthur said "I shall return."

9. Unless you especially want to go to the play I would rather stay home this evening.

10. Sid did you really hit thirty-five home runs one season in high school?

Items in a Series and Coordinate Adjectives

1. Use commas to separate words, phrases, and clauses in a series.

I like apples, oranges, bananas, and pears.
> Use the comma before the *and* unless the last two items go together: Jim's favorite entertainers are the Bravos, James Pawn, and Donna Gilbert and the Tonsils.

The driver lost control of his car and drove it over the guardrail, through the crowd, and down the embankment.

You need to watch your budget when you are constantly in debt, when you have to borrow to cover routine expenses, and when you feel compelled to buy clothes you don't need.

Go to the bookstore, buy an interesting-looking best-seller, and read it over the weekend.

2. Use a comma to separate coordinate adjectives. (Coordinate adjectives are equal adjectives that modify the same noun.)

A college student receives a meaningful, versatile education that will provide a broader view of life than could be obtained by on-the-job training.

Walden is an interesting, thought-provoking book.

Note: Many adjectives that refer to the number, age (old, young, new), origin, size, color, or location of the noun are so closely related to the nouns they modify that commas are not necessary. A useful rule of thumb is that if the word *and* can replace the comma without creating an awkward effect, then the comma is appropriate.

Sandra is a beautiful American girl.
> The sentence would be awkward if it read *Sandra is a beautiful and American girl;* therefore, it would be equally awkward with a comma: *Sandra is a beautiful, American girl.*

There were many satisfied senior citizens when the Social Security increase came into effect.

> The sentence would be awkward indeed if it read, *There were many and satisfied and senior citizens when the Social Security increase came into effect.* Similarly, commas would only be distracting: *There were many, satisfied, senior citizens when the Social Security increase came into effect.*

Practice Sentences 11-3

In the following sentences, insert commas where they are needed.

Example: Go to bed early, get up early, and eat a nutritious breakfast.

1. The customer wanted a good dependable truck.

2. Tommy, Jason and Lewis were the three winners.

3. All he had in his pockets were two quarters and a pocketknife.

4. The company hired an intelligent charming manager.

5. If you cannot sleep, get out of bed, read a book or watch television.

6. The students said it was an unfair even tricky test.

7. The new Spanish teacher spoke with a Southern accent.

8. Drive the car to the shop, park it in front of the service door and explain the problem to the service manager.

9. Sue Ellen is a graceful versatile athlete.

10. Anne told Julian that he was rude to his parents, crude to women and generally obnoxious to everyone.

Nonessential, Parenthetical, and Contrasting Elements

1. Use commas to set off nonessential adjective clauses and phrases. A nonessential (or nonrestrictive) clause or phrase is one that is not necessary to *identify* the noun it modifies.

Karen and Pam, with their bathing suits on and their suitcases in the trunk, headed for the beach.

> The phrase *with their bathing suits on and their suitcases in the trunk* is not necessary to identify the nouns *Karen* and *Pam*.

Mr. Thomas Atkins appears to be very rich, always wearing cashmere topcoats and Brooks Brothers' suits.

> *Always wearing cashmere topcoats and Brooks Brothers' suits* is a nonessential participial phrase placed at the end of the sentence. The phrase is not necessary to identify Mr. Atkins.

The Carthage High School cheerleaders, who were dressed in their cheerleading uniforms, had to be at the stadium an hour before game time.

> The clause *who were dressed in their cheerleading uniforms* is not necessary to identify the noun *cheerleaders*.

Note that essential (or restrictive) adjective clauses and phrases are *not* set off by commas.

The workers participating in the walkout were fired.

> The phrase *participating in the walkout* is necessary to identify the noun *workers*. All workers were not fired, only those participating in the walkout. The phrase restricts the meaning of the sentence.

Students who cheat on tests are not respected by their teachers.

> Teachers do respect most of their students. It is the ones who cheat that are not respected. Thus, the clause *who cheat on tests* is essential and should not be set off with commas.

Adjective clauses beginning with the word *that* are essential.

Daisy Miller bought a novel that was written by Henry James.

Most adjective clauses following proper names are nonessential.

Susan B. Anthony, who was outspoken on the issue of women's rights, is now honored on a dollar coin.

Most adjective clauses following references to one's parents are nonessential.

My mother, who is a fine woman, lives in Portland, Maine.

Sometimes adjective clauses and phrases can be either essential or nonessential depending on what is meant.

The truck driver is very concerned about the Arabian horses, which were killed in the wreck.

> With the comma the sentence indicates that all of the Arabian horses were killed.

The truck driver is very concerned about the Arabian horses which were killed in the wreck.

> Without the comma the sentence indicates that only some of the Arabian horses were killed.

2. Use commas to set off nonessential appositives.

The owner, a self-made man, would not pay any player more than $250,000 a year.

She photographed Mount St. Helens, the only active volcano in the continental United States.

Most one-word appositives are not set off with commas.

My son Tommy is a fast learner.
Roy Rogers' horse Trigger is stuffed.

3. Nonessential titles are set off with commas. Essential titles are not set off.

Some Hemingway short stories, such as "The Killers" and "The Short Happy Life of Francis Macomber," are often anthologized.
   The phrase containing the titles is not essential to the meaning of the sentence.

The Yeats poem "Sailing to Byzantium" is one of the finest poems of the twentieth century.
   The title is essential to the meaning of the sentence; without it the reader would not know which poem by Yeats was meant.

4. Use commas to set off parenthetical elements. (A parenthetical element is any word or expression that abruptly interrupts the flow of a sentence.) Parenthetical elements are not always introducers.

The project, of course, needs more study.
James Rein was unable to finish the book by the deadline, however.

Most writers use commas to set off the longer conjunctive adverbs such as *however, moreover, furthermore, consequently,* and *nevertheless.* The shorter ones such as *also, too, still, then,* and *thus* are not always set off.

Thus the exercise was never actually completed.

5. Use commas with direct quotations to set off expressions such as *he said, she replied,* and *I shouted.*

"The main problem," he said, "is with the compressor."

"The lens is made in Germany," the photographer said, "and it should be just what you need."

6. Use commas to set off contrasted elements.

Give the job to Ensign Davis, not Sergeant Parker.
Margaret could give up cigarettes, but not fattening foods.

Practice Sentences 11-4

In the following sentences, insert commas where they are needed.

Example: Sky King's real name is Kirby Grant**,** not Skylar King.

1. Kay Frost who is a fine landscape painter is a member of the art department of Wilkes Community College.

2. I am currently reading Dickens' novel *Our Mutual Friend.*

3. The only member of the faculty who agreed with the proposal was Dr. Lowe.

4. I asked you to define a tourniquet not a tournament.

5. My mother who lives in Denver is an accomplished pianist.

6. John Pendleton Kennedy's *Swallow Barn* is an important book in Southern literature.

7. Thomas Holley Chivers who was a contemporary of Poe once accused Poe of plagiarizing his poem "Rosalee Lee."

8. My telephone-answering tape which was produced by Radio Shack plays humorous messages.

9. One of the horses which he keeps in his stables is worth $25,000.

10. Scarlett O'Hara who is the central figure in *Gone with the Wind* is an interesting character.

Dates, Degrees, Place Names, and Long Numbers

1. Use commas to set off the items in a date.

On January 5, 1989, Leroy Holrod celebrated his eighty-fourth birthday.

Note: Commas are optional when only the month and year are given.

In May 1988 Nelson Swaim received his D.Ed. degree.

2. Use commas to set off titles and degrees after proper names.

N. P. Acumen, C.P.A.
Dr. Sharon Everett, Dean of Financial Services
Mr. Carl Brim, Chairperson

3. Use commas to set off geographical locations.

South Bend, Indiana, is the home of Notre Dame.

My mother lives at 2102 Seacrest Lane, Duluth, Minnesota.

4. Use commas after every group of three digits, counting from the right in figures of one thousand or more.

2,394
9,643,298
$259,128

Practice Sentences 11-5

In the following sentences, insert commas where they are needed.

> **Example:** On May 14, 1980, John Owens graduated from high
> school in Tupper Falls, Okla.

1. Peg Darcy D.D.S lives in Des Moines Iowa.
2. On September 25 1989 Thomas Quinn Jones Jr. celebrated his first birthday by stepping in the cake.
3. Jessica Chandler Dean of Instruction is a new member of the college staff.
4. Gene went to Las Vegas Nevada and lost $2500.
5. James Key has a Ph.D. in physics but pumps gas in Phoenix Ariz.
6. Ron Chaney Chief Executive Officer receives a salary of $1350000 a year.
7. On Tuesday October 9 1985 Conrad Aimes became a grandfather.
8. Roy Weathers Vice President in Charge of Marketing and Joyce Beamer Vice President in Charge of Advertising occupy adjoining offices.
9. We will be leaving Belmont Miss. on Friday morning and arriving in Baltimore Md. Sunday night.
10. Margaret Hatcher C.P.A. is proud of her new title and her new office.

Unnecessary Commas

Now that you have studied the basic comma rules, you should feel more confident about when to use commas. At this point, however, a reminder of where not to use commas may be helpful. Too often commas are carelessly put in places they do not belong. A comma indicates a pause, but not every pause needs a comma. In fact, there are certain brief pauses that should not have commas. In the following examples, the circled commas are unnecessary.

1. Except when there are intervening elements, do not use a comma to separate a subject from its verb.

> The blind man with the white cane ⊘ walks downtown and back every Sunday.

2. Do not use a comma to separate a verb from its object.

> Betty Ann honestly believed ⊘ that she could defeat her boyfriend in a wrestling match.

3. Do not unnecessarily use a comma before a coordinate conjunction.

> Jennifer is both an excellent golfer ⊘ and a fine tennis player.

4. Do not use a comma to set off most introductory words or short phrases.

> At lunch ⊘ Bob and Jim signed the partnership papers.
>
> In 1964 ⊘ Muriel Thomas graduated from Mount Park High School.
>
> Today ⊘ forty men completed their annual two weeks of training camp.

5. Do not use commas to set off restrictive phrases, clauses, and appositives.

> The men ⊘ putting up the fence ⊘ are with the local building supply company.
>
> People ⊘ that drink too much ⊘ often have serious family problems.
>
> John Gardner's book ⊘ *Grendel* ⊘ received many favorable reviews.

6. Do not use a comma before the first item in a series or after the last item.

> Barbara reads such books as ⊘ *Evelina, Emma,* and *Middlemarch.*
>
> Not surprisingly, Barbara is an intelligent, sophisticated, and poised ⊘ woman.

Practice Sentences 11-6

Circle the unnecessary commas in the following sentences.

Example: People ⊙ that talk too much ⊙ often say very little.

1. Lanny likes books such as, *Walden, Huckleberry Finn,* and *For Whom the Bell Tolls.*

2. The women, planting the shrubbery, got hot and thirsty.

3. Marci is both a good teacher, and an astute businesswoman.

4. Jeff believed, that buying a riding lawnmower would make yardwork fun.

5. John Milton's greatest poem, *Paradise Lost,* was unrecognized in 1667.

6. Tony is a young, handsome, talented, player on the tour.

7. In 1865, President Lincoln was assassinated by John Wilkes Booth.

8. The woman in the Rolls Royce, drives to the Sea Pine Manufacturing Co. every morning.

9. Yesterday, a man and his two daughters were injured in an automobile accident.

10. The man, who lives in the large house at 1512 East Elm Street, is seventy-four years old.

Review Exercise 11-A   Using Commas Correctly (I)

Insert commas where they are needed in the following paragraph.

Example: Ralph C. Montgomery**,** Jr.**,** has an identity crisis.

1. Vance went to the library which is across the street from the auditorium to do some research. *2.* He read about Oliver Wendell Holmes Jr. author of *The Common Law*. *3.* Then he got interested in Oliver Wendell Holmes Sr. a physician and poet. *4.* After he had taken numerous notes on these two men he selected a volume on Emily Dickinson. *5.* Ms. Dickinson who is usually described as being a recluse is a fine poet. *6.* She writes on such topics as death love religion and nature. *7.* At her best she is a precise insightful poet with a gift for expressing herself in a unique and graceful manner. *8.* After reading a few poems by Emily Dickinson Vance looked at the work of a novelist. *9.* George Eliot a pseudonym for Mary Ann Evans is an outstanding representative of Victorian writing. *10.* Vance who was enjoying his research thoroughly learned that Ms. Evans used a man's name because she knew the books would sell better if the public thought they were written by a man.

Review Exercise 11-B   Using Commas Correctly (II)

Insert commas where they are needed in the following paragraph.

Example: My mother **,** who lives alone **,** leads a full life.

1. Trying to understand the game better Beverly played over fifty games of backgammon yesterday. *2.* Today her boyfriend the person who taught her how to play backgammon challenged her to a game. *3.* By the time Beverly had played three rolls of the dice he realized he was in for a battle. *4.* He had taught her the rules but she had obviously learned strategy somewhere else. *5.* Beverly analyzing every move carefully got her runners out and established a block around her bar point. *6.* Her boyfriend Paul Shaw on the other hand was not having good luck with the dice. *7.* He had blots on such key points as B5 B6 B7 and B8. *8.* Beverly who was determined to show Paul how much she had improved put three of his pieces on the bar. *9.* Since she had established a prime block in her inner board Paul couldn't get his last piece off the bar before Beverly had borne off all her pieces. *10.* Beverly was proud of having backgammoned Paul but he refused to play with her anymore.

12

Semicolons

The semicolon is an important mark of punctuation. It is not used often, but when it is used, it must be used correctly. A reader will expect equal grammatical constructions on either side of the semicolon. If they are not there, the reader will be confused.

1. Use the semicolon between main clauses not connected by *and, or, nor, but, yet,* or *so.*

> *The Music Man* is a fine musical; its best-known song is "Seventy-Six Trombones."

> Most employees are covered by medical insurance; however, relatively few are covered by dental insurance.

2. Use semicolons to separate main clauses that themselves contain commas.

> Betty Collins, a most unlikely candidate, was nominated on the first ballot; but, she told reporters, the party would be pleased with her nomination when she won the election in November.
>> The coordinate conjunction *but* indicates the break between the main clauses. Since the break between main clauses is more important than the breaks indicated by the four commas, the conjunction needs a semicolon before it to stress this importance.

Though there is no absolute rule for when the coordinate conjunction needs a semicolon before it at the break between main clauses, an acceptable practice would be to use the semicolon before a coordinate conjunction connecting main clauses when there is a total of two commas in the main clauses. This could mean two commas in the first main clause, two commas in the second main clause, or one comma in the first main clause and one comma in the second.

> **Two commas in first main clause:** Andrew Carnegie, as well as John Rockefeller, made a fortune from the American capitalistic system; and Carnegie became one of America's most famous philanthropists.

Two commas in second main clause: Quite a few writers rebel against establishment values; but many of these authors, surprisingly enough, are shocked when the establishment rejects their revolutionary ideas.

One comma in both the first and second main clauses: Evaluating the track conditions closely, the trainer decided the horse should run; but the valuable animal received a debilitating injury, unfortunately.

3. Use semicolons to separate items in a series that itself contains commas.

Mr. William Engel was accompanied by his son John Engel, a buyer for Nichol's Mills; his daughter Joan Shaw, an executive with Person's Bank; and his wife, a board member of the Utah Power and Light Company.

A reminder: Do *not* use the semicolon to connect unequal grammatical constructions.

Having judged all the evidence available to him at the courthouse; James decided that the real estate cooperative was a rip-off.
The semicolon is used *incorrectly* to connect a participial phrase to a main clause.

Although the governor said he feared the decision would contribute to inflation; he kept salaries at the same level as the previous year.
The semicolon is used *incorrectly* to connect a subordinate clause to a main clause.

The incumbent tried hard to get the votes of all state employees; a task that he could never accomplish.
The semicolon is used *incorrectly* to connect a main clause to a noun modified by an adjective clause.

Review Exercise 12-A   Using Semicolons Correctly (I)

Insert semicolons where they are needed in the following paragraph.

Example: Scott likes the idea of having an answering machine; his wife
hates the devices.

1. Nikki is five years old her brother Jason is eight. *2.* Their mother
sends them outside to play in the summertime they always complain
at first. *3.* Many times their mom turns on the sprinkler this cools
them off even on the hottest days. *4.* Unfortunately, the house does
not have enough water pressure the sprinkler only sprays a stream
three feet high. *5.* One day Mom was taking a shower Jason turned
the sprinkler on. *6.* Mom screamed at the top of her lungs there was
nothing but hot water with the sprinkler on. *7.* Mom was not pleased
with her son he has not played in the sprinkler for a week. *8.* Now he
explores the neighborhood, rides his bike, and plays soldier, but he is
never ready to come back inside when he is called. *9.* He does get
annoyed at Nikki she plays in the sprinkler and makes faces at him.
10. One day he cut the water off to the sprinkler when Nikki looked
down to see what was wrong, Jason turned the water back on.

Review Exercise 12-B   Using Semicolons Correctly (II)

Insert semicolons where they are needed in the following paragraph.

Example: Some colleges have an open door admissions policy**;**
         however, others have strict admissions requirements.

1. Typing is a useful course for any college student to take however, not many do. *2.* Most professors do not like to read handwritten papers therefore, they insist that all papers be typed. *3.* Students who can't type, therefore, are forced to rely on friends who can these friends are not always available. *4.* Clearly, knowing how to type can make you more independent you will be able to prepare your work when it needs to be done. *5.* Today's word processors make typing a less strenuous task all corrections are made on a monitor before a single word is printed. *6.* There is little time wasted with erasers and liquid White Out furthermore, there is no need to retype an entire page because of an error in one line. *7.* The same word processor can even use different printing wheels this enables you to use pica, elite, or proportional spacing. *8.* Since word processors are more electronic than mechanical, they are often cheaper than conventional typewriters the prices of word processors are coming down all the time. *9.* Word processors are generally easier to use than conventional typewriters margins, page length, spacing, etc., are set automatically. *10.* With a word processor you can do your own work you might be the friend others rely on to use it efficiently, however, you still need to know how to type.

Review Exercise 12-C   Using Semicolons Correctly (III)

In the space provided, rewrite each sentence, correcting the semicolon errors.

Example: Although Adolpho studied hard for the English test; he did
not do well.

Although Adolfo studied hard for the English
test, he did not do well.

1. John impulsively bought the new running shoes; even though he knew he couldn't afford them.

_____

_____

2. Thinking she would have plenty of time to return to the problem; Sue skipped number 3 and went on through the test.

_____

_____

3. Elise wanted to return to New Orleans; her favorite city in the United States.

_____

_____

4. Donna wanted to see her paper; even though she already knew her score.

_____

_____

5. If Timothy can get off work in time; he would like to go to a movie.

_____

_____

6. Corbin had to go to the dentist; because he chipped a tooth.

   _____

   _____

7. After the storm passed through Whiteville; there wasn't a tree left standing.

   _____

   _____

8. Because Alex is very tall; he has trouble sleeping in regular hotel beds.

   _____

   _____

9. Demont buys only Zenith television sets; the kind his father preferred.

   _____

   _____

10. The air conditioner wouldn't run; because the filter was filthy.

   _____

   _____

13

Apostrophes

The apostrophe is a somewhat distracting mark of punctuation, and it is not used consistently by all writers. Some languages avoid the problem by having a special ending for possessive nouns. In Latin, for example, the word *terra* means "land" and is used as a subject. When the word is *terrae*, however, it means "of the land" or "land's." Thus Latin uses what is called the genitive case and therefore does not need apostrophes. English could be written without apostrophes, too, but the expressions would be clumsy and wordy:

> the hat of the girl
> the bats of the boys
> the plays of Seneca
>   *Girl's hat, boys' bats*, and *Seneca's plays* would be much better.

Nevertheless, you must realize that English expressions containing apostrophes to indicate possession can be rewritten in phrases consisting of nouns followed by prepositional phrases. Restructuring the expressions in such phrases often helps clarify meaning. For example, if you were asked to put the apostrophe where it was needed in the expression *the guests attire*, you would need to know whether the expression meant "the attire of the guest" or "the attire of the guests." *The guest's attire* means the attire of one guest, and *the guests' attire* means the attire of more than one guest. Once you have mentally restructured the expression in its correct form (noun plus prepositional phrase), you simply put the apostrophe where it belongs.

Also, many expressions containing apostrophes can be rewritten as nouns followed by prepositional phrases, but these expressions are not necessarily possessive. For instance, the expression *tomorrow's assignment* does not mean tomorrow possesses the assignment. Similarly, the expression *a good day's work* does not mean the day owns the work. Such constructions result from the fact that the English apostrophe substitutes for the genitive case of other languages such as Latin. Therefore, the apostrophe in English can be used in the same manner as the genitive case in Latin. Since the genitive case is sometimes used for purposes other than indicating possession, the apostrophe is too. Nevertheless, such an expression as *tomorrow's assignment* can still be rewritten as a noun plus a prepositional phrase: *the assignment for tomorrow*. Remembering that such nonpossessive uses of the apostrophe can be written out in the same manner as possessive constructions should help you better understand the use of the apostrophe.

Not all apostrophes in English even pertain to the genitive case of other languages. Sometimes apostrophes are used to indicate omissions, and sometimes they are used to form plurals. To simplify the uses of the apostrophe, we have divided this chapter into three sections: possession, omission, and plurals.

Possession

1. To form the possessive of most singular nouns not ending in -*s*, add an apostrophe and -*s*.

the mayor's son
the team's coach
the student's test

2. To form the possessive of singular nouns of one syllable ending in -*s*, add an apostrophe and -*s*.

the boss's secretary
Keats's poem
James's car

3. To form the possessive of singular nouns of more than one syllable ending in -*s*, add just an apostrophe.

the mattress' label
Socrates' philosophy
Aeschylus' trilogy

4. To form the possessive of plural nouns ending in -*s*, add only an apostrophe.

the players' contracts
the Smiths' house
the wives' meeting
the Joneses' vacation

5. To form the possessive of plural nouns not ending in -*s*, add an apostrophe and -*s*.

the men's organization
the children's magazine
the women's project

6. Use an apostrophe and -*s* to form the possessive of indefinite pronouns.

> anybody's
> everybody's
> someone's
> somebody's

But notice that no apostrophe is needed with personal pronouns, relative pronouns, or possessive pronouns.

> ours
> > **not** our's
>
> yours
> > **not** your's
>
> hers
> > **not** her's
>
> whose
> > **not** who's
>
> its
> > **not** it's

7. Add an apostrophe and -*s* to the last word to indicate the possessive of compounds and word groups.

> my mother-in-law's bookstore
> anyone else's rights

8. Use an apostrophe to indicate authorship.

> Oliver Goldsmith's *She Stoops to Conquer*
> Herman Melville's *Moby Dick*
> Ernest Hemingway's "The Killers"
> Euripides' *Iphigenia in Tauris*

9. Use an apostrophe and -*s* with a noun or with an indefinite pronoun preceding a gerund.

> Diana Nyad's swimming from the Bahamas to Florida required unbelievable endurance.
>
> Someone's stealing the Christmas bell upset the townspeople.

10. Add an apostrophe and -*s* to the last name in a series to denote possession by two or more jointly.

> Betty and Sue's piano
> Lewis and Clark's expedition

11.   Add an apostrophe and -*s* to each name to denote individual ownership.

John's and Robert's cars
Martha's and Paula's grades
Pam Smith's and Elizabeth Hardy's pianos

12.   Use the form accepted by tradition and law in indicating geographical terms, as well as names of firms, organizations, institutions, clubs, and titles.

Harpers Ferry
Rutgers University
Lions Club
King's College
Gilbert's Fine Furniture, Inc.

Practice Sentences 13-1

Insert apostrophes where they are needed in the following sentences.

Example: The cat's collar is bright red.

1. Sophocles play *Antigone* is in many freshman English anthologies.
2. The shows star was difficult to get along with during the filming.
3. Sherrie and Diannes apartment is quite expensive.
4. Someones mail order purchase was left on the front lawn.
5. The dining room tables finish is in poor condition.
6. The Alexanders home has been vandalized.
7. Samuel Johnsons *Rasselas* is an enjoyable book to read.
8. The faculty members vote clearly showed their support for the proposal.
9. Ladies watches are not as small as they used to be.
10. Margarets helping the injured child was a humane response to an unfortunate situation.

Omission

1.   Use an apostrophe to mark the omission of a letter or letters in a contraction.

don't   (do not)
can't   (cannot)
I'm   (I am)
o'clock   (of the clock)
it's   (it is)
who's   (who is)

Be sure to put the apostrophe in the proper place.

they're, **not** theyr'e
didn't, **not** did'nt

Do not confuse the contractions *it's* and *who's* with the possessive pronouns *its* and *whose*.

It's a beautiful day.
   It's means "it is."

The old car needs its engine overhauled.

Who's at the front door?
   Who's means "who is."

Whose books did you buy?

2. Use apostrophes to indicate the pronunciation of dialectical speech.

Watch you w'en your gittin' all you want. Fattenin' hogs ain't in luck.
Joel Chandler Harris

3. Add an apostrophe where a figure or figures have been omitted.

class of '41 (1941)
spirit of '76 (1776)

Practice Sentences 13-2

Insert apostrophes where they are needed in the following sentences.

Example: Some teachers don't like their students to use contractions.

1. Whos going to the game with you Saturday?

2. Its a reunion for the class of 64.

3. I wasnt able to attend the four o clock meeting.

4. Im not so sure "the good ol days" were really that good.

5. Theyre tired and hot after working in the high heat and humidity all day.

Plurals

1. Use the apostrophe and *-s* to indicate the plurals of letters used as letters.

> His *l*'s look like *i*'s.
> Her *e*'s look like *o*'s.
> There are four *i*'s and four *s*'s in *Mississippi*.

2. Use the apostrophe and *-s* to indicate the plurals of words used as words.

> Mary often confuses her *and*'s and her *an*'s.
> It is hard to tell the difference between his *ploy*'s and his *play*'s.

3. Use an apostrophe and *-s* to indicate the plurals of figures used as figures.

> The printer in the school shop has no more *3*'s.
> The teacher writes *9*'s that look like *7*'s.

4. Use the apostrophe and *-s* to indicate the plurals of symbols and of some abbreviations.

> That model typewriter's #'s and $'s are very close to each other.
> One English professor at Harvard has four *M.A.*'s and two *Ph.D.*'s.

Practice Sentences 13-3

Insert apostrophes where they are needed in the following sentences.

> **Example:** The printer's *I*'s and *l*'s look alike.

1. Caryn made two *B*s and three *C*s last semester.

2. In 1990 State University awarded seven *Ph.D.*s in the English department.

3. Julias 7s look like 9s.

4. The childs *thank you*s sounded like *shank you*s.

5. The publisher would not allow authors to use #s or %s in their manuscripts.

6. On my keyboard it is easy to hit *o*s when I want *p*s.

7. *Sea*s and *see*s are homonyms.

8. Sue has *M.A.*s in history and business.

9. The universitys hiring committee sought candidates with *Ph.D.*s in biological and environmental sciences.

10. The sign looked peculiar since there weren't enough *m*s to spell the full title of the show.

Be careful not to use apostrophes carelessly when the noun is plural and not possessive.

The Joneses are good neighbors.

Review Exercise 13-A   Using Apostrophes Correctly (I)

Insert apostrophes where they are needed in the following paragraph. Add an s *if necessary.*

Example: Herman's cap

1. W.H. Norton new car is a beauty. *2.* Its a 1965 Mustang. *3.* The cars in excellent condition. *4.* Its painted a beautiful British Racing Green. *5.* The Mustangs largely the idea of Lee Iacocca. *6.* Iacoccas thinking was that America was ready for an inexpensive sports car. *7.* The markets reaction proved him correct. *8.* W.H. Norton car looks as if its right off the showroom floor. *9.* Its his pride and joy. *10.* He paid more for his restored car than it cost originally, but he wanted one of Iacoccas original pony cars.

Review Exercise 13-B   Using Apostrophes Correctly (II)

*Insert apostrophes where they are needed in the following paragraph.
Add an* s *if necessary.*

Example: Aeschylus' play

1. Todays homeowner wants a large kitchen with plenty of
cabinets and lots of cabinet space. *2.* Bob Jones built his new home
with these requirements in mind. *3.* He didn't care if the bedrooms
were small. *4.* Unfortunately, Bobs always been fascinated by gadgets.
5. Bobs kitchen is so full of appliances that there isnt any clear
counter space. *6.* Bob even has a microwave that tells the time: "Time
now is two o clock." *7.* The numbers on the coffeemakers digital
clock are hard to read; the 9s look like 7s and the 5s look like 6s.
8. When there isnt an electrical storm in the area, though, the clocks
are accurate. *9.* Lightning causes the clocks to stop, and he doesnt
like resetting them all the time. *10.* When he didnt have counter
space to make a bologna sandwich, he had a yard sale and sold his
appliances.

14

Quotation Marks

Unlike the rules concerning some marks of punctuation, the rules concerning quotation marks are fairly well standardized. The main rule is always, "Quotation marks come in pairs." Whenever you use an opening set of quotation marks, you must remember that a closing set will be required.

Since quotation marks serve more than one purpose, this chapter is divided into four parts: direct quotations, titles, special sense, and with other marks of punctuation. If you follow the rules presented in these four sections, you should not have any trouble using quotation marks correctly.

Direct Quotations

1. Use double quotation marks to enclose direct quotations. Capitalize the first letter of the first word of a quoted sentence.

> Plutarch said, "It is indeed a desirable thing to be well descended, but the glory belongs to our ancestors."

Do not capitalize the first letter of the first word of a quotation if what is quoted is not a complete sentence and the letter would not ordinarily be capitalized.

> Plutarch said that it is fine for us to be descended from famous people but added that the fame "belongs to our ancestors."

Do not use quotation marks to set off an indirect quotation. An indirect quotation reflects the original thought but is not in the exact words of the original. Indirect quotations are often introduced by the word *that*.

> Plutarch said that it was fine for us to be descended from famous people but added that the fame belonged to those who earned it.

2. Use single quotation marks to enclose a quotation within a quotation.

> John said, "Many American soldiers in Vietnam did not agree with Nathan Hale's words, 'I only regret that I have but one life to lose for my country.'"

3.   With a quotation within a quotation within a quotation, double quotation marks are used first, then single quotation marks, and then double quotation marks again.

> "It is a brave man indeed," Jonathan said, "who believes Lieutenant Edward's sentiment: 'Every good soldier agrees with Nathan Hale's words, "I only regret that I have but one life to lose for my country."'"

Quotation marks should not get any more involved than quotations within quotations. When the sentence would be more complicated than that, it should be rewritten.

Note: If you read books or magazines printed in the British Isles or in British territories, you will find that the use of double quotation marks and single quotation marks is exactly the reverse of what has been explained in this chapter. American usage, however, does not permit the use of single quotation marks by themselves except in headlines.

4.   The preferred way of reproducing long quotations is to omit the enclosing quotation marks and indent the entire passage of the quotation about a half-inch. In a typed paper, you should double-space the indented quotation.

> It is interesting that—like Allen Tate, T. S. Eliot, and Ezra Pound— Randall Jarrell never wrote a defense of poetry for the people who felt it needed one. He felt strongly that
>
> > poetry does not need to be defended, any more than air or food needs to be defended; poetry—using the word in its widest sense, the only sense in which it is important—has been an indispensable part of any culture we know anything about. Human life without some form of poetry is not human life but animal existence.[1]
>
> Because he believed poetry was necessary for human existence, he refused to jump on the bandwagon and condemn modern poetry because of its complexity.

5.   A two-line quotation from a poem can be handled in either of two ways.
   The quotation may be incorporated into the text by enclosing it in quotation marks and using a slash to indicate the end of the first line.

---

1. Randall Jarrell, "The Obscurity of the Poet," *Partisan Review* 18 (Jan–Feb. 1951): 67.

Alexander Pope said in his *Essay in Criticism*, "A little learning is a dangerous thing;/ Drink deep, or taste not the Pierian spring." There are many such memorable statements in the poetic essay.

The quotation may be set off from the text and reproduced exactly as it appears in the original (with no quotation marks employed that are not in the original).

Alexander Pope said in his *Essay in Criticism*,

> A little learning is a dangerous thing;
> Drink deep, or taste not the Pierian spring.

There are many such memorable statements in the poetic essay.

6. Longer passages from poems must be set off from the text and reproduced exactly as they are found in the original.

The well-known Scottish poet Robert Burns once wrote:

> My love is like a red red rose
>   That's newly sprung in June:
> My love is like the melodie
>   That's sweetly play'd in tune.

Many English teachers quote the stanza when they are explaining similes to their students.

7. In dialogue the standard practice is to begin a new paragraph with each change in speaker.

"I just don't see how Barbara can sit in front of the TV set all afternoon and watch soap operas."

"I know what you mean. But Jane does the same thing. Sometimes she gets so caught up in the stories that she forgets to pick the kids up at school."

"That sounds familiar. Barbara ruined a ten-dollar roast last week. While the stories were on, she completely forgot about supper, and the roast burned to a crisp."

"That's pretty bad when soap operas hit the wallet."

"Barbara thought so, too. The groceries come out of her budget. She hasn't watched that show again."

Remember to set off such expressions as *he said, she replied*, and *he asked* with commas.

Ellen asked, "Will Paul come to the meeting?"

"Paul cannot attend the meeting today," Jane replied.

"If Paul would come," Ellen said, "we could finish this project today."

Practice Sentences 14-1

Insert quotation marks where they are needed in the following sentences.

Example: Jan said,"Please attend this meeting for us on Thursday."

1. Align the front end, the service manager said, and rotate the tires.

2. Let's get a group together and go to the game on Saturday, Mary said.

3. Janet said that she didn't do well on the test.

4. Get your bags packed, Daddy said, so we can be on our way.

5. Donald said, I read Hemingway's short story The Short Happy Life of Francis Macomber last night.

6. The professor told his colleague: A student kept insisting, Patrick Henry's words Give me liberty or give me death were spoken in a moment of extreme emotional conflict.

7. Bobby, put on a clean shirt before you leave the house, his mother insisted.

8. Nathan Hale said that he only had one life to lose for his country.

9. Your honor, the plaintiff explained, the defendant said I am going to kill you!

10. Cari told her boyfriend, Try to be here on time.

Titles

Books and newspapers do not handle titles the same way. Newspapers use practically no italics at all, whereas books generally use italics for separate publications. The rule presented in this section reflects the usage of reputable book publishers. The general rule is to italicize (underline) the title of a long work and to enclose the title of a short work in quotation marks. Use quotation marks to enclose the titles of newspaper and magazine articles, essays, short stories, short poems, short musical works, and subdivisions of books.

"Dover Beach" is Matthew Arnold's best-known poem.

"The Unparalleled Adventure of One Hans Pfaall" is an interesting short story by Edgar Allan Poe.

One of T. S. Eliot's most famous essays is "Tradition and the Individual Talent."

A series entitled "The Community College: A Better Way" appeared in the *Montgomery Herald.*

The first big hit in America by the Beatles was "I Want to Hold Your Hand."

Part 2 of Herman Wouk's *War and Remembrance* is entitled "Midway."

Practice Sentences 14-2

Insert quotation marks where they are needed in the following sentences.

Example: The next assignment for the class is Faulkner's short story "A Rose for Emily."

1. *Fortune* once published an article entitled Business for the Novice.

2. Many students choose to read Frost's short poem The Road Not Taken in speech class.

3. Virgil's *Aeneid* is a famous Roman epic.

4. Thomas de Quincy wrote a famous essay entitled On the Knocking on the Gate in Macbeth.

5. *The New York Times* blasted the carelessness of oil companies in the article Negligence on the High Seas.

To Indicate Special Sense

1. Use quotation marks to call attention to an unusual word or phrase, a technical term, or a slang or dialectical expression that differs in style from the context.

The minister knew he was "right on" with his advice to the young. An "erg" is a unit of energy.

2. Use quotation marks to suggest that a word or phrase is being used ironically.

Jim's "valuable" prize turned out to be a cheap watch.

The "easy" economics exam caused Jerry to graduate a semester behind his classmates.

Because enclosing an expression in quotation marks really makes it stand out, be sure not to overuse quotation marks to indicate that a word or phrase is used in a special sense. To overuse the device merely weakens its effectiveness.

With Other Marks of Punctuation

1. Place the period and the comma inside the quotation marks.

"You know," the Senator said, "I think I'll run for president."
"Please get off my foot," Kathy asked nicely.

2. Place the colon and the semicolon outside the quotation marks.

One of Poe's best stories is "The Gold-Bug"; the story takes place in South Carolina.

There are four important characters in "The Open Boat": the cook, the captain, the oiler, and the correspondent.

3. Place the question mark and the exclamation point inside the quotation marks when they apply to the quoted matter.

Barbara asked, "Are you ready?"

Did he ask, "What is reality?"

"Tackle him! Tackle him!" the coach shouted from the sidelines.

"Can we stay here?" she asked.
     Notice in the last two sentences that no comma follows a question mark or an exclamation point.

4. Place the question mark and the exclamation point outside the quotation marks when they apply to the whole sentence.

Stop singing "Dixie"!
Do you like "Yankee Doodle"?

Sometimes the proper use of quotation marks can be complicated. For instance, the following sentence contains a quotation within a quotation; the overall sentence is a question but the quotation within a quotation is a statement.

Bob asked his neighbor, "Did my wife say, 'I'm leaving'?"

Practice Sentences 14-3

Put quotation marks where they are needed in the following sentences.

Example: The store owner shouted, "Fire! Fire!"

1. Quentin asked, What club did you use on your last shot?

2. Robert, Charlene said, the boss told me to tell you, Thanks for a job well done.

3. A woman stood up in church and said, Those of you who bring children should keep them quiet during the service.

4. Jill screamed, I made an *A* on my physics final!

5. One of Poe's most famous short stories is The Fall of the House of Usher.

6. The song It's Only Make Believe contains the line, Maybe someday you'll care for me.

7. Just relax! the intern shouted in panic.

8. Thelma asked, Do you like the song Blue Suede Shoes?

9. Sidney, the preacher asked, do you believe in Jesus Christ as your Savior?

10. Of Stephen Crane's short stories The Bride Comes to Yellow Sky and The Blue Hotel, which do you prefer? the teacher asked George.

Review Exercise 14-A   Using Quotation Marks
Correctly (I)

Insert quotation marks where they are needed in the following paragraph.

Example: The author asked the student," Have you read my short story

' Barefoot in the Bermuda Triangle' ? "

1. Mitchell asked Jackie, Have you read Virginia Woolf's novel *To the Lighthouse*? *2.* Yes, Jackie said, I have. *3.* Which of the three sections did you like the best? Mitchell wanted to know. *4.* Jackie replied, I only remember the middle section called Time Passes. *5.* Then she asked, What were the titles of the other two sections? *6.* Mitchell told her that the first section was The Window and the third section was The Lighthouse. *7.* Then he said, I'm not surprised that you remembered the Time Passes section. *8.* That entire portion is beautiful prose describing the passage of time and the indifference of Nature to human suffering, Mitchell explained. *9.* Yes, Jackie agreed, it is. *10.* It seemed to me more like poetry than prose, she said.

Review Exercise 14-B   Using Quotation Marks Correctly (II)

Put quotation marks where they are needed in the following paragraph.

Example: "'The Gambler' and 'Lucille' are two of my favorite songs by Kenny Rogers," Becky said.

1. Jack asked Becky, Have you read Hawthorne's short story Young Goodman Brown? *2.* Yes, I have, she replied. I thought it was excellent, didn't you? *3.* Well, I thought it was a good story, he said, but peculiar. *4.* What do you mean by peculiar? she asked. *5.* The Black Mass for one thing, he told her, and also the bit at the end that it may have all been a dream. *6.* I know what you mean, Jack, she responded, I didn't like that dream cop-out. *7.* I guess I shouldn't complain, though, Jack said. It's probably the peculiar aspect of the story that interests me. *8.* Hawthorne has other short stories that are unusual in one way or another, Becky said. *9.* She continued, Have you read either The Artist of the Beautiful or The Minister's Black Veil? *10.* Yes, I've read both, Jack said, and I thought both stories were good, peculiar but good.

15

Capitalization and Italics

Capitalization

It is difficult to formulate a definitive set of capitalization rules for the English language. Capitalization usage changes with time, meaning, and purpose. The current trend, for instance, is toward fewer capital letters than were used in the past. Just a hundred years ago a newspaper such as *The New York Times* would have capitalized many words that a modern issue of the paper would not. Also, the meaning of a word in the context of a sentence can affect capitalization. You may live on Main Street, for example, but that is only one *s*treet in the town. Capitalization usage varies with purpose, too. Thus newspaper headlines are not always capitalized the same way as newspaper articles. At best, capitalization rules serve only as guides. Since it is important, however, to be as consistent as possible, use capital letters only for a specific purpose and with a particular rule in mind.

In this section the rules of capitalization are divided into three units to make them easier to remember: (1) mechanics; (2) places, times, and kinds; and (3) government and social, publishing and personification.

Mechanics

1. Capitalize the first word of every sentence.

The amateur defeated the professional in the pro-am tournament.

2. Capitalize a word or the first word of a phrase that stands alone like a sentence.

Thanks.
Objection overruled.

3. Capitalize the first word of a direct quotation within a sentence (but not if the quotation is a fragment).

Kahlil Gibran said, "Let there be spaces in your togetherness."
Kahlil Gibran says you must have "spaces in your togetherness."

4.   Capitalize the first word of each line of poetry (unless it isn't capitalized in the original).

> The woods are lovely, dark and deep
> But I have promises to keep,
> And miles to go before I sleep.
>   *Robert Frost*

But some poets prefer not to capitalize:

> it's just like a coffin's
> inside when you die,
> pretentious and
> shiny and
> not too wide
>   *e. e. cummings*

5.   Capitalize a common noun when it is used alone as a well-known short form of a specific proper name.

> the Gulf (Gulf of Mexico)
> the Capitol (in Washington, D.C.)

6.   Capitalize the interjection *O* and the pronoun *I*.

> Come forward, O dear friends; I need your help.

7.   Capitalize all proper nouns and adjectives.

> Faculty Senate
> Surry Community College
> Louisville Country Club
> Lookout Dam

But notice:

> a college
> an avenue
> a dam
> a democracy

8.   Capitalize the first word and any nouns in the salutation of a letter.

> Gentlemen
> Dear Mr. Smith
> My dear Gloria

But only the first word of the complimentary close is capitalized:

> Very truly yours
> Sincerely yours

9. Capitalize calendar designations.

Monday
August
Thanksgiving Day

But notice:

twentieth century
winter

10. Capitalize the abbreviations of many titles and degrees and some common one- or two-letter abbreviations.

James Alfred Draughn, Ph.D.
Theodore N. Swaim, Jr.
TV, CB, F (Fahrenheit)

11. Capitalize the numerals used to refer to organizations or to periods of time. Spell out numerals preceding a name. Often, numerals following a name are put in Roman numerals.

First World War
Second Army
World War II
Edward VII
Fifty-first Congress

12. Capitalize expressions of time such as *A.M., P.M., A.D.,* and *B.C.* (Some writers prefer not to use capital letters for *a.m.* and *p.m.*)

55 B.C.
6:20 A.M.

Practice Sentences 15-1

Supply capital letters where they are needed.

   Example: The class meets every Tuesday night.

   1. churchill downs in louisville, kentucky, is the site of the kentucky derby.

   2. the united states entered world war ii in 1941.

   3. christmas day is a sad time for many lonely people.

   4. in 55 b.c. julius caesar invaded england.

   5. it was f.d.r. that said, "we have nothing to fear but fear itself."

   6. the lincoln memorial in washington is very impressive.

7. the meeting will begin promptly at 10:00 a.m.

8. the temperature was 3°f this morning.

9. steve's mother said, "please close the door."

10. dry wells is a ghost town.

Places, Times, and Kinds

13. Capitalize geographical terms.

Hudson River
Irish Sea
Pike's Peak
Rocky Mountains
Lake Erie

But notice:

the Erie and Huron lakes

14. Capitalize descriptive terms used to designate a definite region or locality.

the North Atlantic States
the South
Eastern Hemisphere
the Promised Land

Directional parts of states are not capitalized, however.

eastern Kentucky
southern Idaho

Also, compass points are not capitalized when indicating direction.

The Smiths drove west for ten miles and then headed northwest for the next twenty-five miles.

15. Capitalize the names of specific streets, roads, highways, toll roads, etc.

Highway 66
Road 2249
West Virginia Turnpike

16. Capitalize proper names.

John Conklin
Spain
Paris

17.   Capitalize the derivatives of proper names used with a proper meaning.

Miltonic style
Jeffersonian democracy
Spanish
Parisian
American

Words derived from proper names but that now have independent meanings are not capitalized.

china (meaning *porcelain*)
pasteurize
bohemian
volt

18.   Capitalize nouns of kinship when used as substitutes for proper names.

I would like to introduce you to Dad.

But do not capitalize nouns of kinship that are preceded by an article or a possessive.

She is my mother.

19.   Capitalize a course of study only if the name of the subject is derived from a proper noun or if you are referring to a specific course title.

French
German
Piaget's Theory of Cognition
History 101
Shorthand II

But:

history
shorthand

20.   Capitalize the word *the* only when it is part of an official name or title.

The Hague
The Tempest

But the word *the* is not generally capitalized in references to newspapers, magazines, vessels, and company names:

the *Atlantic Monthly*
the *U.S.S. America*
the *Winston-Salem Journal*
the Fuji Film Co.

21. Capitalize the scientific name of a genus but not the name of a species.

Acer saccharinum (genus and species)

22. Capitalize religious feast, festival, and fast days as well as historic events and eras.

Feast of the Passover
the Renaissance
Yom Kippur
Christmas Day
Battle of Salamis
Korean War
the Middle Ages
the Treaty of Versailles

23. Capitalize names for God or the Trinity, both nouns and adjectives, and pronouns referring to the Deity.

the Messiah
Our Father
His mercy

24. Capitalize words that refer to the Bible or other sacred writings.

Holy Bible
Genesis
Koran

Practice Sentences 15-2

Correctly supply capital letters where they are needed.

Example: I think highway 601 is dangerous to travel at night.

1. brian score is a state senator in idaho.

2. jane andrews saw pike's peak for the first time when she was thirteen.

3. the bible discusses the promised land.

4. eddie hernandez has taken history 101, history 102, and sociology 304 all this summer.

5. susan has worked for the ibm corporation for over twenty years.

6. the controversial editorial about ted turner appeared in the *atlanta constitution*.

7. spanish, french, italian, and portuguese are all romance languages.

8. many historians consider the treaty of versailles to be a causative factor in the origin of world war ii.

9. oliver wendell holmes and james russell lowell were instrumental in establishing the *atlantic monthly.*

10. brigham young university is a fine school for quarterbacks.

Government and Social, Publishing and Personifying

25. Capitalize the names of administrative, legislative, and judicial bodies and departments.

> House of Representatives
> Supreme Court
> Department of Commerce
> General Assembly of North Carolina

26. Capitalize the names of organizations, political parties, alliances, institutions, religious groups, races, movements, classes, nationalities, athletic teams, civic groups, etc.

> Lions Club
> Young Men's Christian Association
> Republican party
> Princeton University
> Catholics
> Jews
> Women's Liberation Movement
> Dallas Cowboys

But:

> democracy
> club

27. Capitalize any titles preceding a person's name.

> President Kennedy
> King Charles
> Ambassador Smith
> Professor Wiles

28. Capitalize a common-noun title immediately following a name or used alone as a substitute for it to indicate preeminence or distinction.

> Jim Rawlings, Governor
> the President (of the United States)

the K̄ing (referring to a specific one)
the P̄ope

29.   Capitalize the first and last words of the titles of books, articles, student compositions, etc., and capitalize all other important words (nouns, verbs, adjectives, and adverbs). Do not capitalize articles (*a, an, the*) or short (four letters or less) prepositions or conjunctions.

> *Gone with the W̄ind*
> *Ā Raisin in the S̄un*
> "Ān Analysis of R̄oderick Ūsher"

But notice:

> "The Man Ā̱gainst the Sky"
> *Desire Ūnder the Elms*
>   The̱ prepositions *against* and *under* contain five letters or more.

30.   Capitalize trade names, variety names, and names of market grades.

> Corning W̄are (trade name)
> Ḡolden D̄elicious apple (variety)
> ŪSDA C̄hoice (market grade)

31.   Capitalize all personifications. (Personification is the granting of human attributes to abstract ideas and inanimate objects.)

> Suddenly and unexpectedly, D̄eath crept into the room during the night.
> The C̱hair recognizes the representative from Guilford County.

Practice Sentences 15-3

Supply capital letters where they are necessary.

> **Example:** $\overset{M}{m}$ary served in the $\overset{H}{h}$ouse of $\overset{R}{r}$epresentatives for two terms.

1. herman wouk scored two hits with *the winds of war* and *war and remembrance.*

2. i like the morning flower pattern for everyday china.

3. the oakland a's are trying to get into the playoffs.

4. *invisible man* is a fine novel by ralph ellison.

5. the woman thought death stalked her constantly.

6. "the cask of amantillado" is a short story by poe.

7. eliot ness worked for the treasury department.

8. michael jordan is a star for the chicago bulls.

9. have you ever read the book *my brother was an only child*?

10. carla thinks professor reece is an excellent teacher.

Italics (Underlining)

There is no definitive set of rules for the use of italic type. Different publishers follow different rules. Nevertheless, the rules presented in this chapter generally reflect the usage recommended by the *U.S. Government Printing Office Style Manual* and most authorities. In typewritten and handwritten papers you should underline in all cases where printers use italics.

1. Italicize all titles of separate publications (books, magazines, newspapers, plays, long musical compositions, long poems, etc.).

U.S. Government Printing Office Style Manual (book)
Rosencrantz and Guildenstern Are Dead (play)
Paradise Lost (epic poem)
La Bohème (opera, long musical work)
Moby Dick (novel)
U.S. News & World Report (magazine)
the *Chicago Tribune* (newspaper)

2. Italicize the names of ships, trains, aircraft, and spacecraft.

The *Queen Elizabeth II* is a beautiful ship.
Lindbergh's *Spirit of St. Louis* was small and fragile.
The moon-mission of *Apollo II* will never be forgotten.

3. Italicize the titles of motion pictures and works of art.

Star Wars was a movie with magnificent special effects.

Michelangelo's *David* is one of the most famous sculptures in the world.

Leonardo da Vinci's *Mona Lisa* is perhaps the most famous painting in the world.

4. Italicize the Latin names of genus and species.

Osmunda cinnamomea (cinnamon fern)
Canis familiaris (dog)

5. Italicize foreign words and expressions.

raison d'être (French for "reason for being")
e pluribus unum (Latin for "from many, one")

Note: Many foreign words and expressions are so commonly used they are said to be Anglicized; such words and expressions are not italicized:

> patio (Spanish)
> hors d'oeuvre (French)
> bona fide (Latin)

6.   Italicize a letter, word, number, or expression when it is spoken of as such or used as an illustration.

> The *i*'s on that make of typewriter look like *l*'s.
> The words *adapt* and *adopt* confuse many readers.
> Please form your *Z*'s and *3*'s distinctly.

7.   Italicize sparingly to emphasize a word or expression.

> Write all essays in *ink*!
> *Do not overuse italicizing* in this manner.

Review Exercise 15-A   Using Capital Letters Correctly

Supply capital letters where they are necessary by crossing out each incorrect lowercase letter and writing the capital above it.

Example: Âbraham Ĺincoln

1. linda wright is thinking about her upcoming marriage. *2.* she is proud of her name and the well-established family business, wright food distributors. *3.* if she follows marital tradition her new name will be linda mounce. *4.* she knows her fiancé todd mounce is proud of his name and his reputation as editor of the *boston herald.* *5.* she thought about having a hyphenated name, wright-mounce or mounce-wright. *6.* but then linda realized that hyphenated names are often too long to fit on many forms that have to be filled out. *7.* she knew that even her own macintosh computer at home would clip off some of the letters. *8.* she told the professor of her marriage and the family 201 class that always taking the husband's last name wasn't fair. *9.* professor martin agreed and suggested that she discuss her feelings with todd. *10.* linda decided to do that when she saw him friday night.

Review Exercise 15-B   Using Italics Correctly

Underline everything in the following paragraph that would be italicized.

Example: <u>Moby</u> <u>Dick</u>

1. Tommy sailed to New York on the SS <u>Nancy</u>. *2.* He took current issues of <u>Time</u>, <u>Newsweek</u>, <u>U.S. News & World Report</u>, and <u>Foreign Affairs</u> with him. *3.* He also took the novels <u>Middlemarch</u>, <u>Emma</u>, and <u>The Mill on the Floss</u>. *4.* Naturally, he planned to read the <u>Wall Street Journal</u>, <u>The New York Times</u>, and the <u>Washington Post</u> daily as well. *5.* At the newsstand of the SS <u>Nancy</u>, he bought a copy of <u>The Collected Short Stories of Nathaniel Hawthorne</u>. *6.* The first two stories he read were "Rappacini's Daughter" and "Ethan Brand." *7.* He preferred both of these stories to Hawthorne's novel <u>The House of the Seven Gables</u>. *8.* He decided to rest his eyes after reading four hundred pages of <u>Middlemarch</u> and went to the Cinema Room to see <u>Birth of a Nation</u> and <u>Citizen Kane</u>. *9.* The next day he read three hundred more pages of <u>Middlemarch</u> and saw the Hitchcock thriller <u>The Rear Window</u>. *10.* That evening he met a beautiful woman who loved to read and watch classic movies, and he returned to his cabin to watch taped reruns of <u>The Love Boat</u>.

Review Exercise 15-C *Using Capital Letters and Italics Correctly (I)*

Supply capital letters and underlining where they are needed in the following paragraph.

Example: *J. B. B A H G*
J. B. Bury's <u>A History of Greece</u>

1. oliver goldsmith was an outstanding eighteenth century writer. *2.* some say that if it were not for samuel johnson the second half of the century would be known as the age of goldsmith. *3.* goldsmith wrote fine works in different literary genres. *4.* he wrote a fine autobiographical novel entitled the vicar of wakefield. *5.* his poem "the deserted village" is noted for its characterizations. *6.* she stoops to conquer is a full-length play that is still being performed. *7.* goldsmith was also an accomplished essayist. *8.* the citizen of the world contains many of his essays. *9.* he also was a hack writer of grub street. *10.* that means he wrote many works of questionable quality because he needed the money.

Review Exercise 15-D   Using Capital Letters and Italics Correctly (II)

Supply capital letters and underlining where they are needed in the following paragraph.

Example: u s s c
̶u̶s̶s̶ ̶c̶onstitution

*1.*marie recently developed an interest in renaissance art. *2.* she began keeping a list of her favorite works. *3.* she likes leonardo da vinci's famous portrait entitled mona lisa. *4.* her favorite artist, though, is michelangelo. *5.* she especially likes his statue david and his painting on the ceiling of the sistine chapel. *6.* marie also likes the work of raphael, especially his painting the school of athens. *7.* she has titian's portrait man with the glove on her list. *8.* other items are michelangelo's statue moses and raphael's painting galatea. *9.* marie likes the work in marble by donatello, especially the two statues st. mark and st. george and the dragon. *10.* marie certainly shows good taste in her selections.

16

Abbreviations and Numbers

Abbreviations

Standard English usage is rather conservative and permits few abbreviations. As might be expected, there is little consistency in the abbreviations it does accept. Also, the acceptability of abbreviations varies according to the purpose of the writing. For instance, a chart in a technical report and the bibliography of a scholarly article will use far more abbreviations than the standard prose of most popular magazines and books written for a general audience. Naturally, the audience aimed at will largely determine the acceptability of abbreviations. Technical matter aimed at specialists who share a similar background and who are expected to know the jargon of the field contains numerous abbreviations. In fact, the abbreviations, symbols, and equations of some technical writing are practically a form of shorthand. On the other hand, abbreviations are kept to a minimum in popular magazines such as *Time*, *Newsweek*, and *Reader's Digest*. In these magazines the purpose is clarity. Your compositions for your English class are written in standard English. Like popular magazines, you should have clarity as a goal. You do not want to use any abbreviations that might confuse your reader.

Though lists of acceptable abbreviations might differ greatly from one magazine to another, some conventions in abbreviating have developed over the years. This chapter presents the conventions most often accepted in standard English writing for nontechnical audiences.

1. Use the abbreviations *Mr., Mrs., Miss, Ms., St.,* and *Dr.* whenever these titles precede a proper name.

Dr. Alice Smith
Mr. Jones
Mrs. Alistair
Ms. Frances Ingram
St. Christopher

2.   Use the abbreviations *Gen., Sgt., Prof., Gov., Rev., Hon., Sen., Rep.,* and *Capt.* if the title is followed by a first name or an initial as well as a surname.

> Gen. George Patton
> Rev. J. Hutton
> Prof. H. Kissinger

But:

> Captain Adams
> Sergeant Brown

3.   Use the abbreviations *Jr.* and *Sr.* when preceded by a proper name.

> William E. Edmonds, Jr.
> Edward J. Pendleton, Sr.

4.   Use the abbreviations *D.D., Ph.D., M.A., B.A., M.D.,* and *C.P.A.* when preceded by a proper name or alone if the context is clear.

> June R. Mandell, Ph.D.
> William C. Ludwig, C.P.A.
> He earned an M.A. degree before he sat for the C.P.A. exam.

5.   Use the abbreviations *Co., Corp., Inc., Bros., Ltd.* and symbols such as the ampersand (&) in describing business firms only when the abbreviations are part of the legally authorized name.

> Grosset & Dunlap, Inc.
> Jones Bros. & Co.
> Radio Corp. of America
> A & P Company

6.   The abbreviations *i.e., e.g., cf., et al., etc.,* and *vs.* or *v.* may be used in any type of writing.

i.e.	(that is)	et al.	(and others)
e.g.	(for example)	etc.	(and so forth)
cf.	(compare)	vs. or v.	(versus)

> The artist brought several examples of his craft, e.g., silver pitchers and pewter sconces.

7.   Use the following abbreviations for states when they immediately follow any capitalized geographic term. Alaska, Hawaii, Idaho, Iowa, Maine, Ohio, and Utah are spelled out in full. Do not abbreviate the name of the state when it stands alone.

Ala.	Kans.	N. Dak.	S.C.
Ariz.	Ky.	Nebr.	S. Dak.
Ark.	La.	Nev.	Tenn.
Calif.	Mass.	N.H.	Tex.
Colo.	Md.	N.J.	Va.
Conn.	Mich.	N. Mex.	Vt.
Del.	Minn.	N.Y.	Wash.
Fla.	Miss.	Okla.	Wis.
Ga.	Mo.	Oreg.	W. Va.
Ill.	Mont.	Pa.	Wyo.
Ind.	N.C.	R.I.	

Albany, N.Y.
Nashville, Tenn.
Portland, Maine
Provo, Utah
Little Rock, Ark.

But:

She was born in South Carolina.

8. Use the abbreviation *U.S.S.R.* (Union of Soviet Socialist Republics), but spell out the names of all other countries.

in Brazil
in London, England
in the U.S.S.R.

9. Use the abbreviation *U.S.* as an adjective but not as a noun.

U.S. Navy
U.S. Government Printing Office
in the United States

10. Use the abbreviations *A.D., B.C., A.M., P.M., no.* or *No.*, and the symbol $ only with dates or figures.

A.D. 1066
350 B.C.
4:50 P.M.
$100
No. 3

11. Use the abbreviation *D.C.* for District of Columbia.

Washington, D.C.

12.   Use abbreviations for things normally referred to by their capitalized initials.

CB
TV

13.   Use commonly accepted acronyms (words derived from the initial letters or syllables of successive parts of a term).

Amoco (American Oil Company)
UNESCO (United Nations Educational, Scientific, and Cultural Organization)

Practice Sentences 16-1

Correct all abbreviation errors.

              General   *President*
Example: ~~Gen.~~ McArthur and ~~Pres.~~ Truman were not close friends.

1. Doctor Chuck Barris left the operating room at four A.M.

2. Juneau, Alask., and Bismarck, Nor. Dak., are both capital cities.

3. Corp. Davis will soon be promoted to gen.

4. Honduras is in C.A.

5. One famous Eng. novelist wrote about the poor in Victorian England.

6. There were a staggering no. of applicants for the open position.

7. Thad Sanders, Junior, was the best driver on the team.

8. The computer I use was mfd. by International Business Machines.

9. When my neighbor transmits on his cb radio, the picture on my tv looks like a snowstorm.

10. Rome first invaded Eng. in 55 bc but didn't attempt to settle there until ad 43.

14.   Spell out months, days of the week, and units of measurement.

Monday
September
Mary is nearly six feet tall.
163 pounds

15.   Spell out the words *street, avenue, boulevard, road, square, court, park, mount,* and *river* used as an essential part of proper names.

Fifth Avenue
Hampton Court
Washington Square
East Boulevard

16. Spell out the names of courses of study and the words for *page, chapter, volume, part, book,* and *canto.*

I studied physical education and chemistry.
page 15
Chapter 3
canto XXXI

17. Spell out first names.

George Washington
    not Geo. Washington
William Penn
    not Wm. Penn
Thomas Jefferson
    not Thos. Jefferson

18. For an abbreviation that is not generally known, write out the full form in parentheses immediately following its first use.

b.h.p. (brake horsepower)
F.S.L.N. (Sandinista National Liberation Front)

19. Do not use a period after chemical symbols.

$C_8H_{15}N$
H_2O

20. Do not use a period after initials of military services and specific military terms.

USN	United States Navy
MP	Military Police
MIA	Missing in Action
AWOL	Absent Without Leave
PX	Post Exchange

21. Do not use a period after the acronyms of certain governmental agencies or call letters of television and radio stations.

DOE	Department of Energy
FBI	Federal Bureau of Investigation
CIA	Central Intelligence Agency

WXII   television station call letters
WB4EIV   amateur radio operator's call letters

Practice Sentences 16-2

Correct all abbreviation errors.

Example: Louis jumped twenty-fou~~r ft.~~ *feet* in the long jump competition.

1. My call letters are W.B.4.E.I.V.

2. The bag of fertilizer weighed fifty lbs.

3. Ch. 4 has three pgs. that are badly burned.

4. Thelma lives on 6th St.

5. Wm. Brown is a history prof. at the local college.

6. The chemical symbol for hydrochloric acid is H.Cl.

7. The C.I.A. is not supposed to operate in the United States.

8. The meeting is scheduled for Mon., Sept. 12.

9. The pizza restaurant is on E. Blvd.

10. John lost fifteen lbs. in Oct.

Numbers

There seems to be a growing trend these days toward the use of more figures in writing. It is a known fact that readers can comprehend figures more quickly than they can comprehend the written-out forms of numbers. And, of course, figures are vastly preferable in much technical and scientific material. Nevertheless, some rules governing the use of figures are applicable in most standard English prose written for the general reader; those rules are presented in this chapter.

   1. Use figures for numbers that require more than two words to spell out.

   153
   4,289

But notice:

   twenty-four
   ninety-six
   ten

   2. Use figures for time designations used with A.M., P.M., B.C., and A.D.

   8:01 A.M.
   55 B.C.

11:53 P.M.
A.D. 1066

But **not:**

ten A.M.
thirty-three B.C.

3. Use figures in addresses.

Route 2
1128 Belgrade Drive
P. O. Box 531
Room 374

4. Use figures for most dates but not all.

May 1849
January 5, 1946 or 5 January 1946
August ninth or the ninth of August or August 9 or August 9th
the sixties or the 1960s or the 1960's
the twentieth century
1600 or 1632–1638 or 1632–38
from 1941 to 1945

But **not:**

May, 1849
    The comma is not needed.

January 5th, 1946
    Do not use *th* when the year follows.

from 1941–1945
    From must be accompanied by the complementary word *to.*

5. Use figures for serial numbers.

Newsletter 63
page 154
Chapter 4
paragraph 2
Document 12

6. Use figures (normally Roman numerals) to differentiate kings, emperors, and popes with the same names.

Edward VIII
Charles V
Elizabeth II
Boniface VI

7. Use figures (generally Roman numerals) in denoting vehicles.

Courageous II
Pioneer I
Apollo IX

8. Use figures (Roman numerals) to designate family members of the same name.

Ralston M. Ounce, III
John R. Dobbins, IV

9. Use figures to designate local branches of labor unions and fraternal lodges.

Teamsters Local 391
American Legion Post 266

10. Use figures to designate state and interstate highways.

North Carolina 52
Interstate 77

11. Use figures with decimals, degrees, percentages, money, and proportion.

35.6 inches
longitude 51°05′01″ W
33 percent
$912.69
odds of 4 to 1

12. Use figures with game scores, election results, statistics, and items in a series.

a score of 50 to 6
a vote of 321 to 9 against
4 hammers, 7 screwdrivers, and 1,268 nails

13. Use figures in parentheses to repeat numbers in legal or commercial writing.

The cashier keeps two hundred (200) dollars of ready cash on hand.

or

The cashier keeps two hundred dollars ($200) of ready cash on hand.

Practice Sentences 16-3

Make any necessary corrections in the use of numbers.

Example: Jane traveled almost the entire way on Interstate ~~Forty.~~ 40

1. Becky was born on June 16th, 1964.

2. The new elementary school is located at three-five-one Albert Drive.

3. Paragraph twelve needs to be rewritten to avoid sexist language.

4. Henry 8th had 6 wives.

5. Teamsters Local three-nine-one has been quiet for the last few years.

6. The television show ran from 1974–1984.

7. Elections in the 5th Congressional District are usually close.

8. Some historians doubt that the Declaration of Independence was actually signed on July 4th, 1776.

9. The Lakers lost to the Bullets ninety-eight to ninety-five.

10. Chad purchased one hammer, two saws, fifteen boards, and one thousand two hundred fifty-seven nails.

14.   Large round numbers may be either spelled out or put in figures.

thirty million dollars
$30,000,000
$30 million

15.   Spell out numbers beginning sentences.

Ninety men volunteered for the assignment.
Five percent of the Conservative Party are actually Marxists.

When possible, rewrite sentences so that numbers do not come at the beginning.

16.   Spell out ordinal numbers preceding the noun of successive dynasties, governments, and governing bodies.

Third Reich
Eighty-second Congress
Twelfth Dynasty

17. Spell out ordinal numbers less than one hundred that designate political divisions and military units.

Fifth Congressional District
Third Ward
Ninety-fourth Precinct
Second Army
Forty-fifth Regiment
Seventeenth Battalion

18. Spell out numbered streets under one hundred.

Fifth Avenue
Thirty-second Street

19. Spell out numbers designating churches or religious organizations.

First Presbyterian Church
Seventh-day Adventists

20. Spell out numbers preceding the expression *o'clock.*

eight o'clock

Practice Sentences 16-4

Make any necessary corrections in the use of numbers.

    Example: Election returns from the 9th district were lost. *[handwritten: Ninth D]*

1. One mile is 1760 yards.

2. The 42nd Regiment is ready to go.

3. The fire started at 8 o'clock at night.

4. The offices of Flagler & Sharp are located on 7th Avenue.

5. Norbert is to meet the preacher at the 1st Baptist Church tonight.

6. There were 2523 suggestions in the suggestion box.

7. 93 percent of the women favored the new maternity leave policy.

8. The 99th Congress was embroiled in controversy.

9. 15 couples returned from their vacation early.

10. The concert is scheduled to begin in the park at 2 o'clock.

Review Exercise 16-A   Using Abbreviations Correctly

Correct all abbreviation errors.

       11:00 A.M.
Example: ~~11 a.m.~~

    1. Bottle Bailey is a member of the 15th battalion. *2.* Sgt. Bailey loves his work. *3.* He is from Walnut Cove, Sou. D. *4.* The Army gives Sgt. Bailey a chance to travel. *5.* Last year he was in Charleston, Sou. Car., New Orleans, Louis., and Paris, Fr. *6.* This year he has already been to London, Eng., and Rome, It. *7.* Not only that, the Army has trained Bottle beyond his h.s. education. *8.* Sgt. Bailey learned enough chem. to make gunpowder and a smoke bomb. *9.* Though he is unable to be home at Xmas, Sgt. Bottle Bailey likes the Army fine. *10.* However, he would prefer to rise a little later than 4:30 in the A.M.

Review Exercise 16-B   Using Numbers Correctly

Make any necessary corrections in the use of numbers.

Example: on 23rd Street
(Twenty-third)

1. The wedding is to be in the 1st Baptist Church of Dobson. *2.* It is to be at 7 o'clock on Friday, June 30th, 1989. *3.* The bride, who lives at five-three-one Haney Road, has already planned the ceremony. *4.* She wants a small wedding with only 23 guests. *5.* She told the pianist she wanted hymn forty-one played as the guests were seated. *6.* She asked that the minister conduct about a 15-minute service. *7.* 250 dollars was all she planned to spend. *8.* The reception was scheduled for eight in the P.M. *9.* The couple will live at thirteen-thirteen Mockingbird Lane. *10.* It is the 2nd marriage for both, and they are excited.

Review Exercise 16-C   Using Abbreviations and Numbers Correctly (I)

Make any necessary changes in the use of abbreviations and numbers.

Example: 4:00 ~~in the~~ A.M.

1. Wm. Draughn is very precise about his daily schedule. *2.* He gets up each morning at 5:30. *3.* Then he jogs 3 miles on a course he laid out around the neighborhood. *4.* Back at home he eats 2 bowls of Raisin Bran and drinks 1 glass of orange juice. *5.* He takes a shower that lasts exactly 5 minutes. *6.* By 8 o'clock he is sitting in his first class. *7.* At 1:30 in the P.M. he attends his p.e. class. *8.* By four P.M. he is back at home. *9.* He studies for at least 4 hrs. each night. *10.* He began setting such schedules for himself on Jan. 5th, 1990, following intestinal surgery.

Review Exercise 16-D *Using Abbreviations and Numbers Correctly (II)*

Make any necessary changes in the use of abbreviations and numbers.

Example: ~~Wed.~~ *Wednesday* afternoon at ~~5:00~~ *five* o'clock

1. Early Mon. morning at four-thirty A.M. a crime was committed in Dobbins, Oh. *2.* Apt. Thirteen of the Harrison Apartment building was broken into. *3.* Det. Andrews of the Dobbins Police Dept. investigated. *4.* At the scene Det. Andrews found a bare apt. and blood in the bathroom sink. *5.* She also found two pks. of matches from the Highway Four-Twenty-One Truck Stop. *6.* Det. Andrews proceeded to the truck stop and found Mister Wm. Smith, owner of Apt. Thirteen. *7.* Wm. Smith told the det. that nothing had been stolen and no one had been harmed. *8.* He said his furniture was repossessed by Taylor Dept. Store on 5th St. *9.* Wm. Smith then told Det. Andrews that the blood in the sink was from where he had cut himself shaving. *10.* By 8:30 in the A.M. Det. Andrews declared the case solved.

17

Other Marks of Punctuation

In this chapter we present the punctuation marks that have not previously been discussed. The punctuation marks in this chapter are no less important than other punctuation marks that may have more rules governing their usage. In fact, some of the marks discussed here are so specialized that any incorrect use of them could confuse your readers.

Periods

1. Use a period to mark the end of a declarative sentence (one that makes a statement) or a mildly imperative sentence (one that expresses a command or makes a request).

> Matt Davis is the best blocker on the team.
> The sentence makes a statement.

> Please close the door.
> The sentence makes a request.

> Open the glove compartment and get my gloves.
> The sentence expresses commands.

But a strongly imperative sentence needs an exclamation point.

> Put your hands over your head and lean against the wall!

2. Use a period to mark the end of an indirect question. Words such as *when* and *what* often introduce questions that are asked so indirectly that no question mark is necessary.

> The Dean asked me when I could come by and speak with him.
> Martha asked what Bob had said about her.

3. Use a period to mark the end of a polite request, even if it is worded as a question. Business letters often reflect this use of the period. When a businessperson asks a question in a letter, the intent is often more a mild imperative than a question. Also, in such cases the answer is generally assumed to be *yes*.

Will you reply by return mail.
Will you see that the shipment is adequately insured.

4. Use a period for most abbreviations.

Mrs.
Dr.
P.M.
A.M.
etc.
e.g.

Use only one period if a declarative sentence ends with an abbreviation.

The new economics professor is from Washington, D.C.

Use a question mark or an exclamation point after the abbreviation period if an interrogative sentence (one that asks a direct question) or an exclamatory sentence (one that expresses strong feeling or surprise) ends with an abbreviation.

Is the pitcher from Charlotte, N.C.?

Don't hop a train to Chicago, Ill.!

Use whatever punctuation mark would normally be used to follow an abbreviation period inside the sentence.

Some writers use many abbreviations such as *i.e., e.g.,* and *etc.*; other writers, however, do not favor such Latin abbreviations.

5. Use a period to separate dollars from cents in writing figures.

$1.29
$36.94

6. Use the period as a decimal point in writing figures.

98.6°
16.8 percent
$15.6 million

Practice Sentences 17-1

Insert periods where they are needed in the following sentences.

Example: Mrs. Ruth Herman will lecture on "Mead and Samoa."

1. Penny asked me if she could borrow $10

2. Please leave the room

3. Will you please credit my account for the returned merchandise

4. Evening classes at the college begin at 7:00 PM

5. Dr Jackson can see you today at 10:00 AM

6. The receipt for twenty-eight dollars and thirty cents should be written as $2830

7. Did you have a chance to visit with your sister in Richmond, Va?

8. Please close the window, Charles

9. Rev Van Rinegold is supposed to drop by today at 2:00 PM

10. Rick asked the coach if the team had been selected yet

Leaders and Ellipses

There are several instances where "multiple periods" are employed in writing.

Some printers use leaders (a line of periods) in the table of contents of a book to guide the reader's eye from a chapter title to the page on which the chapter begins.

Some printers use three centered periods (or asterisks) to indicate the omission of long passages (a paragraph, a page, or even several chapters). In the following passage, the second paragraph of a three-paragraph letter from Samuel Johnson to James Macpherson has been left out.

Mr. James Macpherson—I received your foolish and impudent note. Whatever insult is offered me I will do my best to repel, and what I cannot do for myself the law will do for me. I will not desist from detecting what I think a cheat, from any fear of the menaces of a Ruffian.

. . .

But however I may despise you, I reverence truth and if you can prove the genuineness of the work I will confess it. Your rage I defy, your abilities since your Homer are not so formidable, and what I have heard of your morals disposes me to pay regard not to what you shall say, but to what you can prove.

You may print this if you will,
Samuel Johnson

The most common use of multiple periods is the ellipsis. The ellipsis mark is three spaced periods in a row. It is sometimes, as in mathematics, used to indicate that a series, pattern, or listing continues on beyond the last item cited.

The boy counted to one hundred: 1, 2, 3, 4 . . .

Sometimes an ellipsis is used to indicate the passage of time.

It was a beautiful morning . . . a cloudy afternoon . . . a stormy evening.

By far the most important use of the ellipsis mark, however, is to indicate that part of a quotation has been left out. Since quotations are normally supposed to be reproduced exactly as they appeared in the original, the ellipsis mark is important in that it lets you alter the quotation by omitting part of it. You should familiarize yourself with the following two rules:

7. If the omission occurs at the beginning or in the middle of a sentence, use three periods.

". . . Wanting both government and liberty the writer . . . pointed out the relationship between the two."

Sometimes the ellipses at the beginning of a quotation are omitted.

8. If the last part of a quoted sentence is omitted or if entire sentences of a quoted passage are omitted, add a fourth period.

Original quotation: Literature is my Utopia. Here I am not disfranchised. No barrier of the senses shuts me out from the sweet, gracious discourse of my book-friends. They talk to me without embarrassment or awkwardness.
—Helen Keller

Quotation with ellipses: Literature is my Utopia. . . . No barrier of the senses shuts me out from the . . . discourse of my book-friends. They talk to me without embarrassment or awkwardness.

Ellipses should not be used to alter the meaning of the original source. If a reviewer says, "I do not think the book is very good," it would be misleading of you to reproduce the quotation leaving out the word *not*, "I do . . . think the book is very good."

Brackets

Like ellipses, brackets can be useful in reproducing quotations. Ellipses permit us to omit words from quotations; brackets permit us to add words. Do not confuse brackets [ ] with parentheses ( ). Parentheses are used to enclose parenthetical material in your own work, whereas brackets are used to add your own parenthetical comments, corrections, and additions to the passage you are quoting.

1. Use brackets to enclose an explanation that is inserted in quoted material and that is not part of the original text.

> James Macke wrote, "She [Emily Dickinson] is the best female poet America has produced."

> The newspaper reported, "Sebastian Coe now holds the world's record for each leg in the Triple Crown [800 meters, 1,500 meters, and the mile]."

2. Use brackets enclosing the Latin word *sic* (meaning "thus") following errors in fact, spelling, punctuation, or grammar to indicate that you know the errors are present.

> The book stated, "Abraham Lincoln was assassinated on April 14, 1965 [*sic*]."

> The student wrote "The English coarse [*sic*] was very difficult."

3. You can correct some errors in the original text by enclosing the correction in brackets.

> The division manager wrote the owner, "You should get Roger Boyd inste[a]d of Bill Tompkins."

> The newspaper summarized the election results with the headline, "McDonald To Be New Pres[id]ent."

Practice Sentences 17-2

In the following sentences, insert brackets where they are necessary.

> **Example:** The biographer wrote, "He [William Shakespeare] was born in 1564."

1. The article stated, "This year's Nobel Prise *sic* was awarded to William Faulkner.

2. The student concluded his paper by saying, "This poet's work Ezra Pound's is too obscure for me."

3. Carmen Gordon wrote in her column, "The project this man has in mind to build a dam three miles above the town would be disastrous to our community."

4. The student wrote, "Alot *sic* of this work is meaningless to us."

5. Sally told her friend, "I think she Emily Brontë wrote a masterpiece in *Wuthering Heights.*

Colons

The colon is a rather formal mark of punctuation. Some writers prefer not to use it. Nevertheless, there are some situations where the colon is the most appropriate mark of punctuation to use.

1. Use the colon to introduce a series of examples or a list of items.

There are three kinds of extrasensory perception: telepathy, clairvoyance, and precognition.

Many schools are organized in the following way: grades 1–6, grades 7–9, and grades 10–12.

2. Use the colon to introduce a long formal statement, quotation, or question.

The book made one irrefutable point: Every good scholar is a good listener.

Speaking of labor, Abraham Lincoln said: "Labor is prior to, and independent of, capital. Capital is only the fruit of labor, and could never have existed if labor had not first existed!"

This is the real question: Should the judiciary be given more power than the President and Congress?

3. Use a colon after the formal salutation of a business letter or speech.

Dear Mr. Tolbert:
Ladies and Gentlemen:

4. Use a colon between the chapter and verse of a biblical reference.

Genesis 46:3
Job 11:20

5. Use a colon between the title and subtitle of a book.

College English: The First Year
Poe: A Collection of Critical Essays

6. Use a colon to separate hours from minutes in time references.

12:58 P.M.
6:45 A.M.

7. Use a colon to indicate that an initial clause will be further explained by the material that follows the colon. In such constructions the colon could be substituted for the expressions *namely* and *for example.*

The local government was famous for its inefficiency: the city councilmen were always duplicating the work of the county commissioners.

Be very careful not to confuse this use of a colon with the normal use of a semicolon. Though the two marks of punctuation may resemble each other in appearance, they do not serve the same function.

8. Do not use a colon between a preposition and its object.

Incorrect: He has always thought highly of: Henry James, Fyodor Dostoyevski, and Gustave Flaubert.

9. Do not use a colon after a verb, after the word *that*, or after the expression *such as.*

Incorrect: John has always enjoyed: tennis, golf, basketball, and handball.
Correct: John has always enjoyed tennis, golf, basketball, and handball.

Incorrect: His problems are: awkwardness, nervousness, and shyness.
Correct: His problems are awkwardness, nervousness, and shyness.

Incorrect: Martha enjoys some of America's classics, such as: *The Deerslayer, The Scarlet Letter, The Adventures of Huckleberry Finn, Moby Dick,* and *Light in August.*
Correct: Martha enjoys some of America's classics, such as *The Deerslayer, The Scarlet Letter, The Adventures of Huckleberry Finn, Moby Dick,* and *Light in August.*

Practice Sentences 17-3

In the following sentences, insert colons where they are needed.

Example: Exodus 5:17

1. There are several appliance manufacturers I like G.E., Sunbeam, and Waring.

2. *Essential College English A Grammar and Punctuation Workbook* is a text used in this course.

3. My alarm went off at 930, but I was supposed to be at work at 800.

4. There are three ways to do the job the right way, the wrong way, and the boss's way.

5. Jim is always thinking about wine, women, and song.

6. I am partial to three types of cars Mercedes, BMW, and Porsche.

7. On Wednesdays Bob has the following schedule physics at 830, English at 930, and history at 1230.

8. The letter to Mr. Dennis began, "Dear Sir Greetings from the IRS."

9. *The Savage God A Study of Suicide* is an interesting book by A. Alvarez.

10. Ray had to meet the repairman at 345 P.M.

Exclamation Points

Exclamation points should be used sparingly. Their correct uses are few and limited. An overuse of exclamation points makes them ineffective.

1. Use an exclamation point to express emphasis, surprise, or strong emotion.

The book advised—idiotic though it seems!—that everyone should strive for celibacy.

What an unbelievably ignorant remark!

"I'm in pain! I'm in pain! Please help me!"

2. Use the exclamation point to express a command or to make a fervent plea.

Pick your toys up this instant!

Please just let me be!

3. Use an exclamation point after strong interjections.

Ouch! That bowl was really hot.

Man! That was a close call.

Question Marks

Though a question mark is generally considered a terminal mark of punctuation (one that comes at the end of a sentence), it may appear within a sentence. But in any event, be sure not to overuse the question mark. The mark should be used sparingly and in accordance with the rules presented in this section.

1.   Use a question mark after a direct question.

Did Orville Wright make the first successful flight?

Robert asked, "Is there any pay increase based on merit?"

Darius—or was it Xerxes?—beat the waves to make them obey his command.

Will I run? is the question every untested soldier asks himself.

But notice that a question mark is not used after an indirect question.

Mary asked what you were going to wear.

2.   Use the question mark with what would ordinarily be declarative or imperative sentences to indicate doubt.

Close the windows?

I have been in the hospital for two days?

3.   Use question marks to indicate a series of queries within the same sentence.

Who will survive? the oiler? the captain? the cook? the correspondent?

Which form of government do you prefer? communism? fascism? capitalism? socialism?

Practice Sentences 17-4

Supply exclamation points and question marks where they are needed in the following sentences.

Example: Get me out of here*!*

1. Are you going to buy the children a dog

2. Jane—or was it Sue—received a pin for perfect attendance.

3. You must eat those vegetables before you can leave the table

4. Ronna asked if she could be of assistance.

5. Do you want me to have your car filled up with gas

Dashes

Some writers and teachers consider the dash an amateurish mark of punctuation. And though the rules in this section indicate correct uses of the dash, you are advised to use the dash sparingly.

1.   Use a pair of dashes to set off a parenthetical expression that you want to emphasize.

> New York, Los Angeles, and Denver—but not Phoenix—are all acceptable convention sites.

> If you do get the book finished on time—and I expect you to try—give me a call immediately.

> Louis Diat—formerly a famous chef at the Ritz—published a book called the *Basic French Cookbook*.

2.   Use a pair of dashes to indicate an abrupt change in thought or tone.

> San Francisco—Mom, I wish you could be here—is a wonderful place.

> Words like *sesquipedalian* and *onomatopoeia*—two-dollar words that aren't worth two cents—pervade scholarly writing.

3.   Use a pair of dashes to set off an interpolated question.

> Abraham Lincoln—or is it George Washington?—is generally recognized as America's greatest president.

4.   Use a pair of dashes to set off a parenthetical element that contains commas.

> Four tragedies—*Hamlet, Macbeth, King Lear,* and *Othello*—are generally considered Shakespeare's best plays.

5.   Use a dash between an introductory series and the main part of the sentence that explains it.

> Homer, Virgil, Dante, Shakespeare, Goethe—these were the men who made up his list of the world's greatest poets.

6.   Use a dash to introduce a word or group of words that you want to emphasize.

> There is one thing Bob enjoys more than eating—golf.

> If we had some ham, we could have some ham and eggs—if we had some eggs.

7.   Sometimes a dash is used to indicate the omission of letters.

> Representative G—is not likely to be well received when he returns to the district.

> Sometimes Ed can be one genuine son of a b—.

8. Sometimes dashes are used to suggest a stuttering or halting speech.

I—er—really don't know what to say.

P—P—Please b—b—bear with m—m—m—me.

9. Sometimes the dash is used in dialogue to indicate an unfinished word or statement.

> Margaret said, "I don't care what you w—"
> "Margaret, now just calm down," her husband warned.

> "Little Jimmy was our whole life and now—" the bereaved mother burst into tears.

Practice Sentences 17-5

Insert dashes wherever they are needed in the following sentences.

Example: Greg stuttered, "B— B — Bob, I— I c— c — can't
    g— go."

1. Beth or was it David? contracted severe spinal meningitis last year.

2. "She doesn't study, yet she expects" the teacher burst out angrily.

3. "She er can't find the authorization slip for the news release right now, sir," the secretary said.

4. Three couples Ted and Marie, Kenneth and Joy, Tim and Linda went to the movie in Brad's new van.

5. Only one chore remains to be done feeding the dog.

6. Cindy, Sharon, and Barbara but not Joanie were chosen to dance in the school musical.

7. "Your daughter uh Mrs. Daley uh is in the hospital," the boy stammered.

8. Today thank goodness it's Friday! I must get a lot of work done.

9. Dennis, Ron, Joey, Clint, and Mike these are the most studious boys in the class.

10. Governor T will probably not run for reelection next year.

Parentheses

The main purpose of parentheses is to set off incidental explanatory information. Commas, dashes, and parentheses can all be used to set off parenthetical information; but the three punctuation marks are used in different ways. Commas are used to set off information that is closely related in thought and structure to the sentence in which the parenthetical information appears. Commas are mild separators; they neither emphasize the parenthetical element nor de-emphasize it. Dashes, however, are used to set off more abrupt parenthetical elements. Dashes are informal marks of punctuation that really emphasize whatever is being set off. Parentheses, on the other hand, are used to set off information that is primarily provided for clarity or for the reader's information. Parentheses are noticeable marks that should not be overused. Parentheses tend to de-emphasize the information that is set off.

> Ralph Waldo Emerson, one of the transcendentalists, is a major figure in American literature.
>> The commas are used here to set off the qualifying element in the least obtrusive manner.

> Ralph Waldo Emerson—an outstanding Lyceum lecturer—is a major figure in American literature.
>> The dashes are used to emphasize the interpolated information.

> Ralph Waldo Emerson (see also his contemporary Henry David Thoreau) is a major figure in American literature.
>> The parentheses are used to de-emphasize the parenthetical information that is inserted merely for the benefit of readers who might be interested.

1. Use parentheses to enclose incidental explanatory matter.

John Adams (1735–1826) was the second president of the United States.

Sentence fragments (see Chapter 7) are very annoying to readers.

The date of President Kennedy's assassination (November 22, 1963) has been forgotten by many Americans.

2. Use parentheses to enclose a numerical figure used to clarify a spelled out number that precedes it.

The dental bill was ninety-eight dollars ($98).

The book entitled *Byron's Complete Poetical Works* costs twenty-five (25) dollars.

3. Use parentheses to enclose a fully spelled out term in order to clarify an abbreviation that precedes it. Do this only the first time the abbreviation is used.

MIA (Missing in Action)

UNRRA (United Nations Relief and Rehabilitation Administration)

4.   Use parentheses to enclose numbers or letters that designate each item in a series.

The camp Bobby wants to go to is (a) too expensive, (b) too far away, and (c) too poorly supervised.

Five of America's most famous golfers are (1) Bobby Jones, (2) Ben Hogan, (3) Sam Snead, (4) Arnold Palmer, and (5) Jack Nicklaus.

Note: In your writing try to avoid this usage, as it tends to make your papers mere catalog lists.

5.   When the parentheses do not enclose a whole sentence beginning with a capital letter, place the necessary commas and periods after the closing parenthesis.

In *On the Origin of Species* by Charles Darwin (1809–1882), the author discusses the process of natural selection.

Your evidence (most of us consider it invalid) is purely circumstantial.

6.   When the parentheses enclose a whole sentence beginning with a capital letter, place the period or other terminal punctuation mark just before the closing parenthesis.

Are car salesmen really ethical? (For that matter, are any sales-men truly ethical?)

Answer one of the three questions. (Be sure to write neatly and in ink!)

Sandra did not like her physical science teacher. (But then Sandra hasn't liked any science teacher since she failed science in the seventh grade.)

Practice Sentences 17-6

Insert parentheses where they are needed in the following sentences.

Example: Frederic Remington (1861–1909) is famous for his paintings of the Old West.

1. The lawyer's document the one explaining the settlement left both parties dissatisfied.

2. The financial reports see attached statements verified that the company was in trouble.

3. The legal speed limit on the open highway in all states is a 45 mph, b 55 mph, or c 65 mph.

4. Josephine received twenty dollars $20 when her first poem was published.

5. Your arguments most of which are illogical do not convince me at all.

6. The major power consumers in a home are 1 heat, 2 air conditioning, and 3 hot water heaters.

7. Many members of SAMLA the South Atlantic Modern Language Association are noted scholars.

8. I can't believe Freddy paid five hundred dollars $500 for that pistol.

9. The Italian artist Benvenuto Cellini 1500–1571 wrote a fascinating autobiography.

10. Colonel William Barret Travis see also David Crockett and James Bowie commanded the Texas forces during the siege of the Alamo in 1836.

Slashes (Virgules)

1. Use the slash to indicate alternative expressions.

During the 1960s many colleges offered a pass/fail grading system.

The job requires a knowledge of typing and/or shorthand.

2. Use the slash to indicate the end of a line of poetry when running two lines of a quoted passage in with the text.

Referring to the battles of Lexington and Concord, Ralph Waldo Emerson wrote, "Here once the embattled farmers stood / And fired the shot heard round the world."

In "The Deserted Village" Oliver Goldsmith said, "Ill fares the land, to hastening ills a prey, / Where wealth accumulates, and men decay."

Practice Sentences 17-7

Insert slashes where they are needed in the following sentences.

Example: The faculty and/or students will be off for July 3rd and 4th.

1. The English poet Robert Herrick wrote, "A sweet disorder in the dress Kindles in clothes a wantonness."

2. Carl took Astronomy 101 on the pass fail system.

3. William Wordsworth said, "She was a Phantom of delight When first she gleamed upon my sight."

4. The doctors and or the nurses may use the lounge downstairs.

5. Edgar Allan Poe opens his poem "The Sleeper" with these lines: "At midnight, in the month of June, I stand beneath the mystic moon."

Hyphens

Compound Words

1. Use a hyphen to connect two or more words serving as a single adjective before a noun.

The medic administered mouth-to-mouth resuscitation.

A two-thirds majority will be required to pass the bill.

Henry Price is not a well-known poet.

But notice that the hyphen is generally omitted when the adjective does not precede the noun it modifies.

John Keats's name is well known.

2. Use a hyphen to form compound nouns of two nouns that show the same functions in one person or thing.

player-coach
secretary-treasurer
AFL-CIO

3. Use a hyphen with numbers from twenty-one to ninety-nine.

thirty-six
eighty-four

4. Use a hyphen to express decades in words.

eighteen-twenties
nineteen-sixties

5. Use a hyphen to indicate a range of numbers.

the years 1832–1837
pages 164–189
Richard Brinsley Sheridan (1751–1816)

6. Use a hyphen to indicate the spelling of a word.

The number is spelled t-w-o and the adverb, t-o-o.

My name is J-o-n, not J-o-h-n.

7. Use a hyphen to prevent confusion in pronunciation when the addition of a prefix results in the doubling of a vowel.

re-elect
anti-imperialist
pre-empt

8. Use a hyphen to join the following prefixes to proper nouns or adjectives.

anti-	anti-German
mid-	mid-America
non-	non-Japanese
pan-	Pan-Hellenic
pro-	pro-Israeli
un-	un-American

9. Use a hyphen to form most, but not all, compound nouns and adjectives from the following prefixes.

all-	all-star
co-	co-worker
cross-	cross-examination
double-	double-breasted
ex-	ex-commissioner
great-	great-grandmother
heavy-	heavy-duty
ill-	ill-conceived
light-	light-hearted
self-	self-concept
single-	single-minded
well-	well-intentioned

Word Division

Use a hyphen to mark the division of a word at the end of a line. The rules for the proper division of words can be complex. In fact, the United States Printing Office publishes a supplement to its *Style Manual* entitled *Word Division*. The volume lists forty-one "wordbreak rules" and has nearly two hundred pages of words separated into syllables. However, most words are divided according to pronunciation. Words occasionally need to be divided to make the right margin look even. It is preferable, however, to avoid dividing a word at the end of a line. When a word must be divided, be sure to put the hyphen at the end of the first line and never at the beginning of the second. Also be sure to consult a dictionary for proper syllabication. The rest of this chapter contains basic word-division rules.

1. Divide words between syllables only.

> feu · dal · ism
> mul · ti · tu · di · nous
> re · in · car · na · tion

2. Do not divide words with fewer than six letters and never divide a monosyllable.

> veto
> only
> breath
> cloud
> though

3. Do not separate a two-letter syllable from the rest of the word.

> in-
> -ed
> -ly

4. Normally, divide a word between double letters.

> reces · sion
> com · municate

If a letter is doubled when adding *-ing*, divide between the double letters.

> refer · ring
> expel · ling

But if the word already ends in double letters before *-ing* is added, divide after the double letters.

> call · ing
> shell · ing

5. Divide words between two vowel sounds that come together.

> residu · ary
> continu · ation

6. Keep suffixes together.

relaxa · tion
persua · sion

7. Do not separate syllables without vowels from the rest of the word.

Wrong: extreme · ly
Wrong: did · n't

8. Do not divide the last word on a page.

9. Do not divide the last word in more than two successive lines.

10. Do not divide abbreviations (*C.O.D., F.I.C.A.*) or numbers written in figures (*$4,045.55*) or short proper names (*Johnson*).

11. Do not divide a person's initials or title (*Mr., Dr.*) from a person's surname.

Practice Sentences 17-8

Insert hyphens in the following sentences where they are needed.

Example: The team's owner-manager was arrested for gambling.

1. There are at least twenty five ways to complete that project.

2. The verb is spelled d e v i s e, the noun, d e v i c e.

3. The team had a pre game meeting in the locker room.

4. The nineteen eighties was a time of political conservatism.

5. Ninety seven people applied for one job opening at the bank.

6. I read pages 491 543 in my history text last night.

7. The man made virus was barely contained.

8. There is much pro Israeli sentiment in the American government.

9. Joel Barlow (1754 1812) is a little known American poet.

10. The day to day figures looked good for the new company.

Review Exercise 17-A   Using the Other Marks of Punctuation (I)

Supply periods, brackets, colons, exclamation points, and question marks where they are needed in the following paragraph.

Example: *American Literature: The Makers and the Making*

1. The Dobson Book Club met at 700 PM 2. The book under discussion was written by Sen Dolph Sanders 3. Everyone enjoyed his book *Intrigue The Other Side of Politics 4.* The members wanted to know how the Senator knew so much about political corruption 5. Could he be dishonest himself 6. In the preface to *Intrigue The Other Side of Politics,* Sen Dolph Sanders said that nearly every politician in Washington was exposed to corruption daily. 7. He also added that most elected officials were honest 8. Of course, members of the book club wanted to believe him, but Wain's book *Temptation The Psychology of Greed* discussed man's innate weakness to temptation 9. What was shocking was how much Sen Dolph Sanders made from his book 10. In the first year he earned over $800,000

Review Exercise 17-B   Using the Other Marks of
Punctuation (II)

Insert dashes, parentheses, slash marks, and hyphens where they are needed in the following paragraph.

Example: Mohandas Gandhi (1869-1948)

  1. F. O. Matthiessen was interested in American literature during the half decade of 1850 1855. *2.* He wrote a book called *American Renaissance* 1941. *3.* The first section of the volume discusses Ralph Waldo Emerson 1803 1882. *4.* The second section is all about Nathaniel Hawthorne 1804 1864. *5.* The third section is entirely about Herman Melville 1819 1891. *6.* The last main section studies Walt Whitman 1819 1892. *7.* Mr. Matthiessen would like to have written a section on Mark Twain 1835 1910, but Twain didn't fit into the 1850 1855 half decade. *8.* Twain's masterpiece *Huckleberry Finn* 1884 was published thirty years too late. *9.* Nevertheless, thanks to Matthiessen's *American Renaissance* the half decade of 1850 1855 has a name of its own. *10.* Matthiessen's *American Renaissance* 1941 is an important volume in the study of American literature.

Review Exercise 17-C   Using the Other Marks of Punctuation (III)

Supply periods, brackets, dashes, exclamation points, question marks, parentheses, slash marks, and hyphens where they are needed in the following paragraph.

Example: thirty-four books

1. Has it rained at least once every week this summer *2.* Every Saturday at about 1030 A M I would plan to mow the lawn only to find a downpour *3.* The yard is getting out of hand 1 the grass is knee high, 2 weeds are taking over the flower beds, and 3 the drainpipes are clogged with underbrush. *4.* With this kind of weather I feel like I'm living in Seattle, Wash , or Portland, Oreg *5.* Last Saturday I put my head out the door and shouted "Enough" *6.* I asked myself, "Will the clouds and rain ever go away" *7.* Mr. Smith, my neighbor, pointed out the good side. *8.* He said the temperatures were lower than normal. *9.* This morning it was only 62 5° instead of the normal 89° *10.* I guess the good Lord determines the precipitation and or the temperature as He sees fit.

NAME _____ CLASS _____

Review Exercise 17-D   Using the Other Marks of Punctuation (IV)

Supply periods, brackets, dashes, exclamation points, question marks, parentheses, slash marks, and hyphens where they are needed in the following paragraph.

Example: Edward FitzGerald(1809-1883)

1. Some of my favorite shows are reruns *2.* A few of them are 1 *Hawaii 5-0*, 2 *Gunsmoke*, and 3 *Spenser for Hire*. *3.* Robert Urich, who played Spenser, always emphasized that his name was spelled S p e n s e r like the poet *4.* Spenser's main co star in each episode was usually Susan Silverman and or Hawk *5.* The stars of later *Gunsmoke* episodes were 1 Matt 2 Kitty, 3 Festus, and 4 Doc *6.* Did you know that Dennis Weaver played a character named Chester Good in the old black and white episodes of *Gunsmoke* *7.* Are you aware that *Hawaii 5-0* was the longest running police drama on television *8.* Steve McGarrett a Capricorn by the way was a hard nosed leader of the state police *9.* He and his trusted friend "Dan'O" solved a new case every week *10.* Now a cliché, it is true that McGarrett concluded many shows with the expression, "Book'm, Dan'O"

Review Exercise 17-E Supplying All Marks of Punctuation (I)

Supply all punctuation needed in the following paragraph.

Example: " Have you read Faulkner's short story 'A Rose for Emily'?" she asked .

1. Julias history teacher asked the class, What was the cause of the Civil War *2.* Dudleys answer was that the War was caused by slavery and/or economics *3.* Another student said The Civil War was caused by geographical factors *4.* Ronnas response was that the South resented the loss of political power it once held *5.* She added Four of the first five presidents were from the South *6.* These are all excellent answers the teacher said but what do you think was the primary and/or major cause *7.* Before researching the topic for this class Madeline answered I had always felt the main cause was economics, but everything I read clearly stated the major cause of the War was slavery *8.* Those were my findings also the teacher said *9.* Then the teacher asked Do you think the War was inevitable *10.* Julia replied Historians do not agree on the inevitability of the War although most of the sources I consulted seemed to believe it couldn't have been avoided at least not for long.

Review Exercise 17-F   Supplying All Marks of Punctuation (II)

Supply all punctuation needed in the following paragraph.

Example: The poets name is spelled S-p-e-n-s-e-r not S-p-e-n-c-e-r.

1. T S Eliot was one of the most influential literary figures of this century *2.* He wrote many famous short poems among them are these three a The Love Song of J. Alfred Prufrock b The Hollow Men and c Journey of the Magi *3.* The poem Journey of the Magi expresses an unusual perspective on the biblical story *4.* Eliot is perhaps more famous for some of his long poems like The Waste Land and Four Quartets *5.* The Waste Land is both influential and controversial many readers dislike the use of multiple languages and the lack of obvious transition between sections *6.* T S Eliot is a fine essayist as well as a poet *7.* His book The Sacred Wood Essays on Poetry and Criticism 1920 contains the well known essay Tradition and the Individual Talent *8.* T S Eliot also wrote influential essays on John Dryden and the metaphysical poets *9.* In addition Eliot wrote some full length plays *10.* Perhaps the most famous was Murder in the Cathedral 1935

Answers to Practice Sentences

Chapter 1

Practice Sentences 1-1

1. They <u>found</u> towels, pens, soap, and many other things.
2. However, they <u>sought</u> one item in particular.
3. Then one student <u>shouted</u> to his friends.
4. He <u>showed</u> them a case of bathroom tissue over in the corner.
5. They <u>loaded up</u>.
6. Each student <u>took</u> at least three or four rolls.
7. They <u>went straight</u> to the main part of the wooded campus.
8. They <u>threw</u> paper to the top of every tree.
9. Unfortunately, the night watchman <u>caught</u> them in the act.
10. The next day in the rain they <u>removed</u> the entire mess.

Practice Sentences 1-2

1. Her specialty <u>is</u> oil painting.
2. She <u>is</u> partial to seascapes.
3. Her favorite <u>is</u> a view of whitecaps at dusk.
4. However, as an artist she <u>is</u> versatile.
5. Her productions in watercolor, acrylics, and even ceramics <u>are</u> famous.
6. Last year she <u>was</u> Artist of the Year.
7. This year <u>is</u> a new challenge for her.
8. Sculpture <u>is</u> the goal.
9. Her bust of Queen Elizabeth <u>is</u> currently on display at the Denver Museum.
10. The only limit on Jane's career <u>is</u> her own imagination.

Practice Sentences 1-3

1. She <u>is building</u> a functional volcano.
2. The frame of the volcano <u>was made</u> of wood.
3. The cone <u>was constructed</u> of papier mâché.
4. When dry, the cone <u>will be sprayed</u> with paint.
5. She <u>has even thought</u> about some moss or even Easter-basket grass on the slopes.
6. She <u>has left</u> a hole in the center of her volcano.
7. A small jar <u>has been placed</u> inside the hole.
8. Mary <u>has placed</u> a mixture of baking soda and water inside the jar.
9. A little vinegar <u>will be added</u> to the baking soda and water.
10. With this chemical mixture her volcano <u>will</u> actually <u>erupt</u>.

Practice Sentences 1-4

1. At first I <u>was planning</u> a career as clerk in a local department store.
2. But I <u>could</u> never <u>earn</u> a good salary in such a position.
3. I <u>would</u> never <u>be promoted</u> in the family-owned business either.
4. So, what <u>can</u> I <u>do</u>?
5. I <u>have</u> always <u>enjoyed</u> working with numbers.
6. In college I <u>could study</u> accounting.

7. An accountant <u>can make</u> a good living.
8. Accountants <u>can help</u> people with their financial problems as well.
9. <u>Would</u> I <u>enjoy</u> a career in accounting?
10. My teachers and my heart <u>are telling</u> me, "Yes."

Practice Sentences 1-5

1. I have heard about the book at school.
   verb: <u>have heard</u>
2. What did you hear?
   verb: <u>did hear</u>
3. Thoreau's book is considered good, but difficult.
   verb: <u>is considered</u>
4. I was told the same thing.
   verb: <u>was told</u>
5. Have you read it yet?
   verb: <u>have read</u>
6. I have just finished it.
   verb: <u>have finished</u>
7. Did you enjoy it?
   verb: <u>did enjoy</u>
8. I was very pleased with Thoreau's masterpiece.
   verb: <u>was pleased</u>
9. Did you find it difficult?
   verb: <u>did find</u>
10. A little, but the book would not have been as good otherwise.
    verb: <u>would not have been</u>

Practice Sentences 1-6

1. <u>He</u> owns several books about furniture styles and periods.
2. Recently <u>he</u> developed an interest in the construction of furniture.
3. This <u>interest</u> led to an interest in woodworking equipment.
4. Now <u>his basement</u> contains numerous tools.
5. Unfortunately <u>his shop</u> has poor ventilation.
6. Sawdust covers everything, including the washer and dryer.
7. <u>His wife</u> prefers to buy her furniture from a store.
8. <u>Curt</u> built a beautiful oak cabinet.
9. The <u>cabinet</u> cost him over $300 to make.
10. His <u>wife</u> saw one just like it in a display window for $195.

Practice Sentences 1-7

1. It had been in Conrad's family for more than a hundred years.
2. The <u>vase</u> had become an antique.
3. The <u>design</u> was now out of fashion.
4. Mythological <u>figures</u> were all around the vase.
5. <u>Conrad</u> became the sole owner in 1963.
6. <u>He</u> was a collector of fine vases.
7. <u>This</u> was his first piece.
8. The out-of-fashion <u>design</u> seemed unique to him.
9. The <u>vase</u> was on a table in his hallway.
10. The <u>vase</u> is still there—after three bumps and one fall.

Practice Sentences 1-8

1. There have been <u>three</u> in our family.
2. My <u>father</u> once collected them.
3. <u>I</u> like the shape of the old beetles myself.

4. Which do <u>you</u> like best, the convertible or the hardtop?
5. <u>Beetles</u> are a little touchy, though.
6. The <u>valves</u> must be adjusted frequently.
7. Did <u>you</u> know that Volkswagen engines are often rebuilt?
8. Nevertheless, <u>beetles</u> have carried a lot of people a lot of miles.
9. Do <u>you</u> remember what <u>people</u> used to call them in the sixties?
10. <u>They</u> referred to VW's as pregnant roller skates.

Practice Sentences 1-9

1. She has already taken all her general college courses.
   subject: <u>She</u>   verb: <u>has taken</u>
2. Last quarter she took pharmacology.
   subject: <u>she</u>   verb: <u>took</u>
3. Wow! Did that course have a lot of math in it?
   subject: <u>course</u>   verb: <u>did have</u>
4. She felt lucky with a C in that course.
   subject: <u>She</u>   verb: <u>felt</u>
5. After pharmacology came med-surg (medical surgery).
   subject: <u>med-surg</u>   verb: <u>came</u>
6. Her main complaint was with the long hours.
   subject: <u>complaint</u>   verb: <u>was</u>
7. But late into the second quarter she began clinical.
   subject: <u>she</u>   verb: <u>began</u>
8. Now she was a real nurse.
   subject: <u>she</u>   verb: <u>was</u>
9. She is responsible for three patients every day.
   subject: <u>She</u>   verb: <u>is</u>
10. All the classroom work has been worth it.
    subject: <u>work</u>   verb: <u>has been</u>

Practice Sentences 1-10

1. Freddy <u>can weld</u> his plow and <u>overhaul</u> the engine on his tractor.
2. Norma <u>drives</u> a school bus and <u>operates</u> her own real estate business.
3. John <u>prepared</u> supper and <u>served</u> it to Marie in the sun room.
4. Aunt Martha neither <u>hears</u> nor <u>sees</u> as well as mother.
5. Jeff <u>handles</u> the ball well but <u>shoots</u> poorly.
6. <u>Does</u> Reverend Brown still <u>visit</u> the hospitals and <u>talk</u> with ill members of the congregation?
7. I <u>dictated</u> and <u>transcribed</u> my own history notes this summer.
8. Andrea always <u>drives</u> the fastest car and <u>spends</u> the most money.
9. The accountant <u>saves</u> his money and <u>keeps</u> excellent records.
10. <u>Can</u> you <u>enjoy</u> a nice evening out and not <u>spend</u> a lot of money?

Practice Sentences 1-11

1. <u>Paula</u> and <u>Jackie</u> both have boyfriends.
2. The girls' <u>mother</u> and <u>father</u> don't mind.
3. <u>Gary</u> and <u>Kevin</u> are nice young men.
4. <u>Gary</u> and <u>Paula</u> have been dating for over two years.
5. <u>Jackie</u> and <u>Kevin</u> have only been going together for eight months.
6. <u>Paula</u> and her <u>boyfriend</u> enjoy bowling.
7. <u>Jackie</u> and <u>Kevin</u> much prefer cruising.
8. New <u>people</u> and neat <u>cars</u> capture their attention on the strip.
9. Bowling <u>balls</u> and <u>scorecards</u> interest the other couple more.
10. But the <u>boys</u> and <u>girls</u> prefer their own company to bowling or cruising.

Practice Sentences 1-11

1. Paula and Jackie both have boyfriends.
2. The girls' mother and father don't mind.
3. Gary and Kevin are nice young men.
4. Gary and Paula have been dating for over two years.
5. Jackie and Kevin have only been going together for eight months.
6. Paula and her boyfriend enjoy bowling.
7. Jackie and Kevin much prefer cruising.
8. New people and neat cars capture their attention on the strip.
9. Bowling balls and scorecards interest the other couple more.
10. But the boys and girls prefer their own company to bowling or cruising.

Practice Sentences 1-12

                      d.o.
1. Bill shoots an accurate shot from the outside.

                                    d.o.
2. Brian, on the other hand, prefers the dunk.

3. They can be an awesome combination at times.

                        d.o.
4. Coach Smith usually wants Brian as the shooter, though.

                      d.o.
5. He likes the high-percentage shot.

                      d.o.
6. Last week, however, Bill hit one from twenty-three feet.

                    d.o.
7. That basket won the game.

8. Bill was the school's instant hero.

                  d.o.
9. He describes the shot to Brian every evening at home.

10. Bill and Brian are brothers.

Practice Sentences 1-13

                  i.o.
1. One student gave his buddy the thumbs up sign.

2. Two others immediately turned in their papers with nothing on them but a name.

                  i.o.
3. The teacher gave the class a lecture on the importance of homework.

                  i.o.
4. One student told the teacher his view of pop quizzes.

                  i.o.
5. Mr. Harper gave that student a lecture on discretion and silence.

                  i.o.
6. Mr. Harper then gave his class a choice.

              i.o.
7. I will not give you any more pop quizzes.

8. But you must be prepared for each class.

9. Several of the students did not like the choices.

i.o.
10. Nevertheless, most students showed Mr. Harper big smiles.

Practice Sentences 1-14

1. Books are his <u>hobby</u>.
2. He has always been a <u>collector</u> of good books.
3. His room is a <u>mess</u>.
4. There are books in his closet, on his bed, and on the floor.
5. Kareem's parents were not usually <u>complainers</u>.
6. But this was the <u>limit</u>.
7. Kareem became a <u>carpenter</u>.
8. He built shelves for all his books.
9. Clutter was a <u>thing</u> of the past.
10. However, Kareem became the proud <u>owner</u> of thirty-six additional books yesterday.

Practice Sentences 1-15

1. It is also very <u>valuable</u>.
2. The pearl handles are <u>genuine</u>.
3. The tang is stamped Case Bros. Cut. Co., Little Valley, N.Y.
4. Knife collectors are <u>aware</u> of its value.
5. But they must be <u>careful</u>.
6. Older Case knives are often not <u>genuine</u>.
7. Some people in the knife business are not <u>honest</u>.
8. Fortunately, most dealers are very <u>reputable</u>.
9. This knife seems <u>genuine</u> to me.
10. I bought it for $850.

Chapter 2

Practice Sentences 2-1

1. <u>Customers</u> like the <u>variety</u> of <u>items</u> in the <u>store</u>.
2. <u>Oils</u>, <u>acrylics</u>, <u>pastels</u>, and <u>charcoal</u> can be found in the artist's <u>corner</u>.
3. <u>Watercolor</u> <u>lessons</u> are available for <u>beginners</u>.
4. <u>Tom</u> teaches these <u>lessons</u> and handles the art <u>supplies</u>.
5. <u>Beverly</u> prefers the <u>crafts</u>.
6. <u>She</u> does <u>needlepoint</u>, <u>cross-stitch</u>, <u>candlewicking</u>, and <u>knitting</u>.
7. <u>She</u> displays her own <u>pillows</u> and <u>sweaters</u> and <u>aprons</u> in the <u>shop</u>.
8. The <u>customers</u>, of course, want to buy these beautiful handmade <u>items</u>.

Practice Sentences 2-2

1. <u>She</u> gave an uncle in Phoenix a beautiful sweater.
2. <u>The</u> Indian designs on it just seemed to suit <u>him</u>.
3. <u>She</u> gave <u>each</u> of his children a pair of slippers.
4. <u>Sherrie</u> gave <u>all</u> in the family a poinsettia.
5. <u>Aunt Leda</u> received a vase with Greek markings on <u>it</u>.
6. <u>John Keats</u> would have been proud of <u>it</u>.
7. <u>She</u> shopped in <u>all</u> of the stores in town for <u>her</u> brother's present.
8. <u>Several</u> of the clerks thought <u>she</u> was crazy.
9. "<u>What</u> is a Hoola Hoop?" <u>they</u> asked <u>her</u>.
10. The hoop <u>she</u> found was listed as a football-throwing target.

Practice Sentences 2-3

Marty recently purchased an expensive assortment of camping supplies for his family. He and his wife plan to go camping on the riverfront property they bought recently. To have ready access to their property, they also bought a four-wheel drive truck. The truck enables them to drive all the way to the riverbank. Marty and his wife and children enjoy fishing and swimming in the river. Last week, however, they got stuck on the land in the four-wheel drive truck.

Practice Sentences 2-4

1. It is not an antique, just old.
2. The red top has several holes in it.
3. The passenger door is barely attached to the rest of the car.
4. The paint job on the car is Postimpressionism.
5. The "chrome" grille looks like the smile of an eight-year-old.
6. The interior looks like something from a Poe room.
7. Of course, little of the original interior remains.
8. The battered dashboard has large holes where instruments used to be.
9. The steering wheel has little plastic still on it.
10. Believe it or not, however, the old bomb still runs.

Practice Sentences 2-5

1. He gave his mother her first dishwasher.
2. His sister received six wine glasses in her pattern.
3. He gave his father a table saw.
4. Of course, he didn't forget about his interests.
5. Bill bought himself a shiny, new Thunderbird.

Practice Sentences 2-6

1. I would have (did, done) the assignment last night.
2. But my little brother (had threw, had thrown) my papers away.
3. He (threw, throwed) them in the hamper.
4. Then he (gone, went) to visit a friend.
5. Fortunately, my mother (saw, seen) the papers.
6. She (ask, asked) me about them.
7. The sight of mother and the papers (brought, brung) a smile to my face.
8. Within an hour I (had drunk, had drank) three beers and (ate, eaten) two pizzas.
9. In this happy condition I (begin, began) work on the assignment.
10. Later I (showed, shown) the F grade to my little brother.

Practice Sentences 2-7

1. Some intoxicated people have seen pink elephants.
2. Robert threw the ball to first base.
3. Laura became very nervous as the clock kept on ticking.
4. The phone rang fifteen times before Mother finally answered it.
5. I have written three letters to that company in the last three months.
6. On that hot day Lorraine drank a liter of gingerale, swallowing continuously.
7. Calvin has rewritten his paper six times.
8. Ryan's teacher has taught him a lot of English.
9. Someone has stolen the dean's fall schedule.
10. Joshua has fallen out of the tree house.

Practice Sentences 2-8

1. I *enjoy* the sport myself. present
2. I once *played* for the Metropolis Muppets. past
3. Each player *had been* individually *recruited.* past perfect passive

4. The coach *was paid* a big salary. <u>past participle</u>
5. The city *will have rolled* out the red carpet for the return of its victorious heroes. <u>future perfect</u>
6. People *will believe* anything. <u>future</u>
7. The Muppets *lost* the first game. <u>past</u>
8. They *were defeated* in all the other games as well. <u>past participle</u>
9. In fact, no Muppet team *has* ever *won* a game. <u>present perfect</u>
10. They *are* the most consistent team in basketball. <u>present</u>

Practice Sentences 2-9

1. He fried the eggs and plugged in the coffeemaker.
2. He sat down and ate.
3. He has now poured his coffee and gone back to the bedroom.
4. He laid out his clothes and shaved.
5. After he completed this, he took a bath.
6. The bath felt good and was relaxing.
7. When he finished his bath, he dressed for school.
8. One shoe was brown and the other was black.
9. His tie did not match the suit he was wearing.
10. Freddy gets out of bed in the morning but wakes up in the afternoon.

Practice Sentences 2-10

1. The bat was made by the Louisville Slugger Company. <u>passive</u>
2. The girl outran the shortstop's throw. <u>active</u>
3. Michael Jordan plays basketball for the Chicago Bulls. <u>active</u>
4. My mother works with an accounting firm in Atlanta. <u>active</u>
5. The company car was sold by the business manager. <u>passive</u>
6. Andrew drove his mother's car into the driver's door of my car. <u>active</u>
7. The bill was padded by the mechanic. <u>passive</u>
8. The batteries in the child's toy ran down in just one week. <u>active</u>
9. The teacher talked to the student about his sloppy work. <u>active</u>
10. The entire crew was blamed by the supervisor. <u>passive</u>

Practice Sentences 2-11

1. Leonardo da Vinci painted the *Mona Lisa*.
2. A victory lap was driven by Richard Petty.
3. *The Rape of Lucrece* was written by William Shakespeare.
4. Ben Cartwright owned the Ponderosa.
5. Rodin sculpted *The Thinker*.
6. A huge box of Valentine candy was bought for Angela by Jerry.
7. Chef in a Box prepared the lasagna.
8. The "woman in red" betrayed John Dillinger.
9. A copy of the test was stolen by an angry student.
10. At three o'clock this morning her bed was made by Mary.

Practice Sentences 2-12

1. I ordered my wife's Christmas gift in July, but I have not received it yet.
2. Danny dunked the basketball, but he broke his finger on the rim.
3. Greg prepared many different dishes, but Martha only ate one.
4. The player declared his innocence, but he refused a drug test.
5. Heather said she really admired Jim, but she refused his ring.
6. The appraiser looked over the car carefully and declared it a total loss.
7. The Express Mail was lost in Chicago, but the postman delivered it on time.
8. The ad campaign was rejected by the company, so Fred redesigned it.
9. Morris dropped the radio, and he repaired it.
10. The manager submitted the proper requisition form, but the boss took no action.

Practice Sentences 2-13

1. Several of the students spent their evenings working.
2. One of the second graders lost his spelling book.
3. If a person wants to cash her check, she should endorse it on the back.
4. We should all write our papers the best we are able.
5. The man repaired the door of his house by himself.
6. People should always strive to do the best they can.
7. The students did their best on the exam.
8. An individual should consider all the factors before making a decision.
9. The man lost his shoe.
10. The woman did a nice job on her own project.

Practice Sentences 2-14

1. If I *were* an author, I would write the "great American novel." subjunctive
2. *Clear* a wide area around the campfire. imperative
3. Carolyn *worked* both the second and third shifts last night. indicative
4. I *wish* I could afford Herman's house on Mockingbird Lane. subjunctive
5. Becky *studied* until 3:00 A.M. for her nursing test. indicative
6. *Keep* your eye on the ball and your left elbow straight. imperative
7. Amy, *did* you *catch* anything in the rabbit gum yesterday? indicative
8. *Send* the children outside to play. imperative
9. If I *were* a police officer, I would work in Hawaii. subjunctive
10. Juan *ran* the mile in under four minutes. indicative

Practice Sentences 2-15

1. She does well in all her classes at school.
2. She easily won the Latin award.
3. Her physics instructor said she did her work efficiently and accurately.
4. In English class she organizes her papers well and expresses herself clearly.
5. Unfortunately, she does not do well in certain activities away from school.
6. She learned painfully that she would not be a famous ballerina.
7. Her first pirouette concluded ungracefully on all fours.
8. Jane ended her dancing career then and there.
9. Where could Jane go from here?
10. She went back to school immediately.

Practice Sentences 2-16

1. They took all the curtains off the wall.
2. Behind the front door they placed a loud buzzer.
3. They loosened the front step with a hammer.
4. It creaked at the least amount of pressure.
5. Before Halloween the students installed a powerful sound system.
6. The tape they played was filled with scary sounds.
7. The students supplied themselves with makeup from the drama department.
8. Strobe lights contributed to the eerie effect.
9. On Halloween night young children were frightened in the house.
10. Some parents were also unnerved in the haunted house.

Practice Sentences 2-17

Individual student answers to this exercise will vary.

Practice Sentences 2-18

1. The company president droned on and on.
2. He said production was up, but sales were down.

3. He threatened that either sales would increase <u>or</u> some sales personnel would be eliminated.
4. He was straightforward <u>and</u> factual.
5. <u>But</u> he was also repetitious.
6. He brought up the same points time <u>and</u> time again.
7. Some of the sales personnel had been slack <u>and</u> they knew it.
8. Some of them already had new jobs, <u>and</u> they were just waiting until their positions became available.
9. Some just listened to the president <u>and</u> laughed.
10. They knew that a $3.5 million profit <u>and</u> a huge untapped market wasn't bad for a small, family-owned business.

Practice Sentences 2-19

1. Mark each part <u>as</u> you remove it from the engine.
2. <u>If</u> you get your tackle together, we can go fishing.
3. <u>Although</u> I made a good grade on the last test, my average is still low.
4. My roommate will be ready to go <u>when</u> he finds his shoes.
5. My printer continues to run paper through it <u>after</u> the power is turned off.
6. <u>Unless</u> you are willing to work hard, do not apply for a job at Western Iron Works.
7. <u>Please</u> do not talk so much <u>while</u> I am trying to think.
8. Jack probably paid too much for that lamp <u>since</u> it is not a genuine antique.
9. Arlene turned Ronnie down <u>when</u> he proposed to her.
10. <u>Although</u> Roy was wearing snake chaps, he was bitten on the hand.

Practice Sentences 2-20

1. <u>Good heavens</u>, Bob, let me help you with that.
2. <u>Ouch!</u> I dropped a hammer on my sore toe!
3. <u>Good grief</u>, Ed, why don't you just ask her if she will go out with you?
4. <u>At least</u> pick up a drill and look like you're doing something, <u>for heaven's sake!</u>
5. <u>Gee</u>, after three days of rain I hope we can finally have our picnic.

Chapter 3

Practice Sentences 3-1

1. He was hunting <u>for squirrels</u>.
2. One ran <u>across the road</u> immediately.
3. He could not get his gun ready <u>in time</u>.
4. Gary hunted diligently <u>for two more hours</u>.
5. He didn't see any squirrels <u>in the trees</u>.
6. Neither did he spot any <u>on the ground</u>.
7. At sundown he walked <u>to his truck</u> and smoked a cigarette.
8. He put the gun <u>in the truck</u> and relaxed.
9. Then a squirrel walked slowly <u>between his feet</u>.
10. Frustrated, Gary threw a rock <u>at the squirrel</u> and went home.

Practice Sentences 3-2

1. Michelle wants *to move this afternoon*. <u>noun</u>
2. Albert married the banker *to get a job at the bank*. <u>adverb</u>
3. The telephone *to be installed* costs $450. <u>adjective</u>
4. *To start as middle linebacker* is Jeff's goal. <u>noun</u>
5. Dee plans *to be president of her own company within six years*. <u>noun</u>
6. *To be perfectly honest*, the food at the new restaurant is terrible. <u>adverb</u>
7. Geneva was interested in all the property *to be sold at the auction*. <u>adjective</u>

8. Brad wants *to be nominated president* of the senior class. <u>noun</u>
9. The man *to be tried next month* is my neighbor. <u>adjective</u>
10. *To make money for his tuition,* Rodney works at <u>McDonald's</u>. adverb

Practice Sentences 3-3

1. Racing down the hill, the children stopped their sled against a tree.
2. Having studied diligently for the test, Craig had a good grade for his reward.
3. Sleeping outside on a cold January night, Angela still wasn't warm enough in the new sleeping bag.
4. Having purchased a new tennis racket, Jason showed no improvement in his game.
5. Having been married for six years, Adrian began to think the ring on her finger was a burden.
6. Finished with the test, the students turned the papers in.
7. Being scientists, the professors studied the white mice.
8. Repaired by the jeweler for $45, the watch Mary owned still failed to keep good time.
9. Determined to do a good job, Paulette painted the house slowly.
10. Spayed at the local animal clinic, the pet Shannon owned was now "safe."

Practice Sentences 3-4

1. Thad, *selected by his classmates,* represented the student body at the convention. <u>Thad</u>
2. The old man left the police station in disgust, *mumbling and grumbling at every step.* <u>man</u>
3. The woman *chosen office manager* was well qualified for the job. <u>woman</u>
4. *Going on break with the class at last,* Missy learned that the other students wouldn't harm her. <u>Missy</u>
5. Kristy, *dressed in a formal gown,* was shocked to find everyone else wearing jeans. <u>Kristy</u>
6. *Driving his father's Cadillac,* Bobby was embarrassed when the car wouldn't start in his girlfriend's driveway. <u>Bobby</u>
7. *Sounding as though he were just learning to talk,* Freddy left the dentist's office with his new set of false teeth. <u>Freddy</u>
8. David, *having slept for eleven hours,* was rudely awakened by his father. <u>David</u>
9. Rebecca, *missing her boyfriend away at college,* got in her car and drove five hundred miles to see him. <u>Rebecca</u>
10. After the performance, the circus janitor cleaned up the mess, *turning up his nose in disgust.* <u>janitor</u>

Practice Sentences 3-5

1. Jim really enjoys *hunting deer.* <u>d.o.</u>
2. The astronomer passed his time by *looking through a telescope.* <u>o.p.</u>
3. *Looking at girls* is a pleasant way to pass the time. <u>subj.</u>
4. Some, however, may prefer *looking at guys.* <u>d.o.</u>
5. Alicia has become a successful lawyer by *preparing her cases thoroughly.* <u>o.p.</u>
6. *Washing clothes* always seems to be done on Wednesdays. <u>subj.</u>
7. Upon *receiving the award,* Herman was so emotional he couldn't speak. <u>o.p.</u>
8. Billy likes *working for charitable organizations.* <u>d.o.</u>
9. *Cleaning your gun afterward* is not the best part of hunting. <u>subj.</u>
10. Becky often thinks about *operating a day-care center.* <u>o.p.</u>

Practice Sentences 3-6

1. *Watching so much TV,* the children seem to be in poor shape. <u>participle</u>
2. They enjoy *looking at all types of programs.* <u>gerund</u>
3. Cartoons, *being their favorites,* seem to be on all day. <u>participle</u>
4. *Watching detective shows and situation comedies* entertains them in the afternoons. <u>gerund</u>
5. They are seldom seen *viewing soap operas or westerns.* <u>gerund</u>

6. *Running and playing around the neighborhood* seem to be things of the past. <u>gerund</u>
7. *Sitting in front of the tube all day,* the children get no exercise. <u>participle</u>
8. *Watching TV programs,* however, is not the only entertainment provided by the set. <u>gerund</u>
9. *Playing computer games like Atari and Nintendo,* the children can stay in front of the tube when there are no programs on of interest. <u>participle</u>
10. To further prevent them from *getting any exercise,* there are, of course, movies and shows on videotape. <u>gerund</u>

Chapter 4

Practice Sentences 4-1

1. <u>Cliff Davis ran the offense for the Hoosiers.</u>
2. <u>He had fifteen assists,</u> but <u>he only scored eight points.</u>
3. <u>Mark Hammonds, Indiana's center, scored thirty-two points,</u> although he only had five rebounds.
4. Although he is not usually a starter, <u>Carlyle Rankin was Indiana's most valuable player.</u>
5. <u>He had twenty-three points, thirteen rebounds, and eleven assists.</u>
6. <u>Carlyle was up for the game</u> because his high school buddy played for Iowa.
7. <u>Carlyle's jump shots in the lane turned the tide in the second half.</u>
8. When the two teams play later in the season, <u>Indiana will need another strong performance by Rankin.</u>
9. <u>Indiana's coach praised Rankin,</u> of course, but <u>he also complimented the team play of Iowa.</u>
10. If Carlyle is healthy next Wednesday, <u>he will start against the University of Illinois.</u>

Practice Sentences 4-2

1. Naturally, I hoped <u>that he would change his mind.</u>
2. There was a line of people <u>that wrapped around the base of the Monument twice.</u>
3. <u>If the line had been a lot shorter,</u> we would have gone to the top of the Monument then.
4. Instead Tommy decided <u>that he wanted to go to the Lincoln Memorial.</u>
5. We saw the Reflecting Pool <u>which leads up to the Memorial.</u>
6. <u>When we were in the Memorial,</u> the seated figure of Lincoln looked enormous.
7. <u>That all Americans will always be free</u> was Lincoln's dream.
8. <u>Because he was only seven,</u> however, Tommy wasn't greatly impressed by such noble sentiments.
9. <u>When we returned to the Washington Monument,</u> the line was much shorter.
10. Tommy was happy <u>as he looked out of the windows atop the Monument.</u>

Practice Sentences 4-3

1. The wings, <u>which were barely attached,</u> were badly rusted.
2. The engine <u>that he thought was sound</u> needed an overhaul.
3. The instrument panel, <u>which looked good to Slim,</u> needed to be replaced.
4. Even the seats <u>that were made of leather</u> fell apart when Slim sat in them.
5. The tail section, <u>which had recently been painted,</u> was hanging on by a prayer.
6. The previous owner, <u>whom Slim had trusted,</u> was no longer in the state.
7. When Slim asked the man <u>who works in the body shop</u> for a repair estimate, the man laughed.
8. The insurance agent <u>that Slim had worked with for years</u> told him to forget it.
9. Slim was beginning to question the wisdom of the purchase <u>that he had made.</u>
10. Slim's wife, <u>who had been with him for twelve years,</u> suggested he sleep in the plane.

Practice Sentences 4-4

1. <u>When the weather was nice,</u> he carried a gas stove, an inflatable boat, inner tubes, and several friends.

2. Nathan and his friends usually stayed until it got dark.
3. The truck was easy to pack up since it didn't have a camper top.
4. Sometimes Nathan went camping by himself because he liked time alone by the river.
5. Once when he was there by himself, a violent thunderstorm came up.
6. Even though the road was muddy, the truck came through fine.
7. One another occasion, Nathan went to the river while there was snow on the ground.
8. Although snow was up to the axle, the truck kept going.
9. Nathan returned home because he got cold.
10. He got stuck in his driveway because he could not see the ice under the snow.

Practice Sentences 4-5

1. Whoever writes the best poem will win the prize.   subject
2. The contract will be awarded to whoever submits the lowest bid.   object of prep.
3. I believe Einstein's general theory of relativity is valid.   direct object
4. The company will pay double time to whoever works on Saturday.   object of prep.
5. A leisurely trip to Bermuda is what I need.   predicate nominative
6. Fred said he was quitting the job in two weeks.   direct object
7. The trained bear can be what the circus needs.   predicate nominative
8. Whomever the astronauts select will be the captain on the next mission.   subject
9. The teacher talked about whatever the students wanted to learn.   object of prep.
10. Carlyle told his supervisor whatever he wanted to hear.   direct object

Chapter 5

Practice Sentences 5-1

1. In June she (was) ill with a temperature of 102°.
2. After this, she (injured) her eye and had to wear a patch.
3. She (had) difficulty (wearing) the patch under her glasses.
4. Finally, she and the doctor (decided) to remove the patch.
5. About that time she (developed) an irritating skin rash.
6. On the way to the dermatologist, she (was struck) by a hit-and-run driver.
7. The police and the sheriff's department (investigated) the accident and (found) witnesses.
8. Priscilla (was) angry in court and (testified) against the man.
9. In the courtroom parking lot, Priscilla (looked) and (looked) but (found) no car.
10. It (had been ticketed) and (towed.)

Practice Sentences 5-2

. 1. He discussed the political theories of Thomas Jefferson⊙and then he contrasted them with the theories of Alexander Hamilton.
2. Professor Hutchins was really getting into the subject⊙but he was interrupted by a student's snoring.
3. Professor Hutchins liked the republican form of government advocated by Jefferson⊙yet he had a totalitarian reaction toward the student.
4. Either explain why you are sleeping in class⊙or get out immediately.
5. The student said the theory was boring ⊙ he explained that he wanted to learn practical politics.
6. Professor Hutchins discussed the matter with his student after class⊙and they agreed to try an experiment.

7. Two weeks would be spent in class on political theory ⊙ then two weeks would be spent on practical applications.
8. Professor Hutchins insisted that some knowledge of theory was necessary to understand what actually occurred in practice ⊙ and eventually the student agreed.
9. The student stayed awake and studied much harder ⊙ but he was still a little skeptical.
10. At a political rally during the second two-week period, the student was fascinated ⊙ but Professor Hutchins was arrested for disorderly conduct.

Practice Sentences 5-3

1. The college president had said [that students could no longer smoke in the cafeteria.]
2. The policy, [which was instituted for health reasons,] seemed dictatorial to the students.
3. [After the president of the SGA opened the meeting,] chaos erupted [because everyone wanted to speak at once.]
4. The president established order and recognized a young woman [that was sitting in the front row.]
5. She said [that she had a right to smoke] [if she wanted to do so.]
6. She was angry [because she felt] [her constitutional rights were being threatened.]
7. Suddenly another student shouted [that he didn't want to get lung cancer from her smoke.]
8. She said [that was as ridiculous as fluorocarbons from deodorant cans destroying the ozone layer].
9. The meeting nearly turned into a riot [until the president suggested a compromise.]
10. Now the cafeteria [where the students eat] is divided into Smoking and No Smoking sections.

Practice Sentences 5-4

1. Mort bought a new car, but he was dissatisfied with it [since it could only go 120 miles an hour on a racetrack.]
2. Sue got her pepperoni pizza, but she sent it back [when she saw anchovies on it.]
3. [Because he was not a very good dancer,] Alfred was uncomfortable at parties; in fact, he was even uncomfortable around girls.
4. Look [before you leap,] or you may regret your move for a long time.
5. The jury members entered the courtroom [when the judge called them,] but they still had not reached a decision.
6. The man said [that he did not agree with the new law;] furthermore, he intended to change it.
7. Arlene looked at houses for days, but she bought the one on Lowe Street [because she liked the floor plan and the location.]
8. William thought [his watch was broken,] but it only needed a battery.
9. Fred purchased a scientific calculator [since he was not good in math,] and his grades improved significantly.
10. Lamont saw the most beautiful girl [he had ever seen,] but she was just a picture in a magazine.

Practice Sentences 5-5

Individual student answers to this exercise will vary.

Chapter 6

Practice Sentences 6-1

1. The baseball pitching machine (throw, throws) balls with great accuracy.
2. My grass (grow, grows) faster than my desire to mow it.
3. The glasses on the bar (is, are) attractive, but cheap.

4. The test questions (is, are) difficult.
5. The Frost twins (pick, picks) apples for their uncle every year.
6. The car dealer (claim, claims) to be honest.
7. The cassette recorder (eat, eats) up all my tape.
8. The coins (is, are) for my soft drink.
9. Roulette (is, are) a more interesting game than many people think.
10. Arnold's son (break, breaks) every toy given to him.

Practice Sentences 6-2

1. Cass (appraise, appraises) diamonds for his father's jewelry store.
2. Psychologists (say, says) everyone has some mental hangups.
3. Mrs. Williams (celebrate, celebrates) the anniversary of her gall bladder surgery every year.
4. Statisticians (say, says) Americans are getting taller.
5. Iris (go, goes) to her aerobics class every Tuesday.
6. Scientists (tell, tells) us not to smoke.
7. Criminologists (attend, attends) all the meetings they can.
8. Bernice (see, sees) her father at least once a week.
9. Mr. and Mrs. Stevens (send, sends) their daughter off to school each morning.
10. Ernest (play, plays) the title role in *The Importance of Being Earnest*.

Practice Sentences 6-3

1. The dog with all the ticks and fleas (need, needs) a bath.
2. The boy with the sad blue eyes (is, are) not really sad at all.
3. Barbara, as well as her friends Alice and Sue, (is, are) going to the meeting in Los Angeles.
4. The Adams Antique Store on the corner of Main and Crutchfield Streets (has, have) old items, but no real antiques.
5. The students in the library (is, are) generally quiet and studious.
6. The chalk purchased by the public schools (come, comes) in six different colors.
7. Many sports fans, including Lorna, (prefer, prefers) basketball to football.
8. Any car with dual headlights (blind, blinds) me at night.
9. Swanson, along with Dale and Henry, (is, are) going to the World 600.
10. A computer with two disk drives (is, are) more versatile than a one-drive machine.

Practice Sentences 6-4

1. My wife, who is also my best friend, (is, are) very reliable.
2. Paige and Angie (is, are) inseparable.
3. Ellen, Kathy, Jack, and Darryll (attend, attends) movies every Saturday.
4. His best friend and companion (is, are) his dog.
5. The goalie on our soccer team and catcher on our baseball team (perform, performs) admirably in both sports.
6. Chicken pox, measles, and mumps (is, are) all common childhood illnesses.
7. Scott and Cheryl (has, have) a good relationship.
8. Mrs. Durallis, who is my neighbor, (sends, send) $50 a week to her son in college.
9. Mr. Rogers and Big Bird (entertains, entertain) children.
10. Alcohol and automobiles (is, are) not a good combination.

Practice Sentences 6-5

1. Both of the men (does, do) well when the pressure is on.
2. Somebody on the staff (wants, want) a new editor.
3. Everyone (is, are) convinced that an annual is worthwhile.
4. Some of the women (goes, go) to the track every morning.
5. Anything (goes, go) in the sport of rugby.
6. No one (likes, like) the aluminum bats used in college baseball.

7. Anyone who knows the rules (thinks, think) chess is a challenging game.
8. Some of the stolen bonds (was, were) recovered.
9. The coach said that anyone who hustles (makes, make) the team.
10. No one (wants, want) to do well more than Harvey.

Practice Sentences 6-6

1. Either Ralph Sheen or Sally Bolts (is, are) going to be the new IBM employee.
2. Neither the Nelsons nor the Cleavers (is, are) on television anymore.
3. Neither the coach nor the players (want, wants) to go back home after the loss.
4. Either the players or the owners (is, are) going to have to back off.
5. Neither the basketball nor the football (is, are) properly inflated.
6. Neither the students nor the professor (is, are) handling the situation well.
7. Either the boss or the employees (is, are) going to be very pleased.
8. Either the postmaster or his son (is, are) to be arraigned on criminal charges.
9. Neither Sally nor her mother (is, are) responsible for the damage.
10. Either the doctor or the nurses (open, opens) the doors every day.

Practice Sentences 6-7

1. Near the drainpipe in the backyard (is, are) the six kittens.
2. Behind the cabinet doors (is, are) a roach the size of your fist.
3. There (is, are) to be a meeting of the minds at the Pentagon this afternoon.
4. Outside in the snow (play, plays) the happy children.
5. There (is, are) a man hard at work in his backyard chopping wood.
6. In a tunnel under the ground (is, are) the men working on the power lines.
7. There (is, are) only one person I feel comfortable with for hours at a time.
8. Behind the hedge (stands, stand) a man with a parabolic reflector.
9. There (was, were) enough tension in the room to coil a spring.
10. Behind the door of the research laboratory (stands, stand) a woman hard at work.

Practice Sentences 6-8

1. The class (is, are) deciding on its senior gift to the school.
2. The faculty (is, are) concerned about the shortage of time in its new exam schedule.
3. The number of freshmen elected at the last induction ceremony (is, are) small.
4. The board (has, have) to complete its budget by next Thursday.
5. The family always (studies, study) its vacation plans carefully.
6. A number of athletes on the team (was, were) suspended because of the drug test results.
7. The committee (is, are) thinking about reconsidering its findings.
8. The number of applicants for the scholarship (was, were) small.
9. The jury (orders, order) its meals at the same time each day.
10. The number of Hispanics attending medical school in Florida (increases, increase) each year.

Practice Sentences 6-9

1. The students usually prefer the professors who (prepares, prepare) their lectures thoroughly.
2. Most people trust whoever (inspires, inspire) them the most.
3. Ambrose Bierce is the man that (defines, define) *positive* as "mistaken at the top of one's lungs."
4. The equipment that (was, were) purchased for the camping trip never arrived.
5. The students who (contributes, contribute) the most to the paper this year will receive the best staff positions next year.
6. The clothes on display at the yard sale are not the ones that (is, are) for sale.
7. The animal that wins the prizes at the dog shows is not necessarily the one that (makes, make) the best pet.

8. An electrical appliance that (has, have) a damaged cord should be repaired.
9. Putting a lot of money into a lawn that is not properly maintained (makes, make) little sense.
10. The conference recognizes the athletes that (does, do) the most for their schools.

Practice Sentences 6-10

1. Seeing *Gone with the Wind* and *Forever Amber* back to back at an all-night drive-in movie (has, have) been a dream of mine for years.
2. Watching too much TV every day (become, becomes) a habit if you aren't careful.
3. Scrubbing toilets and bathtubs (is, are) not my favorite household task.
4. Planning the trip carefully ahead of time (make, makes) for a more enjoyable vacation.
5. Drinking too much alcohol (upset, upsets) your equilibrium.

Practice Sentences 6-11

1. Physics (does, do) not interest everyone.
2. Aeronautics (is, are) a specialized branch of physics.
3. *Gardening News* (is, are) published quarterly.
4. Mumps generally (spreads, spread) very rapidly in a community.
5. Toast and jelly (is, are) not quite enough breakfast for Mike.
6. Economics (is, are) a class I had to study hard in.
7. Joe thinks molasses (is, are) delicious.

Practice Sentences 6-12

1. (That, Those) types of tomatoes are the best.
2. Each man is expected to keep up with (his, their) own equipment.
3. Everyone can keep (his/her, their) weight down if necessary.
4. The article said (this, those) aluminum baseball bats hit the ball fifteen to twenty feet farther than the wooden ones.
5. Each of the women had (her, their) own views about marriage.
6. Someone forgot to turn off (his/her, their) bath water.
7. Each person contributed what (he/she, they) could afford.
8. (These, This) kind of rose produces a small flower.
9. Every member of the faculty expressed (his/her, their) opinion concerning the new attendance policy.
10. It should be easy for either of the two women to prove (her, their) qualifications for the job.

Practice Sentences 6-13

1. The men from the fraternities and the women from the sororities are planning to work at (her, their) Save the Children Festival all day.
2. The president and the students agree that no speed bumps are needed at (his, their) campus.
3. Darlene and her parents go to Shatley Springs every year on (her, their) vacation.
4. Judy and her sister Tina are successful physical therapists in (her, their) hometown.
5. Tim and Todd are having difficulty in (his, their) engineering courses.

Practice Sentences 6-14

1. Either Marie or her two sisters can wear (her, their) mother's clothes.
2. Neither the nurses nor the doctor liked (his/her, their) own suggestions.
3. Neither Ronnell nor Neal felt (he, they) had a chance at the job.
4. Neither the teacher nor the students (was, were) fond of the new administrator.
5. Either Amanda or Margaret will go if (she, they) can.
6. Neither Quinn nor Roman doubted (his, their) ability to do the assignment.
7. Neither the manager nor the players liked (his/her, their) new ballpark.

8. Either the students or the college president will have to alter (his/her, their) stand.
9. Either Stuart or Victor will have to contact (his, their) insurance company about the tree that fell on the fence.
10. Neither the mother nor her children showed up for (her, their) physical examinations.

Practice Sentences 6-15

1. The committee feels it has too many responsibilities on (its, their) shoulders.
2. The clergy proposes to abolish (its, their) former ruling.
3. The mob have (its, their) own spokesperson.
4. The association has established (itself, themselves) a budget.
5. The class know (it, they) must keep quiet.
6. The herd is grazing leisurely in (its, their) pasture.
7. The assembly have repeatedly broken (its, their) rules.
8. That council has decided to extend (its, their) membership policies.
9. That class is very happy with (its, their) new teacher.
10. The jury is presenting (its, their) verdict.

Practice Sentences 6-16

1. The gangster (which, that) lost his gun was in trouble.
2. The tiger (who, which) performed best was very old.
3. She lent her books to the man (who, which) was doing poorly in the course.
4. The woman (that, which) lost her purse was frantic.
5. Anyone (who, which) wants to be well rounded should read as well as exercise.

Chapter 7

Practice Sentences 7-1

1. Rosa began making her mother's birthday present. — complete sentence
2. Cutting out the pattern very carefully. — phrase
3. Being sure not to waste any leather. — phrase
4. One piece of leather having cost her $25. — phrase
5. She was now ready to begin tooling the leather. — complete sentence
6. The design was already drawn on tracing paper. — complete sentence
7. Carefully centering the design on the leather. — phrase
8. She dampened the leather and transferred the design onto it. — complete sentence
9. The stitching being the next step. — phrase
10. Finally, putting on the straps and the hardware. — phrase

Practice Sentences 7-2

1. He was excited about the upcoming car show. — complete sentence
2. Which was to be held in May at the fairgrounds. — subordinate clause
3. He had built the car from the chassis up. — complete sentence
4. Although a few finishing touches were needed on the body work. — subordinate clause
5. The car was just about ready to be shown. — complete sentence
6. When he drove his "new" 1957 Ford Fairlane 500 on the grounds. — subordinate clause
7. He was positive heads would turn. — complete sentence
8. Even though he did not plan to sell the car. — subordinate clause
9. He was curious how much he might be offered. — complete sentence
10. Nothing could compensate him for the time and memories he had in the show-winning car. — complete sentence

Practice Sentences 7-3

1. And being only 5'6" tall was too short for the position.   subject
2. But, nevertheless, was aggressive and hit hard.   subject
3. Mike, being outstanding at his position as a high school player.   verb
4. Had wanted to play for one of the major football schools.   subject
5. The coaches of these schools, however, expressing little interest in him as a prospect.   verb
6. So, therefore, could only do his best with the opportunities available.   subject
7. At Brevard College, having earned a reputation as a hard hitter.   subject
8. Won the conference trophy as Best Defensive Player.   subject
9. Mike, accidentally injurying a player on another team rather seriously.   verb
10. Then and there decided to give up football.   subject

Practice Sentences 7-4

Individual student answers to this exercise will vary.

Chapter 8

Practice Sentences 8-1

1. She always felt close to her grandparents⌒the job is an extension of that relationship.
2. Some of the residents are by no means senile⌒Joan enjoys talking with them.
3. The nursing home residents genuinely love their children and grandchildren⌒unfortunately, some of the children are unkind to their parents.
4. The children never come by to see them⌒this, of course, hurts the residents deeply.
5. Sometimes the children will even try to take control of their parents' estates⌒they say the parents are incompetent.
6. Joan thinks such treatment is awful⌒she tries to help her patients stand up for their legal rights.
7. Many local judges help her⌒they don't like the thought of themselves or their parents being treated that way.
8. There is a brighter side⌒Joan gets to see some of the residents fall in love.
9. Some of the patients feel love at this age is even better than in youth⌒there is a much deeper interest in companionship and in the other person's individuality.
10. Never underestimate the power of love⌒snow on the roof doesn't mean there's no fire in the furnace.

Practice Sentences 8-2

1. When he was in high school, he scored higher than anyone else in the state on a standardized test; he is, of course, very proud of this accomplishment.
2. Quite frankly, he has not found the competition in college that he expected; many of his peers have difficulty with the abstract concepts.
3. He hopes that things will be different when he is an upperclassman; fellow chemistry majors should be more knowledgeable and more motivated.
4. Lamarre enjoys his afternoons in the laboratory; he can see the practical application of the theory discussed in class and in the text.
5. Lamarre's chemistry professor says Lamarre has the most potential of any student he has had in years; he believes Lamarre has a good background and a good attitude.

6. Upon graduation Lamarre plans to do graduate work at MIT; this school was suggested by his professors.
7. Meanwhile, he is studying halogens; he already knows more than most air conditioner repairmen that work with halogens every day.
8. Next week he will be studying the nitrogen family; he has heard the professor brings a container of liquid nitrogen to class.
9. This should be interesting; a rubber ball can be frozen solid by dipping it in liquid nitrogen.
10. The professor let Lamarre dip a rubber ball into the liquid nitrogen; he threw it just over his roommate's head.

Practice Sentences 8-3

1. Many of the stories are said to be based on fact, and there are people who have witnessed the events.
2. The Devil's Tramping Ground is a huge, bare circle in which no vegetation will grow, and it is located in the central part of the state.
3. In the legend of the Devil's Tramping Ground, it is said the Devil removes any objects placed in the bare spot, but no one has ever proved that it is actually the Devil who removes them.
4. Another story, the legend of the Brown Mountain Light, has many explanations, and each one differs in its interpretation of the meaning of the mysterious light.
5. In the mountains of North Carolina, a mysterious light appears, yet there is no apparent reason for the light.
6. Some people say an old slave has come back from his grave carrying a lantern and looking for his master, and a song called "The Brown Mountain Light" relates that version, although that is not the most popular explanation.
7. Another popular legend is of a young girl who hitches a ride with strangers and disappears from their car, yet she always appears on dark, foggy nights and wears a white gown.
8. Apparently, a young girl was killed on a bridge near Chapel Hill many years ago, and ever since that foggy night, she has been trying to get someone to take her home.
9. Many people say they have stopped to pick her up and take her home, but she always disappears without a trace before they reach her home.
10. You should never tell a North Carolinian that these stories are not true, for you may be speaking to someone who has witnessed one of these mysteries.

Practice Sentences 8-4

1. Two days after he bought it there was a heavy downpour; naturally, this was just what Joe had been waiting for.
2. Joe took the umbrella with him to the school cafeteria; he hung it on a peg away from all the other umbrellas.
3. Proud of his fine umbrella, Joe ate an expensive meal; he felt like a real gentleman.
4. After the meal Joe went to get his umbrella; it was gone.
5. Someone had stolen it; the thief now owned an umbrella with Joe's initials on it.
6. Joe was extremely angry; he stole the first expensive umbrella he saw.
7. This was an unusual thing for him to do; Joe isn't a thief.
8. He tried to find the owner in order to return the umbrella; he was unable to do so.
9. He took the umbrella with him to the cafeteria the next time it rained; it was gone when he went to get it after his meal.
10. Joe went to the store the very next day; he bought the cheapest umbrella he could find.

Practice Sentences 8-5

1. Julio ordered a chain saw from a mail-order company; he thought he got a good deal.
2. The saw was supposed to arrive in about ten days; instead it was five weeks before the saw came.

3. Julio went to pick the saw up at the post office ⊙ he was surprised to find three packages rather than just one.
4. Julio figured he was going to have to put the saw together ⊙ this thought didn't please him.
5. At home he opened all the boxes ⊙ each box contained a complete chain saw.
6. He called the company to explain the mistake ⊙ the company representative told him to ship two of them back.
7. Julio found out that it would cost him $87 for the return shipment ⊙ he also learned that his credit card had been billed for three saws.
8. The company representative told Julio he would be reimbursed for return freight ⊙ the two saws were then returned to the company.
9. The saws did not arrive at the company ⊙ the representative told Julio to put a tracer on the return shipment.
10. Eventually Julio's account was straightened out ⊙ he has not ordered anything else by mail.

Chapter 9

Practice Sentences 9-1
1. She is familiar with the computers.
2. Lisa is the only salesperson who has experience on all models.
3. Whoever has a question goes to Lisa.
4. Furthermore, Lisa is a person who is comfortable with all kinds of people.
5. She is definitely my choice.

Practice Sentences 9-2
1. The vice president promoted her to the position of sales manager.
2. The coach told us to hustle.
3. Mother told us girls to get quiet.
4. The man whom he most admired died in an accident.
5. Mrs. Terrill gave me a nice Christmas bonus.

Practice Sentences 9-3
1. Rebecca Martin is the candidate **who** I feel is the best qualified.
2. Correct
3. She will not be easily persuaded by lobbyists **who** are seeking to serve their own selfish interests.
4. In the past Ms. Martin has publicly supported those **who** advocated equal rights for all people.
5. Correct
6. Correct
7. She is the person **who** you may recall did most for the state in upgrading education.
8. Correct
9. She promises to vote her conscience and best judgment, and in so doing she may at times anger those **who** she feels helped her get elected.
10. Correct

Practice Sentences 9-4
1. We were surprised at **their** doing so well.
2. Correct
3. **His** driving the ball 300 yards impressed us all.
4. Correct
5. Correct

Practice Sentences 9-5

Individual student answers to this exercise will vary.

Practice Sentences 9-6

Individual student answers to this exercise will vary.

Practice Sentences 9-7

Individual student answers to this exercise will vary.

Practice Sentences 9-8

Individual student answers to this exercise will vary.

Practice Sentences 9-9

Individual student answers to this exercise will vary.

Practice Sentences 9-10

Individual student answers to this exercise will vary.

Chapter 10

Practice Sentences 10-1
1. My brother reviews his financial affairs carefully.
2. Adrian always takes the same route to school.
3. Gayle sang the hymn beautifully.
4. Wayne took the garbage out quickly before his father returned.
5. Tommy readily admitted that the broken window was his fault.
6. Allison performed the entire ballet gracefully.
7. Gloria confessed quickly to her role in the prank.
8. The teacher returns papers promptly.
9. Ron swiftly grabbed the book when he realized its value.
10. Ronna wanted the problem resolved immediately.

Practice Sentences 10-2
1. Grady's electric sander was expensive.
2. Ralph's dog is ready for the dog show this weekend.
3. The coffee in the cafeteria was bitter this morning.
4. Geraldo's hair looks nice.
5. Beatrice appeared confident after her interview.
6. The project has been ready for nearly two weeks.
7. Benny's new woodcarving was different.
8. The flowers on the table smelled fresh.
9. Sidney seems happy at this college.
10. Mia became enthusiastic about her new job after the first paycheck.

Practice Sentences 10-3
1. Blaine can take notes very (quick, quickly).
2. The lemonade tastes (bitter, bitterly).
3. The table saw cuts (smooth, smoothly).
4. The band saw does not cut metal (good, well).
5. Tony sipped his drink (slow, slowly).
6. The flowers on Margaret's desk smell (fresh, freshly).
7. Percy became (confident, confidently) after the first lap.
8. The professor lectured very (rapid, rapidly).
9. My son looks (careful, carefully) before crossing the street.
10. Your hair looks (attractive, attractively) today.

Practice Sentences 10-4

1. He drives the ball (<u>more accurately</u>, most accurately) than Stuart.
2. He also putts the ball (<u>better</u>, best) than Neal.
3. He is the (more intent, <u>most intent</u>) member of the team.
4. He always listens to instructions (good, <u>well</u>).
5. Furthermore, he is the (better, <u>best</u>) team player.
6. He works (good, <u>well</u>) with his teammates to get the best team score.
7. He is (<u>more serious</u>, most serious) about his game than Michael.
8. Chad has (<u>less</u>, least) trouble with shots from sand traps than anyone in the conference.
9. For one thing, he hits (<u>few</u>, fewest) shots into sand traps.
10. The coach says Chad is the (better, <u>best</u>) golfer he has ever coached.

Practice Sentences 10-5

1. The incumbent hopes to win the **presidential** election.
2. The **Canadian** Mounties are known all over the world.
3. The **judicial** decision was vague and inconclusive.
4. The **gubernatorial** race was won by the newcomer.
5. The **idiotic** policy of forcing everyone to wear ties was enforced.
6. You can easily recognize Fred by his **childish** pranks.
7. For movies rated PG, **parental** guidance is suggested.
8. His company contributed to the **senatorial** campaign.
9. Mr. Borden's company is being sued for practicing **racial** discrimination in hiring.
10. The new **promotional** technique should add millions of dollars to our annual gross sales figure.

Chapter 11

Practice Sentences 11-1

1. Marty installed a new phone jack, and it worked perfectly.
2. Dale's parents do not want him to write a book about his childhood, yet he is determined.
3. Yvonne decorated a cake for a neighbor's wedding, but her family ate it.
4. Gus's father is a highway patrolman, yet Gus was clocked at 160 miles an hour.
5. Allen was a paratrooper in the military, but he won't have anything to do with skydiving.
6. Dana must get the batter out, or the coach will send in a new pitcher.
7. Jerri did not want to go on the fishing trip, yet she went to keep peace in the family.
8. Joanna got soaked in the storm, and she even had her umbrella with her.
9. The child felt sad during the morning recess, but he seemed happier after lunch.
10. Benny thought the medication was too expensive, but it was effective.

Practice Sentences 11-2

1. Since you have a broken finger, I will start the lawnmower for you.
2. Yogi Berra supposedly once told a young ball player, "Your future is all ahead of you."
3. Surprisingly enough, I finished preparing my income taxes in January.
4. Near the car, attendants were estimating the damage.
5. The grass seed not having taken root, the violent thunderstorm washed all the topsoil away.
6. After you go to the bank and deposit your paycheck, why don't you take me out to dinner?
7. In the beautiful green pasture near my neighbor's new barn, his horses are grazing contentedly.
8. Gen. Douglas McArthur said, "I shall return."
9. Unless you especially want to go to the play, I would rather stay home this evening.
10. Sid, did you really hit thirty-five home runs one season in high school?

Practice Sentences 11-3

1. The customer wanted a good, dependable truck.
2. Tommy, Jason, and Lewis were the three winners.
3. All he had in his pockets were two quarters and a pocketknife.
4. The company hired an intelligent, charming manager.
5. If you cannot sleep, get out of bed, read a book, or watch television.
6. The students said it was an unfair, even tricky test.
7. The new Spanish teacher spoke with a Southern accent.
8. Drive the car to the shop, park it in front of the service door, and explain the problem to the service manager.
9. Sue Ellen is a graceful, versatile athlete.
10. Anne told Julian that he was rude to his parents, crude to women, and generally obnoxious to everyone.

Practice Sentences 11-4

1. Kay Frost, who is a fine landscape painter, is a member of the art department of Wilkes Community College.
2. I am currently reading Dickens' novel *Our Mutual Friend*.
3. The only member of the faculty who agreed with the proposal was Dr. Lowe.
4. I asked you to define a tourniquet, not a tournament.
5. My mother, who lives in Denver, is an accomplished pianist.
6. John Pendleton Kennedy's *Swallow Barn* is an important book in Southern literature.
7. Thomas Holley Chivers, who was a contemporary of Poe, once accused Poe of plagiarizing his poem "Rosalee Lee."
8. My telephone-answering tape, which was produced by Radio Shack, plays humorous messages.
9. One of the horses which he keeps in his stables is worth $25,000.
10. Scarlett O'Hara, who is the central figure in *Gone with the Wind*, is an interesting character.

Practice Sentences 11-5

1. Peg Darcy, D.D.S., lives in Des Moines, Iowa.
2. On September 25, 1989, Thomas Quinn Jones, Jr., celebrated his first birthday by stepping in the cake.
3. Jessica Chandler, Dean of Instruction, is a new member of the college staff.
4. Gene went to Las Vegas, Nevada, and lost $2,500.
5. James Key has a Ph.D. in physics but pumps gas in Phoenix, Arizona.
6. Ron Chaney, Chief Executive Officer, receives a salary of $1,350,000 a year.
7. On Tuesday, October 9, 1985, Conrad Aimes became a grandfather.
8. Roy Weathers, Vice President in Charge of Marketing, and Joyce Beamer, Vice President in Charge of Advertising, occupy adjoining offices.
9. We will be leaving Belmont, Miss., on Friday morning and arriving in Baltimore, Md., Sunday night.
10. Margaret Hatcher, C.P.A., is proud of her new title and her new office.

Practice Sentences 11-6

1. Lanny likes books such as ⊙ *Walden, Huckleberry Finn,* and *For Whom the Bell Tolls.*
2. The women ⊙ planting the shrubbery ⊙ got hot and thirsty.
3. Marci is both a good teacher ⊙ and an astute businesswoman.
4. Jeff believed ⊙ that buying a riding lawnmower would make yardwork fun.
5. John Milton's greatest poem ⊙ *Paradise Lost* ⊙ was unrecognized in 1667.
6. Tony is a young, handsome, talented ⊙ player on the tour.
7. In 1865 ⊙ President Lincoln was assassinated by John Wilkes Booth.
8. The woman in the Rolls Royce ⊙ drives to the Sea Pine Manufacturing Co. every morning.

9. Yesterday⊙a man and his two daughters were injured in an automobile accident.
10. The man⊙who lives in the large house at 1512 East Elm Street⊙is seventy-four years old.

Chapter 12

There are no practice sentences in this chapter

Chapter 13

Practice Sentences 13-1

1. Sophocles' play *Antigone* is in many freshman English anthologies.
2. The show's star was difficult to get along with during the filming.
3. Sherrie and Dianne's apartment is quite expensive.
4. Someone's mail order purchase was left on the front lawn.
5. The dining room table's finish is in poor condition.
6. The Alexanders' home has been vandalized.
7. Samuel Johnson's *Rasselas* is an enjoyable book to read.
8. The faculty members' vote clearly showed their support for the proposal.
9. Ladies' watches are not as small as they used to be.
10. Margaret's helping the injured child was a humane response to an unfortunate situation.

Practice Sentences 13-2

1. **Who's** going to the game with you Saturday?
2. **It's** a reunion for the class of **'64**.
3. I **wasn't** able to attend the four **o'clock** meeting.
4. **I'm** not so sure "the good **ol'** days" were really that good.
5. **They're** tired and hot after working in the high heat and humidity all day.

Practice Sentences 13-3

1. Caryn made two *B*'s and three *C*'s last semester.
2. In 1990 State University awarded seven *Ph.D.*'s in the English department.
3. Julia's 7's look like 9's.
4. The child's *thank you*'s sounded like *shank you*'s.
5. The publisher would not allow authors to use #'s or %'s in their manuscripts.
6. On my keyboard it is easy to hit *o*'s when I want *p*'s.
7. *Sea*'s and *see*'s are homonyms.
8. Sue has *M.A.*'s in history and business.
9. The university's hiring committee sought candidates with *Ph.D.*'s in biological and environmental sciences.
10. The sign looked peculiar since there weren't enough *m*'s to spell the full title of the show.

Chapter 14

Practice Sentences 14-1

1. "Align the front end," the service manager said, "and rotate the tires."
2. "Let's get a group together and go to the game on Saturday," Mary said.
3. Janet said that she didn't do well on the test.

4. "Get your bags packed," Daddy said, "so we can be on our way."
5. Donald said, "I read Hemingway's short story 'The Short Happy Life of Francis Macomber' last night."
6. The professor told his colleague: "A student kept insisting, 'Patrick Henry's words "Give me liberty or give me death" were spoken in a moment of extreme emotional conflict.'"
7. "Bobby, put on a clean shirt before you leave the house," his mother insisted.
8. Nathan Hale said that he only had one life to lose for his country.
9. "Your Honor," the plaintiff explained, "the defendant said 'I am going to kill you!'"
10. Cari told her boyfriend, "Try to be here on time."

Practice Sentences 14-2

1. *Fortune* once published an article entitled "Business for the Novice."
2. Many students choose to read Frost's short poem "The Road Not Taken" in speech class.
3. Virgil's *Aeneid* is a famous Roman epic.
4. Thomas de Quincy wrote a famous essay entitled "On the Knocking on the Gate in *Macbeth*."
5. *The New York Times* blasted the carelessness of oil companies in the article "Negligence on the High Seas."

Practice Sentences 14-3

1. Quentin asked, "What club did you use on your last shot?"
2. "Robert," Charlene said, "the boss told me to tell you, 'Thanks for a job well done.'"
3. A woman stood up in church and said, "Those of you who bring children should keep them quiet during the service."
4. Jill screamed, "I made an *A* on my physics final!"
5. One of Poe's most famous short stories is "The Fall of the House of Usher."
6. The song "It's Only Make Believe" contains the line, "Maybe someday you'll care for me."
7. "Just relax!" the intern shouted in panic.
8. Thelma asked, "Do you like the song 'Blue Suede Shoes'?"
9. "Sidney," the preacher asked, "do you believe in Jesus Christ as your Savior?"
10. "Of Stephen Crane's short stories 'The Bride Comes to Yellow Sky' and 'The Blue Hotel,' which do you prefer?" the teacher asked George.

Chapter 15

Practice Sentences 15-1

1. Churchill Downs in Louisville, Kentucky, is the site of the Kentucky Derby.
2. The United States entered World War II in 1941.
3. Christmas Day is a sad time for many lonely people.
4. In 55 B.C. Julius Caesar invaded England.
5. It was F.D.R. that said, "We have nothing to fear but fear itself."
6. The Lincoln Memorial in Washington is very impressive.
7. The meeting will begin promptly at 10:00 A.M.
8. The temperature was 3°F this morning.
9. Steve's mother said, "Please close the door."
10. Dry Wells is a ghost town.

Practice Sentences 15-2

1. Brian Score is a state senator in Idaho.
2. Jane Andrews saw Pike's Peak for the first time when she was thirteen.
3. The Bible discusses the Promised Land.
4. Eddie Hernandez has taken History 101, History 102, and Sociology 304 all this summer.

5. Susan has worked for the IBM Corporation for over twenty years.
6. The controversial editorial about Ted Turner appeared in the *Atlanta Constitution*.
7. Spanish, French, Italian, and Portuguese are all Romance languages.
8. Many historians consider the Treaty of Versailles to be a causative factor in the origin of World War II.
9. Oliver Wendell Holmes and James Russell Lowell were instrumental in establishing the *Atlantic Monthly.*
10. Brigham Young University is a fine school for quarterbacks.

Practice Sentences 15-3

1. Herman Wouk scored two hits with *The Winds of War* and *War and Remembrance.*
2. I like the Morning Flower pattern for everyday china.
3. The Oakland A's are trying to get into the playoffs.
4. *Invisible Man* is a fine novel by Ralph Ellison.
5. The woman thought Death stalked her constantly.
6. "The Cask of Amantillado" is a short story by Poe.
7. Eliot Ness worked for the Treasury Department.
8. Michael Jordan is a star for the Chicago Bulls.
9. Have you ever read the book *My Brother Was an Only Child?*
10. Carla thinks Professor Reece is an excellent teacher.

Chapter 16

Practice Sentences 16-1

1. Dr. Chuck Barris left the operating room at 4:00 A.M.
2. Juneau, Alaska, and Bismarck, N. Dak., are both capital cities.
3. Corporal Davis will soon be promoted to general.
4. Honduras is in Central America.
5. One famous English novelist wrote about the poor in Victorian England.
6. There were a staggering number of applicants for the open position.
7. Thad Sanders, Jr., was the best driver on the team.
8. The computer I use was manufactured by International Business Machines.
9. When my neighbor transmits on his CB radio, the picture on my TV looks like a snowstorm.
10. Rome first invaded England in 55 B.C. but didn't attempt to settle there until A.D. 43.

Practice Sentences 16-2

1. My call letters are WB4EIV.
2. The bag of fertilizer weighed fifty pounds.
3. Chapter 4 has three pages that are badly burned.
4. Thelma lives on Sixth Street.
5. William Brown is a history professor at the local college.
6. The chemical symbol for hydrochloric acid is HCl.
7. The CIA is not supposed to operate in the United States.
8. The meeting is scheduled for Monday, September 12.
9. The pizza restaurant is on East Boulevard.
10. John lost fifteen pounds in October.

Practice Sentences 16-3

1. Becky was born on June 16, 1964.
2. The new elementary school is located at 351 Albert Drive.
3. Paragraph 12 needs to be rewritten to avoid sexist language.
4. Henry VIII had six wives.

5. Teamsters Local 391 has been quiet for the last few years.
6. The television show ran from 1974 to 1984.
7. Elections in the Fifth Congressional District are usually close.
8. Some historians doubt that the Declaration of Independence was actually signed on July 4, 1776.
9. The Lakers lost to the Bullets 98-95.
10. Chad purchased 1 hammer, 2 saws, 15 boards, and 1,257 nails.

Practice Sentences 16-4

1. One mile is 1,760 yards.
2. The Forty-second Regiment is ready to go.
3. The fire started at eight o'clock at night.
4. The offices of Flagler & Sharp are located on Seventh Avenue.
5. Norbert is to meet the preacher at the First Baptist Church tonight.
6. There were 2,523 suggestions in the suggestion box.
7. Ninety-three percent of the women favored the new maternity leave policy.
8. The Ninety-ninth Congress was embroiled in controversy.
9. Fifteen couples returned from their vacation early.
10. The concert is scheduled to begin in the park at two o'clock.

Chapter 17

Practice Sentences 17-1

1. Penny asked me if she could borrow $10.
2. Please leave the room.
3. Will you please credit my account for the returned merchandise.
4. Evening classes at the college begin at 7:00 P.M.
5. Dr. Jackson can see you today at 10:00 A.M.
6. The receipt for twenty-eight dollars and thirty cents should be written as $28.30.
7. Did you have a chance to visit with your sister in Richmond, Va.?
8. Please close the window, Charles.
9. Rev. Van Rinegold is supposed to drop by today at 2:00 P.M.
10. Rick asked the coach if the team had been selected yet.

Practice Sentences 17-2

1. The article stated, "This year's Nobel Prise [sic] was awarded to William Faulkner."
2. The student concluded his paper by saying, "This poet's work [Ezra Pound's] is too obscure for me."
3. Carmen Gordon wrote in her column, "The project this man has in mind [to build a dam three miles above the town] would be disastrous to our community."
4. The student wrote, "Alot [sic] of this work is meaningless to us."
5. Sally wrote her friend, "I think she [Emily Brontë] wrote a masterpiece in *Wuthering Heights*."

Practice Sentences 17-3

1. There are several appliance manufacturers I like: G.E., Sunbeam, and Waring.
2. *Essential College English: A Grammar and Punctuation Workbook* is a text used in this course.
3. My alarm went off at 9:30, but I was supposed to be at work at 8:00.
4. There are three ways to do the job: the right way, the wrong way, and the boss's way.
5. Jim is always thinking about wine, women, and song.
6. I am partial to three types of cars: Mercedes, BMW, and Porche.

7. On Wednesdays Bob has the following schedule: physics at 8:30, English at 9:30, and history at 12:30.
8. The letter to Mr. Dennis began, "Dear Sir: Greetings from the IRS."
9. *The Savage God: A Study of Suicide* is an interesting book by A. Alvarez.
10. Ray had to meet the repairman at 3:45 P.M.

Practice Sentences 17-4

1. Are you going to buy the children a dog?
2. Jane—or was it Sue?—received a pin for perfect attendance.
3. You must eat those vegetables before you can leave the table!
4. Ronna asked if she could be of assistance.
5. Do you want me to have your car filled up with gas?

Practice Sentences 17-5

1. Beth—or was it David?—contracted severe spinal meningitis last year.
2. "She doesn't study, yet she expects—"the teacher burst out angrily.
3. "She—er—can't find the authorization slip for the news release right now, sir," the secretary said.
4. Three couples—Ted and Marie, Kenneth and Joy, Tim and Linda—went to the movie in Brad's new van.
5. Only one chore remains to be done—feeding the dog.
6. Cindy, Sharon, and Barbara—but not Joanie—were chosen to dance in the school musical.
7. "Your daughter—uh—Mrs. Daily—uh—is in the hospital," the boy stammered.
8. Today—thank goodness it's Friday!—I must get a lot of work done.
9. Dennis, Ron, Joey, Clint, and Mike—these are the most studious boys in the class.
10. Governor T—will probably not run for reelection next year.

Practice Sentences 17-6

1. The lawyer's document (the one explaining the settlement) left both parties dissatisfied.
2. The financial reports (see attached statements) verified that the company was in trouble.
3. The legal speed limit on the open highway in all states is (a) 45 mph, (b) 55 mph, or (c) 65 mph.
4. Josephine received twenty dollars ($20) when her first poem was published.
5. Your arguments (most of which are illogical) do not convince me at all.
6. The main power consumers in a home are (1) heat, (2) air conditioning, and (3) hot water heaters.
7. Many members of SAMLA (the South Atlantic Modern Language Association) are noted scholars.
8. I can't believe Freddy paid five hundred dollars ($500) for that pistol.
9. The Italian artist Benvenuto Cellini (1500–1571) wrote a fascinating autobiography.
10. Colonel William Barret Travis (see also David Crockett and James Bowie) commanded the Texas forces during the siege of the Alamo in 1836.

Practice Sentences 17-7

1. The English poet Robert Herrick wrote, "A sweet disorder in the dress/Kindles in clothes a wantonness."
2. Carl took Astronomy 101 on the pass/fail system.
3. William Wordsworth said, "She was Phantom of delight/When first she gleamed upon my sight."
4. The doctors and/or the nurses may use the lounge downstairs.
5. Edgar Allan Poe opens his poem "The Sleeper" with these lines: "At midnight, in the month of June,/I stand beneath the mystic moon."

Practice Sentences 17-8

1. There are at least twenty-five ways to complete that project.
2. The verb is spelled d-e-v-i-s-e, the noun, d-e-v-i-c-e.
3. The team had a pre-game meeting in the locker room.
4. The nineteen-eighties was a time of political conservatism.
5. Ninety-seven people applied for one job opening at the bank.
6. I read pages 491–543 in my history text last night.
7. The man-made virus was barely contained.
8. There is much pro-Israeli sentiment in the American government.
9. Joel Barlow (1754–1812) is a little-known American poet.
10. The day-to-day figures looked good for the new company.

Index